Negotiating the Complexities
of Qualitative Research in
Higher Education

Negotiating the Complexities of Qualitative Research in Higher Education illuminates the complex nature of qualitative research, while attending to issues of application. This text addresses the fundamentals of research through discussion of strategies, ethical issues, and challenges in higher education. In addition to walking through the methodological steps, this text considers the conceptual reasons behind qualitative research and explores how to conduct qualitative research that is rigorous, thoughtful, and theoretically coherent. Seasoned researchers Jones, Torres, and Arminio combine high-level theory with practical applications and examples, showing how research in higher education can produce improved learning outcomes for students, especially those who have been historically marginalized. This book will help students in Higher Education and Student Affairs graduate programs to cultivate an appreciation for the complexity and ambiguity of the research and the ways to think thorough questions and tensions that emerge in the process.

New in this edition:

- Updated citations and content throughout to reflect the newest thinking and scholarship
- Expansion of current exemplars of qualitative research
- New exercises, activities, and examples throughout to bolster accessibility of theory
- A new chapter on "Theoretical Perspectives" and "Challenges in Data Collection"

Susan R. Jones is Professor and Section Head of the Higher Education and Student Affairs program at The Ohio State University, USA.

Vasti Torres is Dean of the College of Education at the University of South Florida, USA.

Jan Arminio is Professor and Director of the Higher Education Program at George Mason University, USA.

Negotiating the Complexities of Qualitative Research in Higher Education

Fundamental Elements and Issues

Second Edition

**Susan R. Jones, Vasti Torres,
and Jan Arminio**

Routledge
Taylor & Francis Group

NEW YORK AND LONDON

Loughborough
COLLEGE est 1909

Second Edition published 2014
by Routledge
711 Third Avenue, New York, NY 10017

Simultaneously published in the UK by Routledge
2 Park Square, Milton Park, Abingdon, Oxon OX14 4RN

Routledge is an imprint of the Taylor & Francis Group, an informal business

© 2014 Taylor & Francis

The right of Susan R. Jones, Vasti Torres, and Jan Arminio to be identified as the authors of this work has been asserted by them in accordance with sections 77 and 78 of the Copyright, Designs and Patents Act 1988.

First published by Routledge in 2006.

CIP data has been applied for

ISBN: 978-0-415-51735-5 (hbk)
ISBN: 978-0-415-51736-2 (pbk)
ISBN: 978-0-203-12383-6 (ebk)

Typeset in Minion
by Apex CoVantage, LLC

To the participants in our research studies and readers of our first edition, thank you for leading us to increased insight, higher quality research, and improved educational practices. In the circle of inquiry, we dedicate this book in gratitude.

Contents

Tables and Figures

TABLES

FIGURES

Preface

The seeds for the first edition of this book were planted through some admittedly bad behavior on our part—passing notes at a professional meeting. We were all members of an editorial board and were reviewing a number of manuscripts professing to utilize qualitative methodology. The subject of our notes revealed that all three of us were concerned about the methodological quality of many submissions we received. We wondered what we might do to improve the methodological goodness of qualitative work. It was important for us to engage with this question by providing an accessible text that also illuminated the complex nature of qualitative work. This was a guiding principle that served as the foundation for the first edition of this book and continues with this second edition. Another primary motivation for the creation of both editions is our belief that the ultimate purpose of conducting research is to create pathways to enhance learning, greater good, and social action. By this, we mean that research ought to result in greater understanding of complex phenomena and that higher education can offer pathways to improved quality of life, particularly for those whose experiences and life situations are understudied and devalued in mainstream society. We wanted to make apparent how research can contribute to this goal.

Why is a second edition of our book on qualitative research particular to the context of higher education necessary? The first edition was written at a time when there were very few good examples of published qualitative research in higher education and student affairs journals. Thankfully this has changed and greater numbers of researchers are using qualitative approaches, although not always in sophisticated ways. This phenomenon requires a new text that reflects these newer methodological developments in the field and the greater sophistication of their use, while also tending to those who are not as knowledgeable regarding qualitative approaches. Second, due to their very nature, good qualitative studies continue to assist those in higher education in meeting learning goals and promoting learning outcomes for students, especially those whose voices have been silenced or made difficult to hear within quantitative research. Also, higher education institutions play a critical role in preparing students as researchers. This occurs through classroom instruction as well as through research endeavors outside the classroom. To meet the growing demands of stakeholders, the public and governing bodies are holding higher education practitioners and institutional researchers accountable to these outcomes and requiring the assessment of educational goals to assure they are being met. Increasingly, such assessments are utilizing both quantitative and qualitative methodologies. Consequently, conducting sound assessment has important implications for institutions in their training of practitioners, administrators, and scholars. Moreover, faculty members who conduct scholarly research, whether qualitative or quantitative, continue to use the higher education context for their work. Other texts have addressed assessment in higher education; our focus is on qualitative research, though we recognize that qualitative methods are often used in assessment work. As qualitative research continues to become a more accepted means of conducting inquiry, it is critical that a common and clear understanding exists of the complexities that encompass qualitative inquiry. In this book, we offer insight into how these complexities are negotiated.

New in This Edition

Our primary goal for this second edition of *Negotiating the Complexities of Qualitative Research in Higher Education* is to provide a high-level introductory text that does not compromise on intellectual depth and theoretical complexity and attends to issues of application and usefulness. As a result of this goal, in this second edition, we have dropped two chapters from the first edition, reorganized the sequence of chapters, and added three new chapters. A related goal was to provide an up-to-date book that incorporates contemporary examples of published research that reflect both methodological issues as well as the challenges facing higher education scholars and practitioners. Thus, much of the material from the first edition is updated to reflect the current thinking and newest scholarship in this area. We also selected examples that demonstrate the complexities of conducting qualitative inquiry in order to challenge readers to both understand the foundations of conducting research and also appreciate the more sophisticated nuances involved. Finally, we increased the number and improved the quality of the exercises, activities, and tables in the text to aid in the application of the material to the research and practice contexts in which individuals find themselves.

As we worked on this new edition, we again sought to mirror the process of "working qualitatively;" that is, we wanted to model the elements of researcher reflexivity and positionality in the book. As coauthors working collaboratively to write a book, we brought to this process our own individual perceptions and experiences; we listened to each other's perspectives, made decisions, and created a common understanding only after challenging and supporting each others' viewpoints. We again reflected on our journeys as qualitative researchers and how the nature of the journey continues to influence our work as researchers.

We acknowledge that we came to this project from different life experiences, learned about qualitative research in different ways, and offered different interpretations of qualitative inquiry. Indeed, our own worldviews influenced all dimensions of this project—we still referred to Jan as the "phenomenological mom" because her very being *is* phenomenological; Vasti is still direct and to the point in her writing; and Susan still uses metaphors to tell a thorough story. In this edition, we disagreed, negotiated, and settled on when and how to use the epistemological concepts of constructionism versus constructivism; if, whether, and when to merge epistemologies in data analysis; and how to respond to other language inconsistencies that still permeate the scholarship on qualitative research. We navigated the tensions through our willingness to receive, sit with, and negotiate differing assumptions, biases, and opinions. We came to a better and deeper understanding of the taken-for-granted aspects of our previous work. However, what continues to sustain us is a commitment to provide a useful text that presents the complexities of qualitative research, including its philosophical and theoretical perspectives, and offer direction for good qualitative work. We did not want to write a simple book because we do not think qualitative work is simple at all. Instead, we hope to cultivate an appreciation for the complexity and ambiguity of this work and ways to think through the questions and tensions that undoubtedly emerge in the qualitative research process.

In acknowledging our differing worldviews, experiences, and training in qualitative research, those using this book may note that chapters are written in different voices and styles. This is most likely because, although we were all involved in the conceptualization and outline of each chapter and in the careful editing of each chapter as it was written, one of us took the lead in writing each chapter. We believe this approach is a strength of the book because it enabled us to synergistically bring multiple perspectives to bear in each chapter as well as to give the reader a glimpse into the great variety of writing styles and strategies associated with qualitative research. Writing the book in this way also enabled us to tap into our strengths and areas of research expertise as well as to stretch into new areas not treated as fully in other resources on qualitative research. We drew heavily on these other sources and do not view our book as the only book on qualitative research that a new researcher should read. Our goal is to help the researcher through the complexities and the nuances of the research process. However, many of the topics we cover are treated in greater depth in other works, and we highly recommend that those be read as well.

Organization of This Book

Although the conceptual approach to the book is one of negotiating complexities, the organizational approach of this edition, similar to the first edition, is intended to mirror the process of designing a qualitative study. All chapters from the previous edition were substantively updated, including reference citations, examples from published research, charts, tables, figures, and exercise/

discussion questions. We added three new chapters and significantly reorganized a fourth. Chapter One, Situating the Research: First Steps, focuses on situating the researcher within a philosophical and epistemological worldview. Meeting the Obligations of High Quality Inquiry is Chapter Two. This chapter is a combination of two chapters in the first edition that we moved earlier in the book to emphasize that issues of quality and trustworthiness need to be considered early in the research planning process rather than at the end. We address the interrelatedness of all elements of the research design and provide a complex analysis of strategies of research effectiveness. Responding to trends in qualitative inquiry, Incorporating Theoretical Perspectives, addressed in a completely new Chapter Three, more thoroughly introduces and explores the role of theoretical perspectives in guiding research design. Here, we include a discussion of several critical theories, such as critical race theory, and the role these theoretical perspectives may play in conducting research. Pinpointing the salience of research questions and methodological approaches, Designing Research and Perspectives on Sampling, Chapters Four and Five respectively, flow from the guidance offered by worldview, theoretical perspective, and standards for good research. Chapter Four is expanded by adding narrative inquiry to the methodological approaches presented (i.e., grounded theory, narrative inquiry, phenomenology, case study, and ethnography). Chapter Five takes the reader through the seemingly straightforward process of identifying participants, or "sampling." In addition, in both Chapters Four and Five, we have integrated attention to different forms of specific methodologies, included information on the ways theoretical perspectives may shift the application of a methodological approach, and added to the number of examples provided. Chapter Six, Challenges in Collecting Data, is another newly added chapter resulting from the fact that expanding technologies are providing ever increasing means by which to collect data. Here, we address how to determine which data collection methods to use, how to write good interview questions, and the use of multiple methods within one study. Each of these areas is presented through the lens of the challenges to researchers as they plan for and conduct the collection of data. Chapter Seven, Issues in Analysis and Interpretation, another new chapter, echoes points made throughout the book about the influence of methodology on interpretation. The chapter focuses on data analysis and addresses issues such as how to make sense of multiple forms of data, coding, dealing with implicit data, and interpreting results. In Chapter Eight, Anticipating and Navigating Ethical Issues, we discuss the ethical issues and complexities that emerge when engaged in qualitative inquiry. We present key ethical principles, such as confidentiality, informed consent, and "do no harm," and then identify the ethical issues that may emerge in every phase of the research process. We conclude the book with a new Chapter Nine, Lessons Learned and Future Directions. In this chapter, we provide new lessons learned that reflect our evolving understanding of qualitative inquiry and identify several future directions that we anticipate will influence qualitative inquiry in higher education.

The end of each chapter includes a series of discussion questions and activities in which readers may engage to advance their understanding of the material covered and the application to the research process. In a new approach from the first edition, these exercises are divided into two categories. The first includes questions and/or activities that relate to the content and concepts presented in the chapters. The second set of questions and/or activities is particular to the research process with the idea that the reader may read the chapters sequentially and, through responding to these questions, be walked through the research design process. All the chapters in the book emphasize the importance of decision making in the research process. Every step of the way, the researcher is making decisions—regarding research questions, who is in the sample, what kinds of questions to ask in interviews, how to analyze data, and so on. Our approach is to emphasize the importance of intentionality in these decisions and the relationship of these decisions to theoretical perspectives and methodological choices. In total, these chapters illuminate the responsibilities qualitative researchers accept when collecting data, the ethical commitments to research participants and those who use research, and the continual obligation of researchers to learn from inquiry.

Negotiating Complexities and Fundamental Elements

We recognize the seemingly contradictory and ironic twist in a title that includes the phrases *negotiating complexities* and *fundamental elements*. *Fundamental* implies building blocks and neat recipes to follow, whereas *complexities* suggest ambiguity; challenges; and troubling, taken-for-granted assumptions. Indeed, we are navigating the space in between simplification and theoretical sophistication. We know there are trade-offs in our approach, but we were guided in our work by an over-arching commitment to produce a text that was useful and accessible to beginning qualitative researchers while also engaging readers in the complex issues that emerge when conducting such research. We hope readers will let us know how we have succeeded in this effort.

Acknowledgments

No book is ever produced as a completely solitary endeavor. Not only were we engaged in a highly collaborative process between the three of us, but we were also supported by others who provided feedback, proofreading, and general expressions of support. One individual who read the entire book (several times) and whose suggestions and feedback were essential to this work is Mei-Yen Ireland, a doctoral student in the higher education and student affairs program at The Ohio State University. Graduate students, colleagues, and some family members read more of the book than they cared to but were very generous in providing feedback as well as technical and logistical support. These individuals include John Arminio, Elijah Howe, and Julie Owen. We are also grateful to the wonderful colleagues who responded quickly and brilliantly to our request for ethical dilemmas they had experienced in their research (these appear in Chapter Eight). These individuals are Elisa Abes, Ebelia Hernandez, Stephen John Quaye, and Kristen Renn. We also thank our anonymous reviewers of the first edition and the proposal for our second edition for their insightful and helpful feedback. Finally, we are appreciative of Heather Jarrow of Routledge who encouraged our second edition and championed its potential. From our colleagues at The Ohio State University, Indiana University, and George Mason University we seek forgiveness for what we left undone while writing this book and give thanks for what we were able to accomplish with their guidance and support.

Susan R. Jones
The Ohio State University

Vasti Torres
University of South Florida

Jan Arminio
George Mason University

1 Situating the Research
First Steps

Many beginnings are precarious. According to Gadamer (1960/1992), "The problem of the beginning is, in fact, the problem of the end. For it is with respect to an end that a beginning is defined" (p. 472). How does a researcher negotiate the precariousness of beginning a study? How does one arrive at a completed, worthy, qualitative study? It is imperative that those who engage in qualitative inquiry address both fundamental and complex defining features. These features include situating the research in a grounding perspective that is congruent with or adds to the research design, including how one designs a research question and selects, interprets, and represents participants. Making appropriate choices about collecting, managing, and analyzing data while also meeting the obligations of conducting high quality inquiry are also fundamental features. Negotiating these complex features determines the quality and worthiness of the research study; yet surprisingly, these features continue to be often overlooked by many researchers who attempt to conduct qualitative studies.

In this first chapter, we discuss navigating these complex features by exploring the fundamental considerations of situating research. To situate a study means to "anchor" it (Jones, 2002, p. 463). This is a decision-making process that involves a series of choices. These choices include selecting a compelling interest, an epistemological grounding, a theoretical framework and perspective, a research question, a purpose (e.g., research, assessment, or evaluation), and a relationship with the topic and participants. We present them in this order as it follows the logic of writing a chapter; however, when designing a study, a researcher typically begins with a compelling interest and research question that drives the other decision making choices. Nonetheless, studies that are not situated or anchored risk running adrift, rambling without direction, or even doing harm to participants or communities. In this chapter, we explore the immediate considerations for negotiating how to situate a study and offer corresponding examples, including the decision making of a fictitious researcher, "Michael," as he situates his study. In subsequent chapters, however, we utilize examples from published research to illustrate the concepts and strategies presented. Because of the variety of design and analytic possibilities, we do not want to suggest through the one example of Michael that there is one right way to approach these considerations. The immediate considerations discussed in this chapter are as follows:

- Situating the study within a compelling interest
- Situating the study within the researcher's worldview
- Contemplating the nature of knowledge and reality
- Situating a study in a theoretical perspective
- Choosing a question that presses upon us
- Researching, assessing, or evaluating

This precarious beginning requires that we start by defining terms most often associated with inquiry and identifying underlying philosophical assumptions. Research is often considered by inexperienced researchers as two opposite types: qualitative and quantitative. Crotty (1998) described the opposition of these terms as the "great divide" (p. 14). Since the 1980s, researchers have been moving away from these oppositional terms. Our dilemma here is whether to use terms that novices will recognize or to use contemporary terms that more accurately depict the complexities of research. We encourage the study and understanding of more complex and descriptive terms but will begin where most inexperienced researchers begin. A discussion on how the broad polarities of quantitative and qualitative research emerged will be instructive, beginning with paradigm. More complex and descriptive terms will be examined later in this chapter and in subsequent chapters.

The Influence of Paradigm on Discourse

Thomas Kuhn (1970) used the Greek term *paradeigma,* meaning pattern or model, to refer to basic patterns that scientists use to interpret data. In this context, he defined *paradigms* as models "from which spring particular coherent traditions of scientific research" (p. 10). He went on to write, "In short, consciously or not, the decision to employ a particular piece of apparatus and to use it in a particular way carries an assumption that only certain sorts of circumstance will arise" (p. 59). He offered a number of examples of scientists whose work was ignored by the established scientific community, thus restricting new understanding. Such scientists have included Copernicus, Galileo, Issac Newton, and Albert Einstein. According to Kuhn, Copernicus did not discover more data; rather, he was able to imagine how the data might fit into a different pattern.

Kuhn employed Joseph Jastrow's famous duck–rabbit picture[1] (see Figure 1.1) as a metaphor of the paradigm shift debate. He concluded that once the viewer has "seen" the new paradigm (or duck–rabbit), it is impossible to forget. This opened the possibility of asking, "What would data look like from

---

1. There is some controversy as to who to credit for this drawing. Some, such as Kuhn, credit Ludwig Wittgenstein (*Philosophical Investigations,* 1953), but Wittgenstein himself credited Jastrow for the drawing published in *Harper's Weekly* in 1892.

Figure 1.1 Duck/Rabbit

another perspective?" "What might the universe look like from the perspective of the sun rather than the earth?" "What new insights can be offered by collecting data from a position of an 'emic,' or insider's view, rather than an 'etic' view of the authority observer?" and "What language best communicates this conceptualization?"

Through calling attention to the different ways of collecting and viewing data, the concept of a knowledge paradigm created an overly simplistic distinction between new paradigm and old paradigm, between rational and mythic, and between quantitative and qualitative inquiry. Many scholars and researchers attack this duality (e.g., Ellingson, 2011; Lather, 2007; Pinar, Reynolds, Slattery, & Taubman, 1995).

In the literature, *paradigm* is rather consistently referred to as a set of interconnected or related assumptions or beliefs, but it is also referred to as *worldview*. How does paradigm relate to worldview? Worldview is the conceptualization people make of their relation to the world. Paradigm, too, is a conceptualization but is more specific to knowledge construction. Likely, one's worldview would contain perceptions about how knowledge is constructed but would also contain perceptions about self, others, and time (Sue, Ivey, & Pederson, 1996). Guba (1990) noted that "the net that contains a researcher's epistemological, ontological and methological premises may be termed a paradigm or interpretive framework" (p. 17).

The language one uses in describing a researchable phenomenon foreshadows philosophy, paradigm, and worldview. There are implications for word choice and contextual language in the research that educators conduct.

Implications for Language

The worldview of the researcher is communicated through language, whether explicitly or implicitly. A differing of opinion exists about whether those whose studies are grounded in a qualitative paradigm should use the same language of the "found world" (e.g., quantitative research) (Smith & Deemer, 2000, p. 885) or create new language. Some scholars, such as Smith and Deemer (2000) and Smith (1993), believed that new language should be used that allows for "moving out from under the shadow of empirical-analytical expectations" (Arminio & Hultgren, 2002, p. 449). However, others, like Lather (1991; 2007), take terms from the quantitative paradigm and transform them to be applicable to other views of knowledge. For example, Lather (1991) offered a "reconceptualization of validity" (p. 66) appropriate for research that is openly committed to a more just social order by advocating for catalytic validity that "by far is … most unorthodox; it flies directly in the face of the positivist demand for research neutrality" (p. 68).

It is important that those engaged in research realize that the language they choose represents and communicates a paradigm and worldview. For many of us, the language of quantitative research has been entrenched in our schooling to the point where we assume that words like *validity, reliability, sampling, correlation, rigor, significance,* and *comparison* have a universal use, but in fact they can represent a particular research paradigm. As interpreters of reality instead of solely being in contact with reality, researchers are responsible for understanding the implications of the language used.

Below are examples of language as represented by each research paradigm:

Quantitative	Qualitative
Variable	Theme, code, category, multidimensionality
Correlate	Interpret, reflect, mutually shaping
Statistical significance	Profound, illuminating
Sample/subjects	Participants, co-researchers, co-travelers
Reliability	Triangulation
Rigor	Goodness, worthiness
Validity	Trustworthiness, catalytic validity
Proof, testing, and control groups	Judgments, perceptions, textual rendering
Results	Discovery, findings, constructing, meaning making
Generalizations	Contextual findings, appropriations
Outlier	Unique
Mechanical features	Morophogenesis (The evolving development of the structure of an entire organism)
Objective positionality	Tending to participants, indwell, human-as-subject, reflexivity
Bias	Perception, influence

It is not our intent to promote the notion of research as polar oppositions. Like Ellingson (2011), we maintain that research methodologies span a continuum.

Ellingson (2011) promoted a continuum that is "anchored by art and science, with vast middle spaces that embody infinite possibilities for blending artistic, expository, and social scientific ways of analysis and representation" (p. 595). She noted too that vocabulary represents such a continuum. The significance of language and word choice cannot be understated. For example, Bhaskar (1979) noted this poignant example of the importance of precise word choice to conveying meaning. Under Nazi rule,

1. Germany was depopulated.
2. Millions of people died.
3. Millions of people were killed.
4. Millions of people were massacred.

Bhaskar (1979) stated that though all four are true, only the fourth is a "precise and accurate description of what actually happened" (p. 76), because only the last implies that the deaths were a part of an organized campaign. "This point is important. For social science is not only about a subject matter, it is for an audience" (Bhaskar, 1979, p. 76). In the first three statements, we must question what is implicitly valued in the attempt to be value free (objective). The fourth statement does not attempt at being value free. But which more adequately describes the event? A more current example of the power of word choice would be terrorist versus freedom fighter.

An example from the literature in higher education is found in the following: "Consequently, compared to their peers with highly educated parents, first-generation students are more likely to be handicapped in accessing and understanding information and attitudes relevant to making beneficial decisions" (Pascarella, Pierson, Wolniak, & Terenzini, 2004, p. 252). How might this quote be viewed differently by the reader if it were said by a first-generation student rather than the researcher? What language does one use about those with whom one is studying? How do these terms represent, re-present, and communicate the relationship? Kezar (2004) commented,

> A student tells me she wants to study the experience of graduate students in the United States who come from other countries. She wants to examine their experience in a foreign place.... [I ask her] What does it mean to use the term foreign? Is she comfortable with this term and its implications in her study? (p. 46)

Words communicate the nature of the relationship between those being studied and the person conducting the study. Words such as *illuminate, explore, discern,* and *meaning* represent an openness to mutual construction and enlightenment (Arminio & Hultgren, 2002), mirroring the purposes of qualitative research. Moreover, Ellsworth (1997) encouraged "troubling" the language to better express what is intended. *Troubling the language* means that words are used in a slightly new or different way in order to challenge the status quo. For example, in an article on the question of criteria of qualitative research, Arminio and Hultgren (2002) asked, "How do we as phenomenologists understand our respons-ability to reframing criteria?" (p. 447). "Respons-ability" troubles the word *responsibility* by highlighting the notion of the ability to respond in the word *responsibility.* This may be considered a "play on words," but this play or troubling extends the "potential of words to spread understanding beyond accustomed boundaries" (p. 452). Jones (2002) also troubled the language to extend meaning potential in her title "(Re)Writing the Word: Methodological Strategies and Issues in Qualitative Research." She wrote,

> To (re)write the word, to engage in research that holds potential for getting closer to what is true about a particular phenomenon, for exhibiting true generosity, and for contributing to the elimination of inequality, those most fully engaged in qualitative research must recognize the complexities in the effort. (p. 472)

The use of "(re)write" emphasizes the importance of revising for deeper understanding that may be lost with the more commonplace use of *rewrite.*

In this section we have defined paradigm and demonstrated how language and word choice align with paradigm. Besides paradigm, there are many other important terms that relate to grounding assumptions. An understanding of these allows for further navigating the complexities in the research processes.

Understanding Terms Necessary in Deciding How to Situate a Study

Crotty (1998) noted a lack of clarity and consistency in some of the fundamental grounding concepts of qualitative research. He wrote,

> Research students and . . . even more seasoned campaigners—often express bewilderment at the array of methodologies and methods laid out before their gaze. . . . To add to the confusion, the terminology is far from consistent in research literature and social science texts. One frequently finds the same term in a number of different, sometimes even contradictory[,] ways. (p. 1)

Similarly, Lather (2007) wrote, "Surveying the various turns in the social sciences, one is struck by the difficulties of deciding on even what terms to feature" (p. 2).

In any case, to negotiate the complex fundamentals of qualitative research, it is important to be familiar with the terms *paradigm, epistemology, ontology, theoretical perspective, literature review/theoretical framework, methodology,* and *method.* Unfortunately, these terms are sometimes defined and used differently by different scholars. These important fundamental concepts are listed in Table 1.1 along with definitions provided by notable research scholars.

Table 1.1 Terms and Definitions From Various Authors

Terms	Creswell 2013	Crotty 1998	Morse and Richards 2002	Patton 1990	Schwandt 2007a
Paradigm	"A basic set of beliefs that guide action" (p. 18, as cited in Guba, 1990).	"Package of beliefs" (p. 35).	"Philosophical paradigms [include] feminism, post modernism, and critical theory" (p. 171).	"A worldview, a general perspective, a way of breaking down the complexity of the world" (p. 37).	"A worldview or general perspective" (p. 217).
Epistemology	"What counts as knowledge and how knowledge claims are justified" (p. 20).	"The theory of knowledge imbedded in the theoretical and thereby in the methodology" (p. 3).	"[A]ssumptions [that] concern the origins of knowledge" (p. 3).		"The study of the nature of knowledge and justification" (p. 87).
Ontology	"The nature of reality" (p. 20).	"Concerned with 'what is' the nature of existence, with the structure of reality" (p. 10).	"[C]oncerns questions about the nature of reality" (p. 3).		Defined under metaphysics and "is concerned with understanding the kinds of things that constitute the world" (p. 190).
Theoretical Perspective		"The philosophical stance informing methodology and thus providing a context for the process and grounding its logic and criteria" (p. 3).		"What distinguishes the discussion of theory … on qualitative methods is the emphasis on inductive strategies of theory development in contrast to theory generated by logical deduction" (p. 66).	

(continued)

Table 1.1 (continued)

Terms	Creswell 2013	Crotty 1998	Morse and Richards 2002	Patton 1990	Schwandt 2007a
Literature Review			Under the heading "Using the Literature Review": "[T]heoretical context . . . places the study in the context of the topic" (p. 189).	"[H]ow others have approached similar concerns" (p. 163).	"Analyzing and synthesizing multiple studies for the purpose of demonstrating their collective relevance for solving some problem" (p. 266).
Methodology	"Procedures of qualitative research" (p. 22).	"The strategy, plan of action, process, or designing behind the choice and use of particular methods" (p. 3).	Defined methodology same as method.		"A theory of how inquiry should proceed" (p. 193).
Method		"[T]he techniques or procedures used to gather and analyze data" (p. 3).	"[S]hare the goal of deriving new understanding and making theory out of data" (p. 13).	"Set of investigative procedures used within a particualr field of study or discipline" (pp. 190–191).	"Permits the evaluator to study selected issues in depth and detail" (p. 13).

You will notice that some authors define terms similarly, some terms are defined differently, and some scholars refer to some of these concepts but not others. *Epistemology* conveys philosophical assumptions about what constitutes knowledge. Some scholars do not refer to epistemology, but those who do define it as the origins, theory, or assumptions about knowledge. Other scholars state what it is that epistemological questions illuminate, some scholars do not mention epistemology, and still others do not define epistemology in their recent works but did so in earlier works. Another set of related assumptions is associated with explanations or questions about the nature or structure of reality or existence. This is referred to as *ontology*. Crotty (1998) noted that issues of epistemology and ontology tend to intersect in that how one defines reality influences what one believes is a viable means of gaining knowledge. For example, can people learn from spirits?

In Table 1.2, we offer a representation of important research terms, but ones we believe to be appropriate in the pragmatic context of higher education. We also offer examples of how they are used. The reader will notice in Table 1.2 that we have replaced the term *literature review* with *theoretical framework* to emphasize the importance of theory. We have differentiated theoretical perspective (assumptions about the nature of knowledge acquisition and existence, see Chapter Three) from theoretical framework (concepts and previous research that inform the phenomenon being studied).

The inconsistent use of the terms *methodology* and *method* is of particular concern. Some authors use the terms interchangeably, defining both as the means by which data are collected. Other scholars differentiate them, with methodology meaning the approach that guides how data are collected and analyzed and method meaning how data are collected. The exclusion of methodology from the discussion of qualitative research has consequences for the worthiness of a study. Methodology is a central concept because it guides the research design. Without attention paid to methodology, the researcher lacks the means by which to appropriately design the study, analyze data, and make sense of findings. We distinguish methodology (which guides research design) from method (the collection of data) while underscoring their relationship. Methodology is discussed in more detail in Chapter Four and method in Chapter Six. Understanding these basic terms allows researchers sufficient grounding to undertake the considerations of situating their study.

Consideration One: Situating the Study Within a Compelling Interest

One of the first considerations in situating a study is to reflect upon what issue or topic is sufficiently compelling that researchers would want to contemplate it more. Researchers must consider, "What is it that presses upon me in a way that necessitates I understand it more? What unknown deters my practice, institution, my community, my society?"

Table 1.2 Jones, Torres, and Arminio's Recommended Definitions With Examples

Paradigm	Epistemology	Ontology	Theoretical Perspective and Framework	Methodology	Method
A set of interconnected assumptions that distinguish between worldviews	Assumptions about the acquisition of knowledge	Assumptions about the nature of reality	Perspective: philosophical (epistemological and ontological) assumptions that guide methodology Framework: suppositions and concepts (e.g., previous research and theories) that inform the phenomenon under study	Informed by epistemology, ontology, and theory, a process that guides study design, implementation, data collection, data analysis, and interpretation	How data are collected
"This section describes briefly (a) the inquiry paradigm used in the study and the researcher's biography, (b) settings and participants, (c) data collection and anlaysis, and (d) trustworthiness" (Kellogg & Liddell, 2012, p. 524).	"The study's epistemological approach was anchored in the constructivist tradition to construct knowledge, meaning, and understanding through human interactions" (Palmer, Davis, & Maramba, 2011, p. 577).	Rarely noted in research in higher education	"Critical race theory is the theoretical perspective of this study .... Critical race theory has been used in higher education research to analyze the Latino college experience .... The theoretical framework for this study was self-authorship .... I chose to solicit narratives through in-depth interviews. This approach fits well with CRT's value of giving voice to people of color" (Hernandez, 2012, pp. 684–685).	"Case study methodology was used to examine a bounded system (Merriam, 2009)" (Quaye, 2012, pp. 546–547).	Usually noted as a heading or subheading

In general, there are two overarching purposes of qualitative research. One is to illuminate and understand in depth the richness in the lives of human beings and the world in which we live. The other is to use new understanding for emancipating practices. Hence, a researcher's compelling interest should reflect at least one of these two intents. The intent should be balanced with what Marshall and Rossman (2011) called the "do-ability" of a study (p. 4), or the feasibility that a study can be completed considering the resources available, purpose, and researcher competence.

Compelling interests that lead to unsettled questions are typically related to our life experiences. This is not to be avoided. Marshall and Rossman (2011) referred to this as the "want-to-do-ability" of a study (p. 5), and as directly related to one of the central features of qualitative research, the researcher-as-instrument (Lincoln & Guba, 1985; Patton, 2002). Qualitative inquiry often requires the researcher to become embedded in a context and responsive to what is happening in that context. There often is, and should be, a relationship between the researcher and the researched. This reflects the passion that later becomes the research question. Critics of qualitative research often refer to this relationship as bias; however, this is a strength of qualitative inquiry. We will address this criticism in depth later in this chapter and in subsequent chapters.

Let's look at an example of situating a study within a compelling interest. In one of his graduate classes, Michael studies campus environments. His reading assignments offer insight into his own experiences of being physically threatened, his privacy compromised, and in general feeling unwelcome on campus. He finds literature that supports and validates his feelings and experiences that safety is a broader notion than physical safety. In a subsequent class on research design, Michael feels compelled to study student safety on campus. Before deciding upon a particular question or its wording, however, Michael has more to consider, including his worldview about the generation of knowledge.

This brings us to consideration two and the question of how one's worldview about knowledge and reality influences research decisions.

Consideration Two: Situating the Study Within the Researcher's Worldview

Researchers often err in deciding upon a research question prematurely. Researchers must simultaneously consider their view about how knowledge is generated and the nature of reality. Jones (2002) noted that conducting qualitative research is both a blessing and a burden. Certainly the enrichment that researchers gain from the research process is one of the blessings, and, as Jones noted, researchers' responsibilities to those with whom they come into contact are significant. The "burden" comes in the need to understand the complexity of philosophy and theory upon which qualitative research and its associated traditions are founded. Negotiating these tensions may at times be burdensome. We encourage researchers to "lean" into these complexities. In fact, avoiding them would be irresponsible. Yet, this "leaning into" takes considerable study. Some practitioners and administrators continue to be reluctant to use theory to guide educational practice, though qualitative research is guided and influenced by philosophy, theory, and "intellectual movements" (Lather, 2007, p. 34). To engage in qualitative research is to pay considerable attention to these.

Worldview, or the conceptualization people make of their relationship to the world, centers on beliefs of human nature, the environment, time, social relationships, responsibility, and control (Hays & McLeod, 2010). Obviously one's worldview can be altered as one matures from life experiences, but it also can house consistent values and concepts. It shapes one's philosophical grounding. In this book, we refer to *philosophy* as a system of fundamental principles that serve as a basis for action (Berube, 1995). Philosophy, the study and search for wisdom, is described as including the elements of logic, epistemology, ontology, ethics, and metaphysics (Brightman, 1964; Durant, 1961; Honderich, 1995). *Metaphysics* at one time referred to the study of the ultimate reality of all things, including the study of existence (ontology) and the study of the nature of knowledge (epistemology). However, Heidegger (1926/1962), the noted philosopher and phenomenologist, contested the notion of an ultimate reality of all things, a grand objective narrative, or representative understanding (Bronner, 1999). Heidegger (1926/1962) wrote, "We do not know what 'Being' means. But even if we ask, 'What is Being'?, we keep within an understanding of the 'is,' though we are unable to fix conceptually what 'is' signifies" (p. 25). Instead, he stressed the necessity to "bring forward the entities themselves" (p. 61).

One's worldview of the nature of existence and knowledge has implications for how one will embark upon a study. For example, believing that existence is an ultimate reality and knowledge a grand narrative, believing that existence is difficult to understand and that existence calls to itself rather than is represented, or believing other notions of existence and reality are important considerations in situating a study. Knowledge creation is influenced in beliefs of knowledge and reality, and they are influenced by culture. As Lather (1991) noted, "Ways of knowing are inherently culture-bound" (p. 2). Consider the traditional Russian wooden doll, where one very small doll is embedded within a small doll, which is embedded in a medium-sized doll, which is embedded in a larger doll; how data are analyzed and the ways in which data are collected are determined by a particular methodology, which is situated within a philosophical stance.

In situating a study within a paradigm and worldview, researchers must become aware of the philosophical stances that inform their perspectives. Some beginning researchers appear to embrace qualitative research while not truly understanding "what it is they claim to be rejecting" or what it is they say they are embracing (Phallas, 2001, p. 10). An exercise to assist you in better understanding your worldview is found in Table 1.3. It describes a series of belief statements listed in four columns. Circle those statements under the columns A, B, C, and D that are most consistent with your own views of knowledge and reality. Is there a preponderance of circles in any one column?

Table 1.3 Worldview Exercise

A	B	C	D
Reality is a physical and observable event.	Reality is constructed through local human interaction.	Reality is shaped by social, political, economic, and other values crystallized over time.	Reality is socially co-created by individuals through the surrounding environment.
The aim of research is to predict and explain, generalizing results.	The aim of research is increased understanding of complex human phenomena to alter existing power relations.	The purpose of research is transformation, and its aim to emancipate so that people are capable of controlling their destiny.	The aim of research is democratization and uncovering what is intrinsically valuable in human life.
Truth is universal and verifiable; findings are considered true.	Truth is an agreement between members of a stakeholding community.	Truth is influenced by history and societal structures.	Researchers cannot know or create truth.
The researcher can and should be objective.	Objectivity is impossible; rather, the researcher serves as an avenue for the representation of multiple voices.	The view of objectivity as a goal is harmful; rather, advocacy is the aim of research.	Researchers should reject objectivity and not force natural science criteria onto social sciences.
Good research is value free.	Values are a means of understanding.	Values are formative.	Values are personally relative and need to be understood.
Researchers study a problem.	Researchers live a question with participants.	Researchers transform with a community by imagining and helping to create alternatives.	Researchers serve as witnesses.
It is through the voice and jurisdiction of an expert that knowledge is gained.	It is through voices and acknowledgment of both participants and a researcher that knowledge is gained.	It is through theoretical perspectives of societal structures in conjunction with the people who are most affected that knowledge is gained.	Knowledge is not guaranteed. Space for the not known allows the exposure of binaries as well as the juxtaposition and paradox of such binaries.
Validity is data that can be duplicated.	Validity is participant and inquirer consensus.	Valid research is that which creates action.	The goal of dissensus is preferred over consensus.
History is progress.			History portrays cultural shifts.

Sources: Bronner (1999); Crotty (1998); Lather (2007); Lincoln & Guba (2000); Lincoln, Lynham, & Guba (2011); Maykut & Morehouse (2001); Pascale (2011); and Pinar, Reynolds, Slattery, & Taubman (1995)

These statements indicate aspects of worldview that will influence views on research. Each column in Table 1.3 depicts a different view or position on knowledge and existence. Consistent with Lather (2007), we have depicted four views here. They are positivism, constructivism, critical, and poststructural/postmodernism. However, Lincoln, Lynham, and Guba (2011) indicated that five positions exist: positivism, postpositivism, critical, constructivism, and participatory. Views of knowledge grounding research are dynamic and seen as a "dizzying array of in-movement shifts" (Lather, 2007, p. 3). It is beyond the scope of this book to delineate the intricate differences of all the views on knowledge and existence or how they intersect; however, we do touch on this later. The point to take away is that these views bring with them assumptions that influence research questions, the purpose of research, the relationships researchers have with their participants, and the interpretation of research findings.

Statements in column A are descriptive of views that knowledge and reality are universal and measurable. Terms associated with these views include *positivism* and *postpositivism* (Crotty, 1998; Lincoln, Lynham, & Guba, 2011), *empiricism* (Smith, 1993), *empirical/analytical* (Coomer & Hultgren, 1989), and *objectivism* (Crotty, 1998), with an emphasis on prediction. In column B, knowledge and existence are perceived and constructed through human interaction and emphasize understanding. The views represented in column B are often associated with the terms *interpretive* (Coomer & Hultgren, 1989), *constructivism* (Lincoln, Lynham, & Guba, 2011), and *constructionism* (Crotty, 1998). Column C depicts the purpose of knowledge as emancipation; meaning of the phenomenon of the study is imposed, imported, or translated by the subject (Crotty). More recently, the purpose has come to also include "discursive categories that articulate collective and social relations" including words that indicate "social locations," such as first generation college student (Pascale, 2011, p. 31). Terms associated with these emancipatory views include *subjectivism* (Crotty), *subjectivity* (Pascale), or *critical science* (Coomer & Hultgren, 1989), *critical* (Steinberg, 2012), and *critical theory* (Lincoln, Lynham, & Guba, 2011). Column D portrays *postmodernism, poststructuralism,* and *deconstruction,* what Lather (2007) called postcritical theories. These acknowledge cultural shifts and embrace an emphasis on social action, situatedness, knowledge as open-endedness, and differing perspectives. The statements in columns B, C, and D are indicative of what is still too commonly referred to as *qualitative research* or included in the *qualitative paradigm*.

Though conducting a study through a constructivist, interpretivist, or postmodern perspective is now more accepted by journal editorial boards; still, many educators and peer reviewers have been schooled only in positivistic methodologies and the philosophy that grounds them. Additionally, grant funding agencies continue to privilege studies with randomized controlled trials (Denzin, 2011). This issue is discussed further in Chapter Nine.

As the differing views represented by Table 1.3 demonstrated, who we are as people encompasses our beliefs about the nature of reality, truth, and knowledge. These beliefs define assumptions about the world and subsequently about the nature of research. Kezar (2004) wrote that researchers should know the philosophy of their worldview well enough to defend choosing it. She continued to write that researchers should

> engage in philosophical questions, write out assumptions about the issue to be studied, investigate one's own role as researcher, consider the purpose of the research from the tradition they are working in, [and] probe what they understand as the nature of reality and how knowledge is developed. (p. 43)

Let's return again to Michael's thoughts as he continues to situate his study. Michael determines that his worldview is more consistent with an interpretive and constructivist view of knowledge. He believes that numbers cannot represent the experience of feeling safe or unsafe. He believes that an in-depth understanding about this phenomenon could best be accomplished through human interaction. As with all researchers, once he has contemplated his worldview, he must now further investigate his epistemological and ontological stance.

Consideration Three: Contemplating the Nature of Knowledge and Reality

In discussing epistemology (the nature of knowledge acquisition) and ontology (the nature of reality), our aim is not to oversimplify what has occurred in the evolution of philosophy over several hundred years. On the other hand, we do not want to burden the reader with philosophical intricacies. Rather, we seek to sufficiently describe the philosophical differences so that the reader can acknowledge that epistemological underpinnings do influence the researcher and research. What follows is a brief discussion of the primary epistemological and ontological frameworks that guide inquiry.

Objectivist Positivistic Empiricism and Postpositivism

Put very simply, what is commonly referred to as *quantitative research* is based upon objectivist epistemology and the linked theories of positivism and empiricism (Crotty 1998; Lincoln & Guba, 2000; Smith, 1993). Objectivism attempts to explain the world by identifying universal law through solely measurable means. Crotty (1998) described objectivism as

> the epistemological view that things exist as *meaningful* independently of consciousness and experience, that they have truth and meaning residing in them as objects ('objective' truth and meaning, therefore), and that careful (scientific?) research can attain that objective truth and meaning. (pp. 5–6)

Auguste Comte was the founder of positivism, the optimistic notion that science leads to progress (Crotty, 1998; Lincoln & Guba, 1985). Positivism and objectivism have come to be mutually reinforcing in that positivism "articulated a search for laws of social life that could stand as equivalents to the natural laws of the physical sciences" (Pascale, 2011, p. 13). Objective claims are true or false independent of what anyone thinks or feels about it such that there is a clear distinction between fact and value (Crotty, 1998). Smith (1993) indicated that to be objective is to detach oneself from one's own interests and depict things as they "really are" (p. 30). Knowledge is what can be found and measured outside of us.

Empiricism is rooted in the idea that people can neutrally observe the world through the five senses (Pascale, 2011). According to Smith (1993), empiricism is the "solution to the knowledge-versus-opinion problem" (p. 5) in that humans have the capacity to not distort observations through the controlled scientific method. By implementing strict procedures, claims can be made and then judged based on evidence.

According to Denzin and Lincoln (2000b) and Smith (1993), the most important aspect of objectivist positivistic empiricism is the belief that truth is universal and can be measured through observation and discovery, proving or disproving a hypothesis. The Enlightenment promoted that what could not be measured or discovered was most likely superstition. Some of the components of objectivist positivistic empiricism were listed in column A in the exercise in Table 1.3. Philosophers most associated with this paradigm include John Locke (Woozley, 1964), who saw the minds of humans as blank slates "devoid of any ideas" (Smith, 1993, p. 27) from which they independently existed in the world, and Max Weber (1958), who believed that researchers and scientists can make a conscious decision to exclude their judgments.

Postpositivism adds a note of uncertainty to scientific findings challenging that observer and observed are independent (Crotty, 1998), whereas positivism views facts as ultimate truth that comes from measurements. While positivism establishes knowledge through verified hypotheses, postpositivism offers probable facts through hypotheses that cannot be determined to be false (Lincoln, Lynham, & Guba, 2011). Creswell (2013) wrote that postpositivist researchers recognize that there can be multiple perspectives and follow structured research processes. Simplistically, postpositivism might be viewed as a bridge between the qualitative and quantitative paradigms. Moreover, there is published qualitative research grounded in postpositivism. For example, many early grounded theory studies were post-positivist in nature because of the disciplinary origins of grounded theory methodology (see Chapter Four for more discussion).

Constructionism, Constructivism, and Interpretivism

Often stated in contrast to the epistemological and ontological views of objectivism, constructionism "posits that knowledge and meaning are always partial, conditional, perspectival—therefore there is no possibility of timeless and universal knowledge" (Pascale, 2011, p. 50). Likewise, Crotty wrote that "What constructionism drives home unambiguously is that there is no true and valid interpretation" (Crotty, 1998, p. 47). Constructionists reexamine taken for granted assumptions (Burr, 2003) and emphasize that meaning is constructed not created (Crotty, 1998). Crotty detailed a story where students were told that a list of authors written on a blackboard was a poem. Students were asked to decipher the meaning of the "poem" (list of words). Several students did indeed offer ideas as to the poem's meaning. Crotty wrote, "The meanings emerge from the students' interaction with the 'poem' and relate to it essentially" (p. 48). In other words, the students constructed the list of names as a poem because they were told it was a poem. Hence, they constructed the poem but did not create a poem.

According to Pascale (2011), constructionism describes the process by which people assign meaning to their world. All reality *"is contingent upon human practices, being constructed in and out of interaction between human beings and their world, and developed and transmitted within an essentially social context"* (Crotty, 1998, p. 42) (italics in original). For example, like all concepts, constructionists believe that the notion of "dog" has been constructed by humans within a social context. The "dog" as family member differs from the "dog" as watchdog and "dog" as sheep herder. There are several types of constructionism, but differentiating them is beyond the scope of this book.

The terms constructionism and constructivism are often used interchangeably (Crotty, 1998; Schwandt, 2007a), but several authors offer distinctions. Constructionism is most often connected to ontology or how meaning is derived through social collective processes (Crotty, 1998; Pascale, 2011), whereas constructivism is more closely associated with epistemology, the nature of knowledge, and how individuals learn and make meaning linking new knowledge to existing understanding (Beck & Kosnik, 2006; Crotty). Relatedly, constructivism is more connected to the natural world and Piagetian psychology; constructionism to the social world and sociology. According to Crotty (1998), constructivism "points up the unique experience of each of us" and social constructionism "emphasizes the hold our culture has on us," hence constructivism "tends to resist the critical spirit, while constructionism tends to foster it" (p. 58).

Interpretivists are "committed to the philosophy of social construction" but believe that the social world is "produced through meaningful interpretations" (Pascale, 2011, p. 22). Interpretivists emphasize meaning people make rather than facts (Pascale). Closely associated with hermeneutics (the science of interpretation), interpretivism seeks to take participants and researchers to a deeper understanding of a phenomenon by uncovering aspects that have been hidden (Crotty, 1998).

Examples in the research of how these terms are utilized include Baxter Magolda, King, Taylor, and Wakefield's (2012) study on decreasing authority dependence during the first year of college. These authors described their work as being grounded in a "constructivist-development tradition," meaning that the authors assumed "self authorship development is socially constructed and context-bound" (p. 420). Palmer, Davis, and Marambga (2011) informed readers that their study's epistemological approach on the impact of family support on the success of Black men at HBCUs was "anchored in the constructivist tradition to construct knowledge, understanding, and meaning through human interactions" (p. 582).

Subjectivism and Critical Theory

Descartes believed that "subjective identity is the mind's awareness of its own representations" (Pascale, 2011, p. 30) but that it is also beyond representation. Subjectivity is also connected to agency or ability to act (Giardina & Newman, 2011; Pascale, 2011). It describes the knower attempting to better understand the world through experiences of those living in the world and understanding that perceptions are not wrong, just different (Abma & Widdershoven, 2011). Crotty (1998) noted that, from a subjectivist point of view, meaning is not created from the interplay between humans, but rather meaning is "imported" (p. 9) or brought into the study. For example, Linder and Rodriquez (2012) grounded their inquiry through the lens of both multiple identity theory and intersectionality theory. Both theories encourage understanding identity in complex ways. Specifically, intersectionality theory offered the researchers "language to discuss multiple identities" and multiple identity theory "allows student affairs professionals to consider intersectionality in the context of student development theory" (p. 394). These theories were not created through the interaction between the researcher and participants; rather, they were used as a lens by which to promote critique and analysis for the purpose of increased understanding, improved praxis, and ultimately liberation.

Unlike positivism, interpretivism, and constructivism, subjectivism suggests that no one can interpret for others. It is only from an inside perspective that one can grasp meaning. Jürgen Habermas (1984) wrote, "What counts as fundamental is not the interpersonal relation between at least two speaking and acting subjects—a relation that refers back to reaching understanding in language—but the purposive activity of a solitary acting subject" (p. 279). Hence, the "I" of the researcher is imperative to acknowledge. Ellingson (2011) noted that subjectivism opens the opportunity for researchers to study their own lives and others. She then listed autoethnography and narrative inquiry as examples of methodologies that utilize subjectivism.

Also with an emancipatory purpose (and discussed in more detail in Chapter Three), Crotty (1998) noted that "the critical tradition . . . is even more suspicious of the constructed meanings that culture bequeaths to us" (p. 59). He went on to note that whereas interpretivists translate the world for greater understanding, critical research interprets to critique. Because some people lack sufficient influence or power to have mastery over their own lives, or because people are afraid of losing the influence and power they have, their communication can be distorted by those with more power. Hence, Habermas believed that just because certain views exist doesn't make them valid (Coomer, 1989). It is through communicative action and discourse that findings are deemed sound. Paulo Freire (1993) was also vitally instrumental in promoting critical thought. He believed that action without first reflecting with others is an empty promise. He wrote that for "people to come to feel like masters of the world explicitly or implicitly manifest in their own suggestions . . . this view of education starts with the conviction that it cannot present its own program but must search for this program dialogically with the people" (Freire, 1993, p. 103). Essentially,

> Critical qualitative research aims to understand itself as a practice that works with people to raise critical consciousness rather than merely describe social reality. A critical qualitative research project will typically be a project in conscientization. It will work with people to make implicit forms of knowing-how into explicit and criticizable forms of discursive knowledge. It will contribute to social change directly and thus not only by informing policy decisions. (Carspecken, 2012, p. 44)

Quaye (2012) used critical race theory (CRT) to ground his study on strategies educators use to prepare for discussions on race. He wrote, "CRT guided this study by enabling me to challenge dominant ideologies, one of which is colorblindedness" and "devote attention to the different ways in which race serves to privilege some and disproportionately create inequitable situations for many others" (p. 546).

Postmodernism, Poststructuralism, and Deconstruction

Lather (2007) lamented that the meanings of postmodernism and poststructuralism are "elusive, and marked by a proliferation of conflicting definitions" (p. 5) but offered her understanding of them. Generally, postmodernism "refers to the material and historical shifts of the global uprising of the marginalized, the revolution in communication technology, and the fissures of global multinational hyper-capitalism," whereas poststructuralism "refers more narrowly to a sense of the limits of Enlightenment rationality" (p. 5). Deconstruction "is both a method to interrupt binary logic through practices of reversal and displacement and an antimethod that is more an ontological claim" (Lather, p. 5). Abes (2009) and Abes and Kasch (2007) aptly demonstrated the impact of constructivism and queer theory as a poststructural perspective on the analysis of lesbian identity development. Utilizing both constructivism and poststructuralism led to not only increased understanding about identity but also about the influence of power, privilege, and oppression on identity formation. Continuing Lather's (2007) promotion of "troubling" (p. 26) theoretical congruence and essentialism, Abes (2009) used a "theoretical borderlands" approach to offer "viable perspectives that simultaneously describe the complexities of development" (p. 150). Lather (2007) illustrated this well when she wrote,

> A very classic move of deconstruction is you identify the binaries, you reverse them and then you use the energy of the reversal to try to get to the third place which is both-and AND neither-nor-both rational and emotional and something that is neither rational nor emotional. (p. 30)

Lather accomplishes this in the poignant book *Troubling the Angels: Women living with HIV/AIDS* (Lather & Smithies, 1997). Lather (2007) stated that the "troubling" in the title signified trying to "walk that fine line between neither demonizing nor angelizing. . .bringing the not-so-pretty stories" as well as the everyday aspects of these women's lives that are similar to the lives of other women (p. 31).

Comparing Epistemologies

Several authors have created charts highlighting the differences noted above using a variety of comparative criteria (e.g., Creswell, 2013; Lather 1991, 2007; Lincoln, Lynham, & Guba, 2011). These charts are dynamic and illustrate a snapshot of current thinking rather than static definitions. The differences are most obvious at their extremes and do not represent "rigid or unchanging differences/boundaries" (Sipe & Constable, 1996, p. 153). We also have constructed a chart (see Table 1.4) with instructive criteria in the context of higher education.

Because higher education values utilitarian knowledge, we have selected the nature of knowledge, knowledge claims, and values as important comparative criteria. We offer the comparison chart as a summary of what we have previously discussed.

Michael discovers that he is drawn to interpretivism in that he is compelled to uncover deeper but hidden nuances of safety and environment. We now turn to theoretical perspective as additional grounding that can inform Michael's research process.

Consideration Four: Situating a Study in a Theoretical Perspective

In Tables 1.2 and 1.4 noting our definitions of terms, we differentiated between theoretical perspective and framework. Here we will further clarify this distinction briefly and the usefulness of each in situating the research, but a more thorough discussion is in Chapter Three.

Theoretical Perspective

A theoretical perspective is "the philosophical stance informing the methodology and thus providing a context for the process and grounding its logic and criteria" (Crotty, 1998, p. 3). The research question or problem is located within a theoretical tradition (Marshall & Rossman, 2011). Broido and Manning (2002) offered that "Research cannot be conducted without the conscious use of underlying theoretical perspectives" (p. 434). There are a number of theoretical perspectives that give direction to research. Because of their number and complexity, we have devoted Chapter Three to their discussion. We acknowledge that, though some scholars refer to these theories as *movements* (Pinar et al., 1995), *philosophical approaches* (Bronner, 1999), *interpretive frameworks* (Creswell, 2013), and *paradigmatic stances* (Sipe & Constable, 1996), we agree with Crotty (1998) and Radhakrishnan (2003) and discuss them as theory.

Table 1.4 Comparing Epistemologies

	Positivism	Postpositivism	Constructionism/ Constructivism	Critical	Postmodern/ Poststructural
Nature of Reality (ontology)	Measure through observation	Imperfectly apprehendable	Outgrowth of human interaction	Perception can be flawed	Reality is co-created by mind and the environment
Values	Value neutral	Value neutral	Participant perspective	Participatory action	Personally relative
Relationship Between Researcher and Participants	Objective	Objective	Facilitator	Passionate participant	Shared research inquiry
Nature of Truth	Universal	Sometimes ambiguous	Individual	Purported truth can be flawed due to the oppressive nature of the world	Power is a factor in what and how we know
Purpose	Predict and compare	Conjecture and falsification	Understanding for improved praxis	Liberation	The form and nature of reality, what is valuable in human life
View of Knowledge (epistemology)	Verify hypotheses	Non-falsified hypotheses	Co-created with participants	Occurs through discourse, requires action, is transformative	Embedded in communities
Knowledge Claims	Claims need to be verified through scientific law	Claims need to be verified through structured process	Claims are made by individuals or groups	Claims present the unpresented	Claims are grounded in experience through interaction with others

Sources: Synthesized from writings of Creswell (2013); Crotty (1998); Lather (1991, 2007); and Lincoln, Lynham, and Guba (2011)

Let us return to Michael. As Michael seeks to refine his compelling interest, he has many questions. He does not know where or how to start and is feeling anxious about the research process. He worries whether he knows enough about his topic and research design to embark upon his study. He seeks out his advisor, who suggests that he look to theory for guidance.

Having done some preliminary reading about poststructural theory, Michael decides that feminist and queer theories offer guidance, not only on how he proceeds with his study but also about the phenomenon of safety itself. By using feminist theory as a lens, Michael is hoping that he might be better able to understand how gender plays a role in feeling safe. He also wonders how the coming-out process described in queer theory might illuminate the struggle with being truly present in a space that is hostile. How is it to come out as oneself in a place where safety is not expected? How is it to continually have to decide whether or how to come out with each new environment?

Theoretical Framework

Whereas theoretical perspective influences how the researcher will approach and design the study and influences how the researcher will approach the topic under study in more abstract terms, the theoretical framework offers suppositions that inform the phenomenon under study and comes from existing scholarly literature. The theoretical framework links the unsettled question to larger theoretical constructs.

Michael looks to campus environment theory to offer him insight into his study. This assists him in refining his question. He decides to use Moos's (1979) work in environment theory and Schlossberg's (1989) work on mattering and marginality to inform his topic. He reads campus environment theory (theoretical framework) simultaneously with feminist and queer theory (theoretical perspective). Both assist him in forming his question. As Michael proceeds, however, he will continually seek out literature to better inform his study. For example, in a study on White Being (Heidegger capitalizes Being), Jan initially gathered information on White racial identity theory, White privilege, authenticity, and guilt and shame to better inform her compelling interest (theoretical framework) while simultaneously looking to Heidegger's notions on phenomenology to guide the design of the study (theoretical perspective) (Arminio, 2001; Arminio & McEwen, 1996). Later, when collecting data through conversations, Jan became aware of the influence that busing to achieve integrated schools had on participants in their meaning making of race. Coles's (1993) work on service and school busing offered revealing insight (additional theoretical framework) of the experience of entering other American cultures by bus. She used this literature to better inform her of her compelling interest after initial data had been collected.

Figure 1.2 depicts philosophical stances and theory along a chronological continuum that inform research and their relationship to each other. Note that this is a snapshot of current understanding, which is dynamic and evolving.

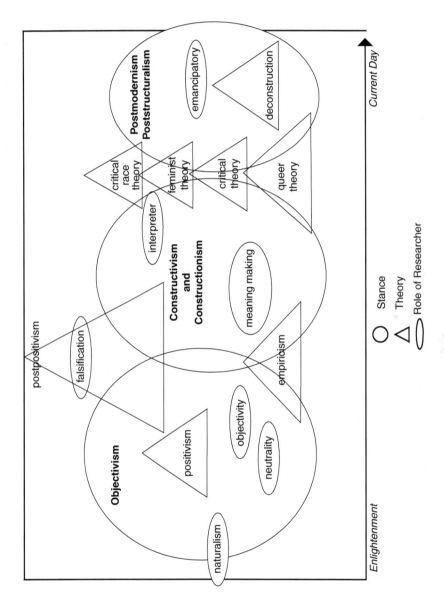

Figure 1.2 Philosophical Stances and Theories That Inform Research

With insights from theoretical perspective and theoretical framework, Michael now seeks to frame his statement of purpose and research question.

Consideration Five: Choosing a Question That Presses Upon Us

> [T]he path to all knowledge leads through the question.
> Gadamer (1960/1992, p. 363)

It is from a compelling interest that those engaged in a study find unsettled questions. Gadamer, a noted philosopher who wrote *Truth and Method,* considered one of the most important works in humanistic studies, noted that questioning is "more passion than an action. A question presses itself on us; we can no longer avoid it and persist in our accustomed opinion" (p. 366). Gadamer cautioned researchers to differentiate between a question and an opinion. A question is "not settled," whereas an opinion is. Several unsettled questions typically emerge from a compelling interest. Often, researchers contemplate a question that is either too broad or too narrow or that may generate several disparate unsettled questions from a compelling interest. A compelling interest offers the opportunity to dwell upon an unsettled question that should lead to a manageable study. Factors of do-ability assist in determining which of the unsettled questions to undertake. Below are samples of compelling interests that led to research questions in studies that have been published. Note that the worldview of the researcher framed how the question was posed.

- A pressing interest in men's identity development led to the questions of "(a) how do college men come to understand themselves as men; (b) how does this understanding of what it means to be a man change over time, if at all; and (c) what are the critical influences on the process?" (Edwards & Jones, 2009, p. 212).
- An interest in understanding how "leaders navigate power conditions" led to the question "How do faculty/staff grassroots leaders work with students to create change?" (Kezar, 2010, p. 452).
- To address the need "for a holistic picture of Latina/o doctoral student experiences. . . . The purpose of this study was to bring to the forefront the voices of Latina/o students in the process of attaining a Ph. D." (Gonzalez, Marin, Figueroa, Moreno, & Navia, 2002, pp. 541–542).
- A compelling interest in exploring lesbian college students' multiple dimensions of identity steered Abes and Kasch (2007) to the questions "What new insights about college students' negotiation of multiple identities are gained through the use of queer theory? What new insights into student development theory might queer theory uncover?" (p. 619).

Let us return to Michael and his efforts at situating his research. Michael has decided that his worldview is consistent with the constructivist and interpretive epistemologies because he has noticed how he learns through interactions with others. He believes that perception defines people's realities and that he is best able to learn about the experience of safety through interaction with others. He wants to "probe deep" with others about their experiences. He wonders how experiences of safety and feelings of inclusion relate. He refines his compelling interest into an unsettled question in language that represents and communicates his worldview: "What is the lived definition of campus safety for students who feel unsafe?"

Consideration Six: Research, Assessment, or Evaluation

For what purpose does Michael engage in this study? Another aspect of situating a study is whether the study is research, assessment, or evaluation. Upcraft and Schuh (2002) admitted that differentiating these may be seen as not very relevant. For our purposes, however, their differentiation is consequential. First, by exposing the differences, we highlight the point that qualitative methodologies can be used in assessments and evaluations, not only in research. Although many institutions have institutional research offices, assessment tasks typically are add-on responsibilities to educators outside of such offices (Ewell, 2002). Furthermore, many staff and administrators in higher education believe they are conducting assessments when in fact they are conducting evaluations. Differentiating these data-gathering activities recognizes the scholarship of assessment (Ewell, 2002).

Briefly, *research* concerns theory: forming it, confirming it, disconfirming it. Research assumes broader implications than one institution or program. *Assessment,* on the other hand, is more focused on the outcomes of participant programs, though this can be very broad as to include an entire institution. It does not infer individual student outcomes. Assessment includes "conceptualizing, planning, implementing, and evaluating the impact or outcomes of a purposeful, intentional event on an identified set of learners" (Keeling, Wall, Underhile, & Dungy, 2008, p. 10). The purpose of assessment is to guide practice rather than relate practice to theory. *Evaluation* is even more particular to a specific program and is concerned with the satisfaction, organization, and attendance of a program. As Figure 1.3 indicates, there is some overlap and the three are related.

For example, a program may be based on a theory particular to adult development that was created through research. Outcomes of the theory-based program are assessed to determine whether adult students are indeed gaining what was intended from the program. Using the assessment outcome data to make judgments about and then changing policy and practices related to the program is evaluation (Upcraft, 2003). The three are not mutually exclusive but rather have a dialectic relationship. Marshall and Rossman (2011) referred to this as the cycle of inquiry, which is depicted by the arrows in Figure 1.3. What is important to remember is that the means of conducting a study (design, sampling, and method for collecting and analyzing data), whether for research, assessment, or evaluation, can be similar, but the purpose of conducting research, assessment, and evaluation differs.

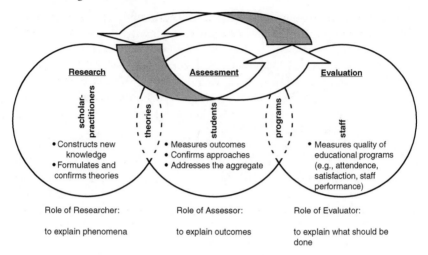

Figure 1.3 Confluence of Research, Assessment, and Evaluation
Sources: Upcraft and Schuh (2002); Upcraft (2003)

Michael has decided to situate his study as research because he is seeking to consider how students experience safety in a broad sense, rather than particular to any one program or institution. The secondary purpose of his study is to confirm theory about safety. In addition, he seeks insight that is beyond a bounded context. He proposes to explore more than just satisfaction or dissatisfaction with safety or who is safe and who is not (evaluation), but rather the questions of what safety is, how it is experienced, when it is not experienced, and why. How do students negotiate being safe? How do they make meaning of safety? Michael now has articulated his compelling question and has determined that his purpose is research. He also must contemplate how it is that he will be with the participants of his research study.

Consideration Seven: Reflecting on Research Positionality

Positionality describes the relationship between the researcher and his or her participants and the researcher and his or her topic. Research paradigm, theoretical perspective, and methodology all influence those relationships.

Fine (1994) believed that positionality does involve decision making on the part of the researcher, including the way in which researchers will represent or, more accurately, re-present participants. What is happening between the researcher and participants during the study? Researchers must consider not only what is said and what was not, but also what was quoted and what was not. What and who is being protected from public view and why? Are power structures being protected at the expense of participants? Are researchers protecting themselves? Are researchers even conscious of what they include or exclude? Lather (2007) called reflection on these questions as the "struggle against omnipotence" (p. 41). Researchers should not be in the position of omnipotence but rather "as witness giving testimony to the lives of others" (p. 41).

This concept is so important to good qualitative work that it will be addressed in several subsequent chapters, particularly in Chapter Two. For now, however, it is important for the reader to know that deciding upon the relationship of the researcher to the researched is one of the fundamental considerations that researchers must make as they embark upon their work.

Michael realizes that his experiences with feeling unsafe shape how he will engage with his participants. He also realizes that his role as researcher and graduate student; his gender, race, and sexual orientation; and his status as a first-generation college student influence the relationship he will establish with his participants. He considers how to engender trust with his participants throughout the research process.

Summary

Situating a study necessitates determining within what epistemology, theoretical perspective, theoretical framework, methodology, and method the question will be explored. Not appropriately situating a study is a frequent mistake made by researchers who believe that qualitative research is simply interviewing a few people and noting common themes. The analogy below may help differentiate phases of situating your study. If you were to consider your study a journey, the fundamental elements would be the following:

Destination: increased understanding about an unsettled question

Map: philosophical and theoretical perspective

Specific routes to take: methodology

Mode of transportation: method

There are several means and routes that will take you to the same destination. However, some routes are appropriate for some modes of travel. For example, you wouldn't travel very far by riding your bicycle on railroad tracks using an atlas as a guide. Yet, sometimes this happens when researchers frame a question not consistent with their worldview or use a method of collecting data that is not consistent with a particular methodology and not grounded in its founding philosophy. Apprentice researchers often find the notion that there are several appropriate ways to explore a question frustrating. Situating an unsettled question in an epistemology, theoretical perspective and framework, and methodology is crucial because often during inquiry questions arise that can only be answered from philosophical, theoretical, and methodological guidance (Maykut & Morehouse, 2001). For example, because narrative studies often emphasize the meaning attached to local environments (Chase, 2011), how participants make meaning of local environments is of particular interest.

A participant may share a poignant story that appears to be unrelated to the compelling interest but that may be included in the research report because of the nature of narrative inquiry.

Often in the research process there are delays along the inquiry journey. They are not always negative. In fact, often delays or detours can lead to unexpected insight. When this occurs, and it will, researchers should use the map (theoretical perspective and framework) and specific routes (methodology) to continue toward their destination.

Exercises

Chapter-related

1. Before reading this book, what would you have listed as main considerations in conducting a qualitative study? How has that changed since reading this first chapter?
2. What implications do your results of the worldview exercise have for you as a reader? As a consumer of research? As a creator of research?
3. Write an "autobiographical rendering" that explores who you are as a researcher. What are your assumptions about research? How did you come to *know* as you do? How were you socialized as a researcher and knower?

Research Process

1. As you consider situating a study, identify your compelling interests. What calls to you about these topics? What intrigues you about them? Which interests are you most willing to explore? How do you hope your research will impact higher education and student affairs?
    *   Circle the interests that "press upon you." Eliminate those for which you already hold a closed opinion. Eliminate those that are too narrow or specific and those that are too broad. Consider the do-ability of your list.
2. Of those interests remaining, draft several questions that translate your interests into research.
3. How do these questions reflect your worldview?

2 Meeting the Obligations of High Quality Inquiry

Many institutions of higher education list critical thinking—using sound criteria on which to base an idea or opinion—as one of the principle goals of student learning (Baxter Magolda, 2001). Judging the merit of inquiry is an outgrowth of the concern with how to distinguish between "true and false appearances" and "belief or opinion," which dates back to ancient Greek philosophers (Smith, 1993, p. 3). Because criteria for judging the worthiness of an argument or a study have traditionally been grounded in the positivistic paradigm, tensions exist related to judging qualitative work. These tensions revolve around the topics below, the exploration of which is the purpose of this chapter:

1. Qualitative studies should be judged on different criteria than quantitative studies. Criteria to determine worthiness include general research guidelines and paradigmatic criteria.
2. Specific selected research traditions in the qualitative paradigm (e.g., grounded theory, case study, phenomenology, ethnography, and narrative) call for following specific guidelines.
3. Recognizing the relationship between researcher and the researched is an essential criterion for judging qualitative research.
4. Criteria can also be derived from complementary methodology, method, and analysis that lead researchers to offer recommendations for the greater good.

More specifically, this chapter addresses general guidelines that inform all research; paradigmatic criteria that include controversies, conflicts, and confluences; and criteria specific to methodological approach.

Adhering to obligations for determining worthiness in research is so imperative that in this second edition we moved this chapter immediately following initial considerations in situating a study. Expectations for worthiness influence research processes subsequently discussed in this book (design, sampling, data collection, and data interpretation). We begin this examination of criteria being clear that, contrary to some criticism of qualitative research, there are standards and obligations required of qualitative inquiry. "Anything" does not go (Smith & Hodkinson, 2008, p. 419). According to Smith and Deemer (2000), poor qualitative work is merely an assertion lacking an articulated grounding that provides a framework for the research design and findings. Even though qualitative work acknowledges relativism, "As individuals, we must make judgments, and as members of social groups, however loosely organized, we must be witness to situations in which our individual judgments are played out with the judgments of other individuals" (Smith & Deemer, 2000, p. 887).

Because qualitative and quantitative research have different purposes, the criteria for judging quality must be reflective of those purposes (Morrow, 2005). For example, judging the worthiness of qualitative inquiry is not determined solely upon whether or not the researcher implemented the correct procedures as in quantitative research (Rossman & Rallis, 2010; Smith, 1993). These researchers might be considered "non-foundationalists," who stress understanding and relationships over the control of prediction (Denzin, 2011, p. 464). Rather, a study's participants, readers, and discipline all are involved in the judgment process through dialogue centering on criteria. Lincoln, Lynham, and Guba (2011) referred to this as "dialogic efforts that are clearly themselves forms of 'moral discourse'" (p. 121). Criteria for judging the quality of research "must be thought of not as abstract standards but rather as socially constructed lists of characteristics" (Smith & Hodkinson, 2008, p. 420). Consensus is reached about judgments of research through reading, dialogue, discourse, and subsequent research. Hammersley (1990) called this a communal assessment. Lincoln (1998) also referred to the community as an arbiter of quality. Our discussion of the communal assessment of research criteria will encompass its language and process; general, paradigmatic, and methodological criteria; and inquiry and relational competence.

The Language and Process of Community Assessment

Several researchers have advocated for the use of the term *goodness* to indicate quality criteria in qualitative inquiry (Arminio & Hultgren, 2002; Lincoln & Guba, 2000; Marshall, 1990; Morrow, 2005; Smith, 1993). This allows for the "breaking out from the shadow" of quantitative criteria and allows "the *qualis* of qualitative work to be pursued on its own terms" (Arminio & Hultgren, 2002, p. 446). The word *qualitative* is a derivative of the word *qualis*, meaning "what it is," but is still judged by what it is not—values and criteria from a positivistic paradigm. The etymology of the word *rigor*, often used to depict the criteria of quantitative work, is stiffness, exactness, and severity (Hoad, 1986). Because qualitative work is grounded on foundations far different from those of quantitative work, it is only reasonable that criteria for evaluating research grounded in different epistemologies be different. However, we must acknowledge that qualitative research is currently under attack by the "audit culture" and "evidence based movement" imposed by some grant funding and government agencies (Denzin, 2011, p. 647; also Smith & Hodkinson, 2008, pp. 411–434). Agencies such as the National Research Council and the Society for Research on Educational Effectiveness are defining all research as that borrowed from medical science. This is research that includes randomized controlled experiments. These agencies and associations promote criteria that are *"foundationalist"* in nature, meaning that all research should be judged by the same criteria (e.g., internal and external validity, generalizability, transferability, confirmability, transparency, and warrantability) (Denzin, 2011, p. 646; Smith & Hodkinson, 2008). Prominent qualitative researchers vehemently oppose this paradigmatic transposing of criteria.

Indeed researchers should pay attention to general guidelines that encompass all research, and also paradigmatic criteria, and criteria for methodological approaches (Morrow, 2005). Figure 2.1 depicts criteria on a continuum from general to more specific.

There are criteria for all research and then criteria that are more specific according to grounding theoretical perspectives and methodological approaches. We will discuss below general guidelines that inform all research; paradigmatic criteria that include controversies, conflicts, and confluences; and criteria specific to methodological approach.

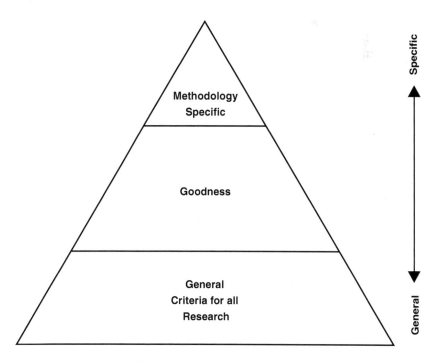

Figure 2.1 General Research Criteria

General Research Guidelines

Regardless of the research paradigm, the following are criteria for determining the worth of any study:

- Consistency must exist between the research question, data collection, and analysis procedures;
- Collection and analysis procedures must be correctly and competently applied;
- Researchers must be aware of the background knowledge of the topic;
- The researcher must differentiate why some conclusions were embraced and others discounted; and
- Researchers must articulate the value of this study to practice in a language that is accessible to a wide range of readers.

First, consistency must exist between the research question, data collection, and analysis procedures. The "research question should drive data collection techniques and analysis rather than vice versa" (Howe & Eisenhart, 1990, p. 6). Second, collection and analysis procedures must be correctly and competently applied. Third, researchers must be aware of the background knowledge of the topic (theoretical framework, as discussed in Chapter One) and background assumptions of the researcher connecting this study with previous studies. For example, "If the results of one study contradict those of another (or several others), then some sort of explanation of why this occurred is in order" (Howe & Eisenhart, 1990, p. 6). Fourth, the researcher must differentiate why some conclusions were embraced and others discounted. Lastly, researchers must articulate the value of this study to practice in a language that is accessible to a wide range of readers. This allows for the necessary opportunity for debate within the discipline. Smith (1993) believed that all research should provide evidence that it is reasonable, responsive to challenges presented during the process, open to others' points of view, and honest.

Now that we have discussed criteria for judging research across paradigms, we will spend significant space differentiating the criteria between paradigms. Specifically, we discuss criteria associated with philosophical and theoretical perspective, trustworthiness, inquiry and relational competence, social identities, positionality, power relations, and reflexivity.

Paradigmatic Criteria

Though the criteria above are appropriate skeletal criteria for assisting in determining the worthiness of a study, as Figure 2.2 illustrates, additional specific criteria must be added to these general criteria: criteria specific to a research paradigm, meaning in simplistic terms differences in qualitative and quantitative research.

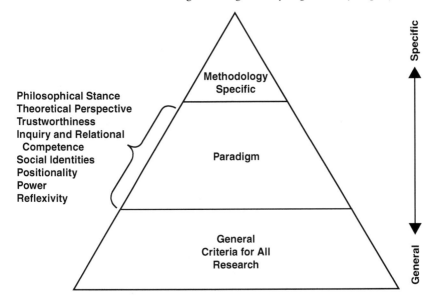

Philosophical Stance
Theoretical Perspective
Trustworthiness
Inquiry and Relational
  Competence
Social Identities
Positionality
Power
Reflexivity

Methodology
Specific

Paradigm

General
Criteria for All
Research

Specific

General

Figure 2.2 General to Specific Criteria

We offer these criteria to provide guidance for conducting inquiry as well as for judging the worth of inquiry.

As a paradigmatic criterion, our obligation as researchers requires that the philosophical stance and theoretical perspective is stated and evidence is provided that what is outlined is actually followed. We have noticed that some published studies do not meet this criterion. Moreover, researchers must embody, discuss, and illustrate the obligations for quality research in a language consistent with the philosophical grounding being used (Arminio & Hultgren, 2002). Again, it is important to keep in mind that, unlike the objective positivistic paradigm, there is no "mechanical-making procedure" (J. K. Smith, 1990, p. 184; also Rossman & Rallis, 2010, pp. 379–391) for determining worthiness of the study. Instead, worthiness is determined by the reader, participants, and by discussion and debates within the disciplinary community (Lather, 2007; Lincoln, Lynham, & Guba, 2011).

The philosophical stance includes whether the study used a constructionist, constructivist, interpretivist, critical, participatory, or poststructural grounding. Study authors would also state the corresponding theoretical underpinnings, including theoretical perspective (e.g., critical race theory or feminism) and theoretical framework (theories or literature that offer suppositions about the phenomenon under study). We would also expect to see references to and quotes from authors from whom the researcher found philosophical and theoretical inspiration and direction.

For example, in her article *The Developmental Dimensions of Recognizing Racist Thoughts* (Torres, 2009), Vasti noted that she used a constructivist, grounded theory approach. In describing their research on how graduate students construct spirituality in preparation programs, Rogers and Love (2007) explained that their research was conducted "from a constructivist paradigmatic stance" and "specifically an interpretivist perspective" (p. 690). They went on to explain,

> Operating from this perspective made sense because we sought to produce descriptive analyses and understandings of the particular socially and idiosyncratically constructed phenomena we were exploring—the place of spirituality in curriculum and pedagogy and the role of spirituality in one's professional identity and practice. (p. 690)

In essence, to meet this criterion, authors must state their philosophical/paradigmatic stance, theoretical framework, and theoretical perspective and show evidence that all are complementary. Together they offer grounding, direction, and insight necessary to implement a study. That being said, Kinchloe, McLaren, and Steinberg (2012) reminded researchers that theory is dynamic; it changes along with perceptions of the world. Freire (1993/1970) wrote that "reality is really a process, undergoing constant transformation" (p. 75) and encouraged educators to go beyond current understanding for the purpose of emancipation. One means to engage in the process of theorizing as going beyond is through the concept of *bricolage*. A bricoleur is one who makes use of many tools that are available to complete a task (Kinchloe et al., 2012). Denzin and Lincoln (2011) offered quilt making and a film montage as examples of bricolage. In regards to research, this means bringing together a "set of representations that are fitted to the specifics of a complex situation" (p. 4). Experienced researchers use the philosophical, paradigmatic, and theoretical tools available to "attack . . . complexity, uncovering the invisible artifacts of power and culture and documenting the nature of their influence not only on their own works, but on scholarship in general" (Kincheloe et al., 2012, p. 21). As mentioned in Chapter One, Abes (2009) and Abes and Kasch (2007) provided fine examples of bricolage. Their studies used "multiple and contradictory theoretical perspectives" (Abes, p. 142), to create new meaning of understanding about identity (this is further discussed in Chapter Nine). The multiple and contradictory theories used were constructivism and queer theory (a poststructural theory). Lather (2007) described her experience in this regard as "my textual practices move toward some place of both/and and neither/nor, where I trouble the very categories I can't think without" (p. 41). However, researchers must first understand paradigmatic and theoretical perspectives before they can piece together multiple and contradictory theoretical tools. Lather (2007) stated that she requires her students to begin their qualitative research experiences utilizing interpretivism as she believes that it was easier for them to apply. In any case, authors must state the philosophical stance, theoretical framework, and theoretical perspective and show evidence that all are complementary unless experienced researchers offer evidence that they are serving as a bricoleur.

The terms most associated with qualitative research criteria are trustworthiness and triangulation. We turn there now to continue our exploration of obligations for high-quality research within the qualitative paradigm.

Trustworthiness

Many readers are most likely familiar with the term *trustworthiness*. This is typically understood as the qualitative paradigmatic means by which to assure a study is of high quality. We also assume that readers are familiar with the traditional obligations of quantitative work—reliability and validity. To break out of the shadow of quantitative research, some qualitative researchers believe that the language used to judge qualitative work should be different than that of quantitative inquiry (Arminio & Hultgren, 2002). However, others such as Kvale and Brinkman (2009) preserve the language of quantitative research. They stated:

> We retain the traditional concepts of reliability and validity, which are also terms in common language—as reflected in sentences such as "Your passport is not valid," "Your argument is not valid," and "Is he reliable?"—with the concept of reliability having not only a methodological but also a moral meaning, as when we speak of a reliable person. (p. 245)

Talburt (2004) viewed validity as confirming " 'real' events in 'real' lives" (p. 81) and so advocated instead for research to "speculate about unexpected connections, relations, and implications. These connections . . . will be necessarily incomplete, tentative, and unverifiable" (p. 92).

Other authors and researchers promote parallel language of criteria. Morrow (2005) offered the following analogous terms:

Table 2.1 Analogous Terms

Quantitative	Qualitative
Internal Valididty	Credibility
External Validity or Generalizability	Transferability
Reliability	Dependability
Objectivity	Confirmability

Furthermore, Patton (2002) paralleled rigor with trustworthiness. Some authors believed that trustworthiness is achieved through the parallel quantitative and qualitative processes named in the chart included here.

Essentially, trustworthiness is associated with confidence in the research findings. Means to demonstrate trustworthiness encourage confidence in the findings. Patton (2002) associated trustworthiness with authenticity and Creswell (2013) with validation. Lincoln, Lynham, and Guba (2011) asked these questions in determining trustworthiness:

> Are these findings sufficiently authentic (isomorphic to some reality, trustworthy, related to the way others construct their social worlds) that I may trust myself in acting on their implications? More to the point, would I feel sufficiently secure about these findings to construct social policy or legislation based on them? (p. 120)

Still other researchers lament that these parallels impose procedure over relational ethics. Talburt (2004) wrote that such parallels strive to find a confirmable truth when finding "new realms of the possible" (p. 93), is the paradigmatic aim. Rossman and Rallis (2010) wrote, "The paramount principles of justice, beneficence, and respect for human beings are often reduced to the procedural matters of gaining informed consent" (p. 382). Hence, their definition of trustworthiness emphasized the relational. They see trustworthiness as "both competent practice and ethical considerations for the participants with the underlying demand that the relational matters" (p. 383). We discuss aspects of inquiry and relational competence that are ways to ensure trustworthiness.

Inquiry Competence

According to Morrow (2005), ways of embracing trustworthiness include credibility, dependability, transferability, and confirmability. *Credibility* occurs through prolonged engagement in the field and the use of others to confirm findings. These others can include research participants (this is typically referred to as member checking), and peer or expert reviews. Lather (2003) stressed the importance of ensuring "face validity," which is "recycling categories, emerging analysis, and conclusions back through at least a subsample of the respondents" (p. 206). However, she cautioned researchers against seeing member checking as verification but rather "as an elaboration on the emerging findings and treated as additional data" (p. 198). Talburt (2004) concurred with Lather's caution and stressed "speculating about unexpected connections, relations, and complications" (p. 92).

Qualitative competence also requires "multi layered" (Morrow, 2005, p. 252) descriptions, or what others refer to as thick descriptions (Talburt, 2004). These are descriptions that are detailed, expressive, and explicit explanations of the phenomenon under study.

To be credible, Morrow believed researchers must offer rationale for why the amount of data collected was reasonable. Beginning researchers often ask "How many interviews must I conduct" or "How many participants must I include?" These are questions asked from the shadow of quantitative research. Researchers are obliged to collect data until there is more than sufficient coverage, where a point of saturation is reached, where no additional data collection is useful. For some research, that may be field work that takes years to complete or an intense immersion experience of a few weeks. Our experience is that researchers err in spending too little time in the field collecting data rather than too much.

Transferability requires that findings are meaningful to the reader. *Dependability* means that the inquiry processes are explicit and include a "chronology of research activities and processes" (Morrow, 2005, p. 252). *Confirmability* requires the researcher to tie findings with data and analysis. Smith and Hodkinson (2008) also offered *plausibility* to this list of what they call "neorealist criteria," "a commitment to believe that there is a real world independent of our knowledge, but that we can never be sure that we have portrayed that world accurately" (p. 414). Plausibility seeks to address whether research findings are likely to be true given current knowledge. Although they described these criteria, Smith and Hodkinson (2008) also resisted procedural criteria, acknowledging:

> Judgments . . . are practical and discursively considered. When we make judgments we generally can specify some of the reasons, but other things seem to be out there—what might be called a surplus of meaning that seems to stand just beyond our grasp, just beyond our ability to completely specify or articulate. (p. 421)

Researchers must offer verification that they did not reshape the data to merely meet their assumptions. As Smith (1993) suggested, "What the reader should see is evidence that the researcher did not rework the data so that it would be in line with the researcher's pre-established framework or theoretical interests" (p. 112). Furthermore, "The researcher must present the best possible case for their claims" (J.K. Smith, 1990, p. 185). The researcher "must document the extent to which theoretical perspectives were altered, revised, or deepened" by the data (J.K. Smith, 1993 p. 113). What were the surprises? Noting changing perspectives between one's early assumptions and one's findings would be such a means through which to document altering or deepening perspectives. So, too, could peer reviews, expert reviews, or human science dialogues, where a researcher consults with a knowledgeable peer, an expert in the field, or a group of both.

Substantiating that an important purpose of qualitative research is to provide an avenue for the illumination of multiple perspectives, Lincoln, Lynham, and Guba (2011) promoted the obligation of *fairness*, meaning that "all stakeholder views, perspectives, values, claims, concerns, and voices should be apparent in the text" (p. 122). They emphasized a commitment to honor marginalized voices so that they are represented. These authors also emphasized the importance of research that prompts action. Lincoln, Lynham, and Guba

(2011) referred to this as *catalytic* and *tactical* authenticities and Lather (2007) as *research* praxis. We discuss praxis in greater detail later.

Demonstrating multiple perspectives is often achieved through *triangulation*, a means of confirming findings through several data collection methods (Creswell, 2013; Denzin & Lincoln, 2011). An example of this would be to authenticate perspectives of interview participants through observation and document review. Some researchers such as Creswell (2011) emphasized the importance of triangulating data as an obligation of worthiness, while others lament its technical nature (Denzin & Lincoln, 2011; Talburt, 2004). The selected methodology guides the researcher as to the appropriateness of triangulating data. Though very important in a case study, it is less important in a phenomenological inquiry and ethnography because it is participants' articulation of their experiences that is paramount.

Having briefly explored aspects of research that Rossman and Rallis (2010) would consider competence criteria (credibility, dependability, transferability, confirmability, fairness, and triangulation), we now turn to relational research competence. Many researchers believe these competences to be more salient in determining the worthiness of a study.

Relational Competence

Relational competence includes important issues such as what researchers bring to the research process (social identities, researcher positionality, power relationships, researcher pre-understanding), the relationship researchers have with participants (reflexivity, or participants as multicultural subjects), and the evolving role of the researcher. Several authors have been concerned with how the "moral principles guiding research practice have become trivialized and proceduralized" (Rossman & Rallis, 2010, p. 380). Lather (2007) called this the crisis of representation. How is it that researchers "decenter [their] authorial voice via unmediated participant voices" (p. 39)? Talburt (2004) too saw technical competence as inappropriately determining the elusive "real story" (p. 92) rather than the more important purpose of research as posing new perspectives of the possible. In beginning to contemplate relational competencies, we propose the following reflection questions that are appropriate for researchers in the context of higher education:

1. Why is it that I am engaged in the present study? What is it about me and my experiences that lead me to this study?
2. What personal biases and assumptions do I bring with me to this study?
3. What is my relationship with those in the study?

These questions are addressed through:

*   self-reflection,
*   reflection with other researchers,

- reflection with participants, and
- reflection on the theoretical perspective and framework (what we know from previous research and related literature).

Researchers must contemplate why it is they are engaged in the study. Arminio and Hultgren (2002) referred to this as "autobiographical rendering" (p. 455). Such rendering illuminates why *I* turn to the question. Because qualitative researchers are the instrument of analysis, especially in interpretive and constructivist designs, their interests, values, experiences, and purpose influence the analysis. Consequently, knowing this autobiographical insight is imperative for the user of the research to understand more about the research context and to make judgments about whether the study meets the obligations of worthiness.

The introduction and literature review sections of a written report offer an opportunity for this autobiographical rendering. Hence, it is no accident that these are written before data are collected. Journaling is another means through which to reflect on why one turns to these questions. Also, before data are collected, researchers need to inform participants as to their connection to the study. For example, in their article examining the spiritual struggle of college students, Rockenbach, Walker, and Luzader (2012) wrote:

> Although space prohibits a fuller treatment of our own spiritual struggle biographies, we have included a few sentences from our reflections to illuminate the perspectives each of us brought to the study. Alyssa identifies as a mainline Protestant Christian who emphasizes the progressive and generative aspects of her faith tradition. Her spiritual struggle has involved observing and experiencing the implications of conflicts between traditional religious beliefs that perpetuate prejudice and exclusivity and social justice values that promote equality, compassion, inclusion, and pluralism. Coretta identifies as a Protestant Christian who focuses on the compassionate and relational components of her faith tradition. As a person of devout faith, Coretta's greatest spiritual struggle involves advocating on behalf of religious and spiritual minorities and members of the LGBT community, particularly in her interactions with other devout Christians. Jordan currently identifies as religiously/spiritually explorative. He was raised in a mainline Protestant church, but withdrew from the community because of ideological differences. Although Jordan does not have a current faith of practice, he has engaged in the historical study of many of the world's religions. Current spiritual struggles for Jordan revolve around his concern regarding elitist rhetoric within different faiths and his belief that truth is not singular but may be represented by multiple interpretations. (p. 58)

As this example demonstrates, the autobiographical rendering does not entail voyeurism where researchers become engrossed in "detailed self analysis" (Lather, 2007, p. 44), but rather offers a sincere sense of what the researcher brings to the research endeavor that is important for the reader to know. To explore more in depth the nature and influences of relational criteria on the research process, four areas of relational criteria will be discussed: (a) social identities, (b) researcher positionality, (c) power relationships and their influence on persons oppressed by social power structures, and (d) reflexivity.

Social identities.   One of the issues that must be integrated into all phases of the research design in order to maintain congruence in the research process is the influence of the researcher's own social identities and the social identities of participants on the research process. This influence is particularly apparent in the interpretation of data and the way in which research participants are represented in the presentation of findings and discussion. The element of power is inherent in the relationship between the researcher and participant and is played out in the interpretation and representation of participant stories. Because of how power operates in U.S. society and the pervasive nature of power, those conducting research both within and outside their own communities and social identities are influenced. This power element requires that the issue of social identities be carefully considered so that researchers recognize their own role and not "hide behind the alleged cloak of neutrality" (Weis & Fine, 2000, p. 34). Social identities

> explain how people's conception of who they are (their self-concept) is associated with their membership of social groups and categories, and with group and intergroup behaviors. [Social identity theory] defines group membership in terms of people's identification, definition, and evaluation of themselves as members of a group (social identity) and specifies cognitive, social interaction and societal processes that interact to produce characteristic group phenomena. (Hogg, 2010, p. 749)

When a research project includes interaction with individuals who belong to one, or more, of these social identities (i.e., race, gender, sexual orientation, social class, and religion), it is critical to consider the impact this may have on the project and decisions the researcher must make. Researchers must pay attention to the role of social identities within the context of any research study. In addition, researchers should understand their own position by examining what social statuses they possess (either visibly, invisibly, or unconsciously) that illustrate power or privilege and recognize how their own social identities might be perceived by those with differing social identities.

Researcher positionality.   One of the "enduring concepts" of feminist research is standpoint research that replaced the "essentialized universalized woman with the idea of the situated woman with experiences and knowledge specific to her place in the material division of labor and racial stratification systems" (Olesen, 2011, p. 130). At the core of feminist research is the belief that there is no one truth or authority (Olesen, 2011). This core belief is the basis for acknowledging the influence of one's own identity and sociocultural history on the research process. An example of this would be when a researcher positions herself according to her race or ethnicity, indicating it as an important element in the research process. For example, Ayala (2000) stated: "The second voice speaks through standpoint theory, where I position myself as a Latino researcher whose interpretations stem from theory and biography" (p. 102). Researchers' positions indicate the influences that come from their own social identities. Acknowledging one's position in the context of the research helps the audience understand the influence of social identities on the research process.

Interpretation of data and representation of participants are linked to the concepts of positioning and standpoint. The notion of understanding one's own position (or standpoint) also describes taking into account the experiences and social identities of those being studied and of the researcher, while considering how societal structures have constrained marginal, oppressed, or dominated groups. Rossman and Rallis (2010) called this "simultaneous awareness of the self and other, and of the interplay between the two" (p. 384). Understanding one's standpoint and position before entering into a research project is imperative so as to guard against hearing, seeing, reading, and presenting results that conform to the researcher's experiences and assumptions about self and other, rather than honoring the participants' voices in the study. A researcher must understand his or her position and power within societal structures in order to attend to her or his potential biases. Researchers must also guard against assuming their experiences are similar to those of their participants. Without reflection on the influence of social identities in the research process, interpretation and representation becomes more about telling the researcher's story and less about staying true to the words and stories of participants. Lincoln (1997) made this point well:

> Research participant's (subject's) words were used to provide evidence of some point which researchers wished to make (indeed, I have chosen particular quotations from my research respondents for exactly and precisely the same reason—to buttress some point of my own interpretation, not necessarily a point of theirs). (p. 43)

It is important to clarify whose story is being told and to illuminate for the reader how the participants' words are being interpreted. How researchers position themselves within a research study is critical to understanding the lens used to interpret the data. Ayala (2000) referred to this as "voicing my position(ality)" (p. 103). She described her voice in this manner:

> I write as a Latina, embodying what Hidalgo (1998) calls an "overlapping insider/outsider status." This affects how I interview, what I find, how I interpret what I find. An insider to the community of respondents I am interviewing, I share the Latino cultural citizenship. . . . My outsider status stems from the stretch of our educational, national, and generational differences. (p. 103)

In a description of her positionality, Ayala is clear how her insider status impacts the research process (approach to interviewing and the interpretation of the data), but she also makes clear what makes her an outsider (education, nationality, and generation). Understanding both positions is important to the research process. Without this understanding, the researcher's assumptions dominate the interpretation and analysis of the research process.

According to Olesen (2011), a commonality about much feminist research is raising the questions "Whose knowledges? Where and how obtained, by whom, from whom, and for what purposes? (p. 129). What she called "transformative feminist thought" moves feminist research from Whiteness in Western frames to postcolonial feminists who question whether traditionally subjugated women will be "forever silenced by . . . elite thought" (p. 130). Consequently, women from within the culture under study should collaborate with the researcher on the research project so that the voice of insiders and outsiders are included in the process. Although intra-group belonging is helpful in understanding different cultures, it is by no means a simple task to be an insider either. When Vasti began her longitudinal work with Latino/a college students, she considered being an insider (Latina) as an advantage in her approach to the research. What she did not expect was the personal reaction that occurred as a result of being an insider. In an article focused on the process of research, Vasti wrote:

> I found myself wanting to be a practitioner rather than a researcher. This desire arose as students told me their stories; some of them resembled my own story. Because this study is on a predominantly Anglo campus, this was the first time several of the freshmen felt comfortable talking about their conflicting feelings and the struggles they were experiencing around the choices they were forced to make about their culture of origin and the environment in which they live at college. (Torres & Baxter Magolda, 2002, p. 479)

These conflicting feelings and reactions caused Vasti to question her stance as a researcher and whether or not she was tending to the students or being more focused on maintaining her role as a researcher. Over time, Vasti established a rapport with the participants in her study that allowed her to explore issues seldom mentioned in the literature. Yet this rapport comes with responsibility to interpret voices in a way that is authentic to *their* experiences. This demonstrates that even when ethnicity and culture are taken into account, the researcher can still experience difficult situations.

One of the elements that is most influenced by differences (and commonalities) in social identities is the analytic and interpretive process. The interpretation of the data is inevitably impacted by our own experiences and worldview. This requires that special attention be given to how our own and the participants' social identities influence what is said and what is understood. For example, in a thesis chaired by two faculty members, both of whom identified as members of the GLBT community, a graduate student explored the experiences of undergraduate students who identified as allies to GLBT students. The researcher considered herself an ally. This identification and positionality as both researcher and ally influenced how she understood what her participants said and how she interpreted their stories. One of her participants told a story about a friend who occasionally told gay jokes. However, the participant rationalized this by suggesting that the friend did not tell jokes in front of gay people and really did not mean to be offensive. Because the researcher so wanted to tell the positive story (her story) of ally behavior, she did not deal with this comment in the initial stages of analysis. Her advisors were able to engage the researcher in conversations about what really constitutes ally behavior. The differences in interpretation are critical to understanding the phenomenon under study and impacts whose story is really being told. The result was a much more nuanced and complex analysis and interpretation of her data that emphasized the situational nature of ally behavior, rather than starting from the premise that her participants were always engaging in ally behavior (Gribbin, 2005).

Other examples might include the study of women without considering the sociohistorical forces that influence societal views of women. Using theoretical perspectives that are focused on majority White students and imposing that perspective on students of color is a frequent and misguided decision some researchers make. Trustworthiness requires researchers to recognize themselves, their relationships with those involved in the study, and their relationship with the topic itself.

Power relations.   Within the qualitative research literature, much has been written about the relationship between the researcher and participants. The literature refers to this connection as the relationship between the knower (researcher) and known (participant) as an evolution of going from a separateness orientation (objectivity) to an orientation where inquiry is a form of interaction that influences both the knower and the known (co-construction of knowledge) (Lincoln, Lynham, & Guba, 2011). One area not always discussed in this literature is the existence of power differences in the self-other relationship.

Privilege and power must be acknowledged in the research process to understand, to the best of our abilities, the experiences of participants from different social identities. Racism, sexism, and other isms yet to be identified are part of the fabric that makes up the national identity of the United States and can only change when power hierarchies are changed (Torres, Howard-Hamilton, & Cooper, 2003). Unfortunately, the current political and funding context pushes researchers to not analyze their positions of power and privilege or recognize their own actions as oppressive (Cannella & Lincoln, 2012). In any case, researchers must acknowledge the potential position of power they hold as researchers and as a result of their social identities. Kincheloe and Steinberg's (2012) concept of "indigenous knowledge" (p. 348), the multidimensional body of understandings, assists in making this connection. They wrote:

> Western scholars dedicated to the best interests of indigenous peoples often unwittingly participate in the hegemonic process. . . . Is the study

of indigenous peoples and their knowledges in itself a process of Euro-peanization? If [researchers] are to operate as agents of justice they must understand the dynamics at work in the world of indigenous people. . . . Western terms . . . inadvertently fragment knowledge systems in ways that subvert the holism of indigenous ways of understanding the world. (pp. 347–348)

Power and social identity is at work, too, when middle and upper class feminist researchers concentrate on issues of great interest to them while ignoring the issues that are salient to poor women.

One example related to power that many researchers take for granted is the use of the informed consent form and the power imbalances this form represents between researcher and participant. Weis and Fine (2000) came to the understanding that "the introduction of an informed consent form requires analysis as much as that which is routinely and easily considered data" (p. 42). They elaborated that rapport can be unraveled when the informed consent form is given to the participant because what the form actually sets out is differential power relationships between researcher and participant. Chapter Eight provides further discussion of the role and ethics of the informed consent form. Nonetheless, it is important to note that the institutionalized human subjects review process of informed consent exists on the assumption of individual autonomy rather than on social contextual ethics or relational research competencies (Christians, 2011).

Power also can inhibit establishing rapport and trust with participants. In his study, Duneier (2004) reflected on his experiences and acknowledged that one cannot

begin with the assumption that special rapport or trust is always a precondition for doing successful fieldwork. And don't be so presumptuous as to believe that you have trust or even special rapport with the people you are trying to write about, even when it seems you do. (p. 209)

This statement articulates the reality that researchers must face when working from a position of power and privilege, particularly in making decisions about how to conduct the study, what to ask participants, how to interpret and represent what they hear from participants, and what implications will be suggested. All of these decisions are made by the researcher and ultimately must be made explicit to the audience in order for those hearing or reading the research to know how a particular phenomenon was investigated and the influences that arose as a result of the interaction between the participants and the researcher.

When Vasti began her longitudinal study on the experiences of Latino/a college students, she used a research team as inquiry auditors during the analysis phase. During this process, a White research team member would interpret a behavior using the norms of the majority White societal status rather than understanding the status of the participant. One example that emerged early on in the study is the understanding of autonomy. For many Anglos (Whites), autonomy entails separation from parents and independent thinking that is not influenced by parents (Erikson, 1968). Within many Latino cultures, separation from parents is not culturally acceptable and independent thinking is seen as making one's choice within the context of the family. These two interpretations of autonomy and the types of decisions first-year Latino/a students relayed in the interview created many challenging and value oriented discussions among the research team. These discussions allowed researchers to explore biases and worldviews. The construction of equal power among all involved occurred when multiple interpretations of autonomy were considered.

Not having a similar lived experience causes a different set of tensions that a researcher must consider and work through. In the example above, the White research team member may have come to understand her culturally biased assumptions about what autonomy is by connecting her own experiences of being misunderstood with how she misunderstood Vasti's Latino/a participants. The use of inquiry auditors is one of the techniques recommended to establish trustworthiness in the research process, and in the example provided, illustrates how issues of trustworthiness are connected to positionality and standpoint.

Uncovering researcher preunderstandings.   What personal biases do I bring with me? This question seeks to underscore the researcher's preunderstandings by acknowledging one's assumptions. Indeed, "It is better to make explicit our understandings . . . to hold them deliberately at bay and even to turn this knowledge against itself, as it were, thereby exposing its shallow or concealing character" (van Manen, 1990, p. 47). Researcher assumptions about the research question should then be triangulated with literature that confirms the researcher's assumptions and literature that contradicts the researcher's assumptions, stating why the contradiction. Again, journaling and the introduction and literature review sections of a written report offer an opportunity for this clarification of assumptions. In this regard, Davis (2002) explained:

> For me, this meant being aware that I might try to make the interview data fit my preconceptions (Self) rather than allowing the participants (Other) to speak for themselves. I am drawn to the study of gender and men due to my own curiosity about the impact of gender on men's development, but I also have political, social, and cultural views related to this topic. I also clearly have biases associated with my own development as a White, heterosexual, Italian American male. As I read transcripts and listened to participants, for example, I had to intentionally avoid relying on initial intuitive interpretations rooted in my own experience. (p. 512)

Reflexivity.   Another relational competence is the necessity of reflecting critically on the human as instrument. This is referred to as reflexivity (Lincoln,

Lynham, & Guba, 2011). How one responds to those involved in the study and the topic itself is probably the most elusive but important criterion of worthy research. This has been the topic of much consideration over time. Ballard (1996) poignantly stated:

> We have critiqued the research method as if it were the foundation of our work. It is now time to look at the ghost in these research machines, that is ourselves. This means focusing on research as an essentially human activity and as therefore embedded in personal, social, cultural, political, historical, spiritual and gendered bodies and contexts. (p. 103)

Cynically, hooks (1990) offered this description of the research process:

> I want to know your story. And then I will tell it back to you in a new way. Tell it back to you in such a way that is has become my own. Re-telling you. I write myself anew. I am still author, authority. I am still the colonizer, the speak subject, and you are at the center of my talk. (pp. 151–152)

Researchers must balance the caution hooks offers of not colonizing participants by "portraying themselves as expert of others' experiences" (Arminio & Hultgren, 2002, p. 455) while making participants the center of researchers' talk. As noted earlier in the section on social identities, researchers have many selves. Obligations to high quality research require that researchers participate in the "process of discovery of the subject (and the problem itself) and discovery of the self" (Lincoln, Lynham, & Guba, 2011, p. 124).

How the researcher recruited, came to know, and think about the participants must be explicit in the explanation of the research design (Lather, 2003). This takes the form of what is referred to as reflexive subjectivity (Lather, 2003). Reflexivity is about

> The micropolitical practices of representation, the meta narratives within which inquiry is embedded, the relation of its questions, and the effectivity of its practices to the sociocultural horizon. (Lather, 2007, p. 44)

A research design must include ways in which researchers will demonstrate to their audience how they situate themselves historically and geographically, as well as their personal investment in the research.

Researchers need to consider how they are going to negotiate the self-other relationship, and then they must divulge it. For example, in an ethnographic study manuscript submitted for publication in a journal particular to higher education, the author had studied a community-building program in a college residence hall. Yet, the author never divulged what role he or she had in the program. Was the researcher a faculty member who taught in the program, an administrator of the program, a parent of a student in the program, a resident of the program, or unaffiliated with the institution? The role of the researcher and his or her relationship to the program and the students influence whether the reader can determine if the findings presented are reasonable.

Marshall (1990) cautioned qualitative researchers from "going native" (p. 194). This occurs when a researcher goes through the motions of, and takes on, a cultural behavior without knowing, understanding, or embracing the underlying reason for the behavior. The researcher takes advantage of the behavior for his or her own purposes, usually to gain access to participants. Kincheloe and Steinberg (2012) described it this way: "What is the difference between a celebration of indigenous knowledge and an appropriation? Too often, Western allies, for example, do not simply want to work with indigenous peoples—they want to transform their identities and become indigenous persons themselves" (p. 341). This could be patronizing or, even worse, lead to harm. The importance of reflecting upon the researcher and participants as intercultural subjects, and the implications for data analysis and presentation, cannot be overstated.

Suggestions about the impact of relational competence on the research process. Throughout this section on paradigmatic obligations of relational competence for high quality research, the constant focus has been on awareness of the researcher's lens. The following suggestions are offered to assist researchers in fulfilling obligations of relational competencies:

- If this chapter is the first time you have heard of the concepts of privilege and power in research, then you need to do much more reading on these issues. Being naïve about these issues can potentially harm participants in a study. As a researcher, it is your responsibility to do no harm.
- Contemplate what social identity groups you belong to and which ones you do not. For example, if you are from a privileged group, it is critical that you explore why you would consider studying a less privileged group. Only through understanding your own privilege can you begin to understand the lack of privilege others can have.
- Articulate to yourself and others why you are choosing to do research on a population that is different from your own social identity. Make sure you are the best person to conduct this type of research. The act of talking/ writing/reading about this decision will allow you to reflect and hear/read yourself speak/write about the issues and promote discussion about your own identity and the identity of participants.
- Make sure you reflect on how your own identity may interact with different social identities and how you will respond to that interaction. Do not assume you will be trusted—that assumption illustrates your privilege and power, not a commitment to increased understanding.
- Insert into the research design elements to ensure that you are conducting a high quality study, as discussed here.
- Acknowledge that there are multiple perspectives to any issue and work to hear and understand those perspectives. Strategies that can be used include who you choose as peer debriefers or inquiry auditors. Care should be given to this choice. Convenience is insufficient.

As mentioned above, discovery of self as well as discovery about the phenomenon being studied is a laudable goal. Vasti's reflection about her interaction with the participants in her study illustrated that "Perhaps the most significant impact of this study has been my own evolution as a researcher" (Torres & Baxter Magolda, 2002, p. 480).

In these sections, we pursued the obligations of worthiness for research in general and qualitative research (spending significant space pointing out both technical and relational competencies), and now we turn to methodological obligations followed by criteria in data collection, analysis, and praxis.

Methodology: The Approach

In addition to paradigmatic criteria, researchers should pay attention to methodological criteria for goodness (see Figure 2.3).

The methodology selected gives more specific direction to a study, which is in turn grounded in a theoretical perspective and paradigmatic stance. The methodology is the approach, plan of action, and design. To meet the obligations of a high quality inquiry, there must be a clear research question or purpose that can be appropriately addressed by the chosen methodology, which offers clarity on how data are collected and the means for analysis. As will be covered in Chapter Four, researchers should rely on methodology for study design and

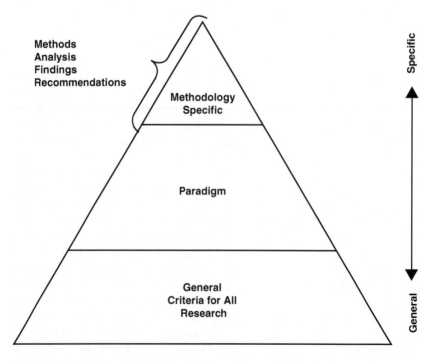

Figure 2.3 Criteria Specific to Methodology

provide evidence of that in the written research report. This includes informing the reader of the methodology by introducing basic principles, historical origins, and methodological experts. We would also expect to see references to contemporary users of this methodology from one's discipline. The researcher must note how the basic principles were followed and applied in the study. A number of methodologies or research traditions (Creswell, 2013) exist in qualitative inquiry. Some researchers err in combining methodologies without an adequate understanding of any of them.

Methodological interests, values, and purposes can account for differences in interpretation and analysis (Creswell, 2013). The analysis of some methodologies is more interpretive and less structured than others. So, for example, we would expect to see indicated in a written report how a hermeneutic phenomenological study is more interpretive than a grounded theory study. Lincoln, Lynham, and Guba (2011) asked:

> Are we interpretively rigorous? Can our co-created constructions be trusted to provide some purchase on some important human phenomenon? Do our findings point to action that can be taken on the part of research participants to benefit themselves or their particular social contexts? (p. 120)

Considering another example, in critical theory, due to its emancipatory aim (Lather, 2007), users would expect to see more emphasis on "an ethical advocacy stance to address injustice and/or inequity" (Shields, 2012, p. 5).

Method: Obligations for Collecting Data

Method, the collection of data, is often confused with methodology. Methodology provides the direction for the method. There must be a clear connection between the methodology (discussed in Chapter Four), how participants will be recruited and selected (i.e., sampling strategy), and how data will be collected. Chapter Five offers a discussion on how sampling decisions are influenced by methodology and Chapter Six explores data collection in greater depth.

In qualitative research, the procedures themselves are not the criteria on which a study is deemed sound, but rather it is the congruency of the theoretical perspective, methodology, and method. For example, how systematic, structured, or unstructured data collection methods are, again, is determined by the selected methodology. Rather than purportedly being value free, the researcher must be clear about what values he or she is acting upon when collecting data and how the chosen methodology and method support those values. Kvale and Brinkman (2009) used the metaphors of miner and traveler to distinguish differing interviewing styles depending upon methodology. Miners see knowledge as buried. It is the researcher's role to dig for it. This is consistent with the search for the essence in phenomenology. The traveler however, "wanders through the landscape and enters into conversations with the people he or she encounters" (p. 48). This type of interviewing is more appropriate for an ethnography.

During and subsequent to data collection is the process of data analysis. Chapter Seven more explicitly incorporates how interpretation and analysis techniques vary, but we touch on criteria of goodness of analysis below.

Analysis and Its Presentation

The word analysis can be traced to the German word analusein, meaning to unloosen or undo (Hoad, 1986). This obligation requires that the text (or data) is undone according to the methodology. The purpose of analysis is to uncover findings that lead to new and increased understanding. Merriam (2009) described the beginning of data analysis this way:

> You read and reread the data, making notes in the margins commenting on the data. You write a separate memo to yourself capturing your reflections, tentative themes, hunches, ideas, and things to pursue that are derived from this first set of data. You note things you want to ask, observe, or look for in your next round of data collection. (p. 170)

Researchers must create a system for managing data. Again, analysis will be guided by methodology, but in general analysis "involves consolidating, reducing, and interpreting" (Merriam, 2009, p. 176). Units of data (small pieces of data important to the study) are combined with other similar topical units of data to create categories. Through processes of writing, discussion, and reflection categories are refined and meaning can be made of the phenomena under investigation. Novice researchers often merely report what was obvious rather than interpret what was illuminated. The latter is much more difficult because it requires a risk or, as Lather (2003) wrote, "credible leaps into the unknown" (p. 205). Researchers must make obvious the difference between reporting and interpreting. For example, in her article *Identity and Learning: Student Affairs' Role in Transforming Higher Education*, Baxter Magolda (2003) offered a lengthy quote from one of her participants, a small portion of which is presented below:

> The whole thought process of just taking stock of where you are in your life. It's like putting your life through a sieve, getting the big awkward chunks out of your life, getting the nice finely sifted residue—it is kind of sorting it all out. What is the essence of you and what isn't? (p. 233)

Baxter Magolda provided this interpretation:

> Dawn's comments reveal . . . [she] was defining a path to follow until new experiences reshape it, processing each new experience in the context of the essence of who she is. Students using this process during college would be less likely to chose [sic] a major because they thought someone (e.g.,

their parents, their peers, society at large) wanted them to and more likely to choose majors and careers consistent with their own values. Doing so would yield less changing majors and perhaps more effective in-depth learning in areas to which students are committed. Better career decisions would enhance students' education and preparation for careers after college. (p. 233)

Though difficult to illustrate without duplicating the entire article, this excerpt demonstrates that interpretation is not a rephrasing of the text. It embraces the text but broadens and deepens understanding of what was said, what it means, and its implications. The depth of the interpretation will be determined by theoretical perspective and methodology.

Important questions to consider in order to comply with obligations of analysis and presentation include the following: Could other reasonable researchers make these same claims? Would others be able to determine how the findings and interpretations were generated? Would others use these interpretations as a basis for their work? Are these interpretations more probable than other interpretations or conclusions? Was the engagement prolonged, the observation thorough, and the meaning thoughtful? Did the researcher grapple with alternative explanations?

In higher education, ultimately researchers conduct research to improve practice. Worthiness for research in higher education necessitates that attention be given to how the research improved practice.

Recommendations From Findings

Once findings have been interpreted and means taken to ensure that they are reasonable, it is up to the researcher to provide ideas about how the study is applicable in practice. Arminio and Hultgren (2002) wrote:

For what purpose do I engage as a researcher in this way? It is not for the sake of research itself that researchers should embark upon this work, but rather to improve the lives of others. Interpretive research is initiated for the purpose of improving the world through more informed action. (p. 457)

Research should not be conducted in an "academic vacuum apart from the outside world" (Lather, 1991, p. xvi). Researchers must connect their findings to applicable recommendations. These recommendations should allow for the empowerment of people and improvement in the quality of life. As Arminio and Hultgren (2002) noted, "Being conscious of goodness asks that . . . research make connections between self, other, and world and offer reflections on what is right to do and good to be as an inquirer" (p. 458). To meet this criterion, inquirers must provide reasonable grounds that results are relevant to their practice.

A concern exists that studies too often focus on a "trivial problem" (Smith & Deemer, 2000, p. 879). Shields (2012) wrote that the role of the researcher is

> to engage the stakeholders on an ongoing basis with the findings and implications of a critical research study, to emphasize [its] authenticity . . . to ensure that people's understandings are indeed changed, and that such new comprehension leads to action that is tactical and strategic. (p. 9)

Researchers should ask themselves questions such as: What are the implications for not just the immediate actors but also a larger circle of others? What are the implications for systems and organizations? Again, it is not for the sake of the inquirer that the study is conducted.

Lincoln (1998) called for researchers to "leap from understanding to action" (p. 18). This occurs by not conducting research that exacerbates social ills or takes needed resources from social institutions (e.g., schools and health care). Lincoln directed researchers to frame "inquiries in such a way as to prompt action" (p. 23). This action also includes the discourse between researchers and practitioners in order to promote local efforts of community involvement. Carpenter (2003) described such action-oriented research as scholarly practice. Examples of scholarly practice based on research would include the development of racial justice allies by Reason, Roosa Millar, and Scales (2005). Also, the work by Jones, Rowan-Kenyon, Ireland, Niehaus, and Skendall (2012) offered important implications of their research on short-term immersion programs that are often students' first significant experience in cross-racial and cross-cultural contexts and that though short, students find poignant. Furthermore, Shupp and Arminio (2012) noted implications for supervision of new professionals using Bronfenbrenner's ecological model, meaning recommendations were offered within the mesosystems and exosystems of institutions.

Summary

As educators, whether faculty members, student affairs staff, or administrators, we must acknowledge, embrace, and integrate the obligations of research goodness. There are general obligations for all research, obligations specific to qualitative research, and obligations that are specific to methodology that coincide with appropriate methods, analysis, and recommendations based on findings. Insight can best be gained from studies that follow these obligations. Arminio and Hultgren (2002) suggested:

> Qualitative research that exemplifies goodness must be an important part of the assessment, research, and evaluation efforts taking place on college campuses, linking [our work] to student learning and offering directions for continuous improvement. Including qualitative research is important not because it might be "trendy," but rather because good qualitative research brings voice and insight forward for all constituents living

complex phenomena, including underrepresented people and their experiences. Using good qualitative work to demonstrate effectiveness allows institutions to realize their mission more fully. (p. 458)

Qualitative work must be judged on what it is, rather than upon quantitative research, which it is not, while understanding that "criteria must be thought of not as abstract standards but rather as socially constructed lists of characteristics" (Smith & Hodkinson, 2008, p. 420). Part of understanding one's own social identities is to reflect on the privileges that come with any one identity and how that is perceived by others, most notably participants in a study. It is our desire to promote more responsible researchers who are aware of their own influence and actively take steps that meet the obligations of high quality inquiry.

Exercises

Chapter-related

1. Select and read a qualitative study. Identify the ways in which the authors demonstrate the strategies discussed in this chapter. In what ways were the strategies sufficient or insufficient?

2. Identify and list the social identities you possess. Adjacent to this, identify the privileges and stereotypes of these social identities. Reflect on how these identities will interact with the proposed focus of your study and the sample of participants you want to research. Be very specific in identifying the potential issues that may emerge as you research either within and/or outside of your own social identities. Ask a colleague to examine your list and make any suggestions. Identify ways to ensure that differing interpretations will be respected within the research process. You may want to use the bulleted points in the section on suggestions.

Research Process

1. Revisit the compelling interests and questions you identified at the end of Chapter One and brainstorm strategies to apply trustworthiness criteria you will want to keep in mind as you design your study.

2. What are you trying to understand about your topic? What do the criteria push you to consider about your topic?

3 Incorporating Theoretical Perspectives

In the first chapter of this book, the process of situating research was illustrated through explanations of paradigm, epistemology, and theoretical framework. Consistent with the process of creating a good qualitative study, the second chapter addressed the elements of researcher positionality and trustworthiness. This chapter will focus on another aspect of the research process that requires decisions to be made related to whether a researcher could, or should, consider the use of theoretical perspectives.

As previously stated, a theoretical perspective is "the philosophical stance informing the methodology and thus providing a context for the process and grounding its logic and criteria" (Crotty, 1998, p. 3). This stance is an element that is critical for some researchers and studies, but perhaps not necessary for all. To determine the necessity or appropriateness of a theoretical perspective, researchers should ask questions such as: (a) What aspect of my compelling interest requires a specific theoretical perspective? (b) Is using a particular theoretical perspective compatible with my chosen epistemology and methodology? and (c) What does using a particular theoretical perspective contribute to the study? This chapter provides some guidance for what should be considered when thinking about questions related to incorporating a theoretical perspective into a research design and the process of making these decisions.

In order to serve as a guide for researchers, the chapter begins with a definition of what theoretical perspectives bring to the research process. Then we provide a concise explanation of various types of theoretical perspectives. While we attempt to organize these perspectives according to their philosophical origins, we acknowledge that the grouping used is a "best effort" and not meant to be definitive. Finally, the chapter ends with emerging tensions and how researchers can be proactive in considering these tensions.

Using Theoretical Perspectives

Theoretical perspectives reflect an individual standpoint about the philosophical tenets regarding sources of knowledge and how this standpoint influences the way data are interpreted. The use of a theoretical perspective within a qualitative study "can lead to a more complex understanding" (Broido & Manning,

2002, p. 437) of what is being considered in the research. Many of the perspectives highlighted within this chapter share an "interest" in questioning issues of power, identity, and what is considered the "norm" (Broido & Manning, 2002). Like the other decisions made thus far in the research process, the tensions that can arise from using a theoretical perspective must be carefully considered by the researcher. While statements about tensions are provided throughout, the final section of the chapter will highlight specific examples.

In this chapter, we attempt to provide descriptions of the changing landscape of theoretical perspectives in higher education research. In the end, it is hoped that researchers will understand the issues involved and potential advantages and limitations of including a theoretical perspective within a research study.

Understanding When the Research Prompts the Use of Theoretical Perspectives

As the need increases to understand the experiences of diverse populations and the policies that influence programs that reach out to marginalized groups within higher education, the use of theoretical perspectives emerges as a useful approach to help in the analysis of data and to convey findings through different lenses. An interest in questioning the status quo is at the heart of most theoretical perspectives, although not all, since some qualitative researchers may adopt more traditional positivist epistemology or a constructivist developmental lens. A critical theoretical perspective promotes a view of the "human world and social life within that world" (Crotty, 1998, p. 7) and takes into account the cultural, symbolic, economic, and political power that influences the lives of individuals oppressed by those in the majority, often times seen as those in power. Bringing to light the experiences of oppressed participants can prompt the need to more explicitly express one's theoretical perspective and emphasize how social, cultural, or economic aspects influence the interpretation of data.

In many ways, these critical theoretical perspectives further critique the historical relationship between researcher and knowledge, or truth, by recognizing the researcher's view of societal influences on what is considered knowledge. Although the idea of questioning the status quo may be attractive to many researchers, the use of theoretical perspectives should be considered within the context of epistemology and methodology selected for the study. For example, a researcher using a positivist epistemology, which includes the belief that truth exists, would experience a major tension using a theoretical perspective with philosophical tenets focused on truth as socially constructed. Therefore, a positivist researcher would find great tension when using critical race theory as a theoretical perspective because of its foundation around understanding the world through the lens of racism. If truth does exist for positivist thinkers, then how can varying social constructions of race attached to racist ideas be integrated into one truth?

However, before we move on to discuss critical theoretical perspectives to which many researchers in higher education and student affairs are drawn, we comment briefly on the evolution of incorporating theoretical perspectives. As noted, theoretical perspectives gained attention through the increased interest of turning a critical lens on research designs and analysis of data. Many researchers in higher education studying student development situated their studies in what is referred to as a constructivist developmental approach, which emerged from positivist worldviews about how development occurred and should be studied. In an insightful article, Baxter Magolda (2004) chronicled her evolution as a researcher as well as the evolution of her views of epistemological reflection as moving from positivist to constructivist. She wrote the, "Evolution of my conceptualization of the construct is due to a complex interplay between my meaning-making as a researcher, the study participants' meaning-making as young adults, and the implications of the intersection of these two sets of meaning-making for how I conducted the longitudinal study" (pp. 31–32). The methodological implications of this evolution led Baxter Magolda to narrative inquiry rather than relying on a measure of epistemological reflection using Perry's scheme. This shift resulted in the foregrounding of her participants' constructions of realties and meaning-making rather than a more distanced analytic approach. We mention Baxter Magolda's work here both because the theoretical perspective of constructivist developmentalism is prevalent in higher education and student affairs research and because her experience is an excellent example of the purpose and value of researcher reflexivity. In her case, such reflexivity led to the shifting of theoretical and methodological assumptions guiding her work and influencing her results. Although constructivist perspectives are not critical in nature, they do bring to the forefront of analysis the voices, experiences, and meaning-making of participants, including those whose stories have been underrepresented in the research.

In another example of blurring boundaries when theoretical perspectives are considered, some researchers are pursuing the integration of critical approaches with quantitative designs. A New Directions for Institutional Research text titled *Using Quantitative Research to Answer Critical Questions* (Stage, 2010) and a growing number of scholars are employing the critical framework of intersectionality (which will be discussed further later in this chapter) to both quantitative and qualitative designs. For example, Bowleg (2008) examined research addressing intersectionality and the measurement, analysis, and interpretation challenges that result from both quantitative and qualitative designs. Similarly, Warner (2008) discussed quantitative approaches to studying intersectionality advocating the use of "explanatory variables, or those that are hypothesized to be the underlying causes behind the effects that demographic variables have on study outcomes" (p. 461). Finally, Museus and Griffin (2011) explored the promise of intersectionality to research in higher education, again suggesting the utility of quantitative, qualitative, and mixed methods approaches that address populations on the margins and structures of inequality. All of these examples point to the importance of knowing when integrating theoretical perspectives into a research design is appropriate and how such a decision connects the elements of the design, including the interpretation of results.

We now turn to an introduction of several critical theories that may be integrated into research designs. To provide insight, each of the perspectives described in this chapter are complemented with succinct descriptions of the tenets from the philosophical tradition that influenced how the ideas behind the perspective emerged. The perspectives presented include critical theories as well as the more contemporary perspectives such as critical race, postmodern, and post-structural theories.

Critical Theories

Researchers who consider themselves critical theorists are interested in responding to the historical events of the day (Ingram, 1990). The philosophical thoughts leading to critical theories date back to the ideals begun in the French Revolution and the Enlightenment that focused on equality and human rights. While many books are dedicated to the philosophical tenets of critical theories, we provide a brief overview to place the theories within historical philosophical tenets that contributed to the current understanding of critical thought.

Although some of the historical beliefs start earlier, we begin with Kant's influence on the German philosophical tradition (Ingram, 1990). In the spirit of building on previous work, Kant's critical philosophy was linked to Karl Marx's critical social theory by Georg Hegel who made the claim that "reason is an objective historical force" which should be considered "dynamically or developmentally" (Ingram, 1990, p. 11). With the understanding that historical forces are influenced by those living the experience, Hegel contributed one of the central ideas of critical theories—that an understanding of society encompasses a subjective appreciation of relationships, historical features, and cultural understanding. Marx broke away from Hegel's ideas because he believed that universal interest could be mediated by corporate entities. These professional and business associations could put their own corporate or class interest ahead of the public good. For this reason, there were real and unavoidable conflicts and tensions around what constitutes the ideal public good. In essence, some groups in society were oppressed by these corporate interests (Ingram, 1990).

Over the years, the ideological beliefs of critical theory were diluted, and student movements and economic conditions gave rise to the need to consider the "nature of the relationship between culture, the state and social movements" (Morrow, 1991, p. 31). As a result, critical theory is incorporating aspects that make it more applicable to today's research rather than only being philosophical (Morrow, 1991). Although the critical theories in current higher education research are somewhat distinctive from the philosophical aspects of critical theory, they are focused on challenging the dominant ideology in some way, much like Marx's ideals. Tierney and Rhoads (2004) pointed out that critical perspectives share similarities to other traditions and developed five premises that scaffold how higher education research should be considered when adopting a critical lens:

1. Research efforts need to be tied to analyses that investigate the structures in which the study exists;
2. Knowledge is not neutral. It is contested and political;
3. Difference and conflict, rather than similarity and consensus, are used as organizing concepts;
4. Research is praxis-oriented; and
5. All researchers/authors are intimately tied to their theoretical perspectives. We are all positioned subjects. (p. 327)

These premises illustrate what researchers using a critical lens would need to consider during the research process and provide thoughtful and applicable guidance for embarking on research framed by critical theory.

The following section offers concise explanations of several critical theoretical perspectives seen within research in higher education.

Critical Race Theory

The use of critical race theory (CRT) emerged from legal studies as a result of race and racism not being sufficiently addressed in legal research. The goal of CRT is to critique the slow pace and unrealized promises found within the civil rights legislation and thus challenge ongoing racism in the legal system (Taylor, Gillborn, & Ladson-Billings, 2009). CRT is influenced by the literature in multiple disciplines, including law, education, social science, and ethnic and women's studies (Solórzano & Yosso, 2002). Because we are concerned with the use of CRT within higher education, we will focus on how educational researchers describe these tenets and what is expected of researchers when using CRT in their research.

Within educational research, CRT offers "an explanatory structure that accounts for the role of race and racism in U.S. society" (Yosso, Parker, Solórzano, & Lynn, 2004, p. 2). The five central tenets described below represent the foundational ideas behind CRT:

1. Racism is normal and not unusual in U.S. society. This makes it a part of the social order, as it appears both normal and natural within the U.S. (Ladson-Billings, 2009; Yosso et al., 2004). This tenet requires that researchers using CRT approach data with a goal to unmask and reveal racism in the various systems that are within society (Ladson-Billings, 2009). This tenet also acknowledges the layers of subordination based on gender, class, immigration status, surname, accent, and sexuality.
2. The interests of Blacks are accommodated only when there is a convergence with the interest of those in power (Taylor, 2009). Interest convergence suggests that gains for the underserved will not likely happen unless there is some

furthering of the material interest of those who are in power. Others bring attention to this interest convergence as a way to highlight the need to have a commitment to social justice (Yosso et al., 2004). In this sense, CRT scholars work towards the elimination of racism and empowerment of subordinate groups.

3. Because U.S. social systems are based on White people having certain rights to property and capital, CRT is grounded in the historical context that the past influences interpretations of what happens today (Taylor, 2009). This is also referred to as the challenge to the dominant ideology. By considering the historical context, CRT researchers understand social systems with more nuance and challenge policy changes through the lens of privilege and power (Yosso et al., 2004). Within this tenet, the CRT scholar would approach traditional views of objectivity and neutrality as camouflaging self-interest, power, and privilege.

4. The use of narrative to "redirect the dominant gaze, to make it see from a new point of view what has been there all along" (Taylor et al., 2009, p. 8) allows for the experiences of those who were previously marginalized to be legitimized. This can also be called the centrality of experiential knowledge (Yosso et al., 2004). In order to draw on the lived experiences of persons of color, the CRT scholar uses methods such as story-telling, family histories, narratives, and testimonies.

5. Disciplinary boundaries are not as essential as analyzing race and racism within the historical and contemporary context. This transdisciplinary perspective allows CRT to be used beyond disciplinary boundaries (Yosso et al., 2004).

Within higher education, CRT scholars have considered a variety of topics, including educational policies (Harper, Patton, & Wooden, 2009; Solórzano & Yosso, 2002), the experiences of students (Solórzano, Ceja, & Yosso, 2000), and faculty work (Delgado Bernal & Villalpando, 2002; Jayakumar, Howard, Allen, & Han, 2009). Other chapters in this book offer additional examples. One of the common uses of CRT in higher education is as a lens for examining educational policies. Using CRT, Harper, Patton, and Wooden (2009) were able to "offer a critique of the progressive and regressive policy efforts associated with African American student participation in higher education" (p. 392). In their study of access policies and African American students, Harper, Patton, and Wooden (2009) provided a critical view by conveying the interest convergence and historical racism seen within the development of such policies.

Buenavista, Jayakumar, and Misa-Escalante (2009) used CRT to assert that "the stereotype and generalizations of Asian Americans is a manifestation of a larger racial agenda that serves to maintain the dominance of whites in the United States" (p. 71). Using CRT, these scholars highlighted the "liminality of Pilipinos" (p. 75) by explaining how this group of students is positioned between "two states that are characterized by ambiguity" (p. 75) and perceived as both foreigners and colonial subjects. This dynamic is reflected in their college experiences as they are considered second generation college students, yet they have parents who do not understand nor can help them navigate the U.S. higher education system. The historical aspects combined with the scrutiny of political labor practices underline how using CRT provided a more nuanced view of Pilipino students and captures a critical view of how society labels and views these students.

LatCrit

LatCrit emerged from CRT with an additional concern about the progressive sense of Latino/a pan-ethnicity (Delgado Bernal, 2002). Aspects of the pan-ethnic label are the common experiences of colonization from Spain and the influence of European power. LatCrit emphasizes characteristics like speaking the Spanish language and experiencing the historical/legal components of immigration—elements that are sometimes lost within CRT. In addition to the tenets of CRT, LatCrit considers the Eurocentric perspective and the use of this perspective in labeling Latino/as in the U.S. This Eurocentric, colonialist perspective is equated with White superiority, capitalism, and scientific intelligence (Delgado Bernal, 2002). As a result, the narratives of indigenous ideals and the borderland are neglected.

LatCrit within the higher education literature is often used in conjunction with CRT. Studies focused on Latino/a college students (Villalpando, 2003) encompass cultural concerns and provide insights into how their experiences may be understood. In her study of student protests and the development of political consciousness, Hernandez (2012) used CRT and LatCrit to make sure there was "a more intensive investigation of how the social world influences individual development" (pp. 698–699). She contributes the critical perspective by linking activism with development and providing "further depth and complexity to understanding Latino development and self-authorship theory in the three dimensions" (Hernandez, 2012, p. 698).

The use of LatCrit alongside CRT is common and often seen within higher education research. Other studies of Latino/a college students have used CRT to look at the college access pipeline. One such study is Sólorzano, Villalpando, and Osequera (2005), who examined Latino post-secondary educational progress. Their reasons for choosing CRT as a theoretical perspective are that it "explores the ways in which 'race-neutral' laws and institutional structures, practices, and policies perpetuate racial/ethnic educational inequality" (p. 274). This statement illustrates how using CRT allows the researchers to consider specific "structures, practices, and policies" (p. 274) that contribute to Latino educational progress.

TribalCrit

TribalCrit also emerged from CRT and "is rooted in the multiple, nuanced, and historically- and geographically-located epistemologies and ontologies found in Indigenous communities" (Brayboy, 2005, p. 427). The commonalities between Indigenous communities' epistemologies and ontology include the view that oral stories are not separate from knowledge and therefore legitimate sources of data. Brayboy (2005) articulated the nine tenets of TribalCrit as including the following:

1. The acknowledgement that colonization of native cultures is endemic to how society has treated Indigenous communities;
2. Policies towards Indigenous peoples are ingrained with "imperialism, White supremacy, and a desire for material gain" (p. 429);
3. "Indigenous peoples occupy a liminal space" (p. 429), which influences the nature of identity;
4. Tribal sovereignty, autonomy, self-determination, and self-identification are central desires of Indigenous peoples;
5. Using TribalCrit provides new meaning of culture, knowledge, and power;
6. Assimilation has guided both governmental and educational policies that affect Indigenous peoples;
7. "Tribal philosophies, beliefs, customs, traditions, and visions for the future are central to understanding the lived realities of Indigenous peoples, but they also illustrate the differences and adaptability among individuals and groups" (p. 429);
8. Stories told are legitimate sources of data and are real ways to explain ways of being; and
9. "Theory and practice are connected in deep and explicit ways such that scholars must work towards social change." (p. 430)

Within higher education, Castagno and Lee (2007) used TribalCrit to view Native mascots at a Midwestern University. According to Castagno and Lee, TribalCrit "provides a more culturally specific and hence accurate perspective on issues relating to Indigenous people and communities" (p. 4). TribalCrit as a theoretical perspective allows for the voices of Indigenous students to emerge more clearly.

Although more prevalent in legal studies, some education scholars have begun to integrate critical perspectives by combining the tenets of CRT with other philosophical traditions. Berry (2010) used Critical Race Feminism (CRF) to consider engaged pedagogy and Misawa (2010) considered QueerCrit when looking at adult and continuing education. Though these perspectives are not as prevalent in higher education, they are mentioned here as potential resources for researchers.

Postmodernism

As a reaction to an emphasis on rational, reasoned, and positivist scientific ideals, postmodern researchers abandon the subject-object separation previously expected (Broido & Manning, 2002). As stated in Chapter One, postmodern perspectives focus on the historical and global issues of those marginalized and how research can examine the power and privilege exerted by some groups (Broido & Manning, 2002). Postmodernism emphasizes the importance of historical moments in time and works against grand or metanarratives that essentialize experience and society (Schwandt, 2007a).

Postmodern perspectives share certain aspects with critical theory in the sense that both consider the research process as being located within power structures, and the social identities of the researcher and participant influence the findings (Broido & Manning, 2002). Researchers using a postmodern perspective embrace the ambiguity that comes with abandonment of previously held beliefs about certitude and continuity (Crotty, 1998). As a result, postmodernism does not privilege any one authority nor support the idea that reality is socially constructed (Kincheloe & McLaren, 2000). This idea opens postmodern researchers to the criticism that the meaning of this social construction is influenced by ethnocentric views of history that can be internalized by the researcher (Kincheloe & McLaren, 2000; St. Pierre, 2011).

As an example of the use of this perspective in higher education, Tierney (1997) described culture from a postmodern perspective as "not waiting 'out there' to be discovered and 'acquired' by new members" (p. 6). In his study of promotion and tenure processes, Tierney focused on understanding organizational socialization and how institutions could "develop policies that contribute to the successful socialization of faculty into the academy" (p. 2). Providing the insight that culture "is the interpretation the organization's participants give" to knowledge and processes while working together, Tierney sought to understand academic culture and how it could be reconfigured during the socialization processes of promotion and tenure. This postmodern perspective allows culture to move beyond defining the world and towards an understanding that culture is being constantly changed by processes and represents the "hopes and dreams" of what the organization might be in the future (Tierney, 1997, p. 6). Using this postmodern perspective, Tierney (1997) provided this potential interpretation:

> One radical interpretation might be that we have a postmodern culture operating within a modernist framework: conflict and discontinuities exist because people do not know what is expected of them. Of consequence, they fall back on their own interpretation of how to fit within the culture. Yet such an interpretation is unpersuasive if the outcome is assimilation; ultimately, the recruits learn how to teach, work with students, and participate in the community according to the implicit mores of the organization. My point here is to suggest that postmodernism highlights the inherent contractions that exist within modernist frameworks so that we might be able to develop academic communities that honor difference rather than assimilation. (p. 14)

Post-Structuralism

Though sometimes used interchangeably with postmodernism, the post-structural perspective is distinctive (Crotty, 1998; St. Pierre, 2011). Emerging from the French philosophical traditions, post-structuralism "critiques the scientific pretensions of structural tendencies in all disciplines" (St. Pierre, 2011, p. 615). For this reason, the deconstruction of discourses, as reflected in the ideas of foundational theorist Derrida, is a way to realize justice (St. Pierre, 2011). In addition, strict definitions and descriptions are elusive and not constant; therefore, they are not desired. These ideas allow researchers using this theoretical perspective to question power structures and deconstruct what is known or accepted. Though not always used within this configuration, the two post-structural perspectives covered here are Feminist Perspectives and Queer Theory.

Feminist Perspectives

Feminist theories may be employed in qualitative studies in a variety of ways. Schwandt (2001) argued that "There is no single feminist epistemology" (p. 92). However, the social construction of gender throughout history allows feminist researchers to deconstruct and reframe theories "to better explain the gendered nature of behavior" and how participation as well as relationships are marked by gender (Broido & Manning, 2002, p. 442). A researcher using a feminist perspective brings to the research process a "sense of oppression in a man-made world" (Crotty, 2003, p. 182). This can be referenced as a feminist standpoint, which consists of understanding the feminist values, cause, and the purpose of bringing the issues to light in a way that is different from others—specifically men (Crotty, 1998, p. 182). Patricia Hill Collins (2000) described the "seamless web of economy, polity, and ideology as a highly effective system of social control" for women (p. 7).

Patti Lather made a unique contribution in feminist research by publishing books that illustrate the findings of a research study using a feminist lens (Lather & Smithies, 1997) and then the methodological learning she gained from that study (Lather, 2007). In *Troubling the Angels* (1997), she used feminist experimental ethnography to consider women living with HIV/AIDS. In *Getting Lost* (2007) she focused on exploring "the context of feminist research methodology" (p. viii). This unique combination allows the reader to view how one feminist researcher has grappled with the "anxieties that haunt feminist ethnography" (p. 146) and questioned the universal acceptance of reflexivity as a trap that needs to be considered as a troubling aspect of the research process. While readers may be tempted to draw a concise synopsis, *Getting Lost* is a book that must be considered as a whole and is highly recommended to researchers interested in feminist perspectives.

The web of economic, political, and ideological control referenced by Collins (2000) is even more pronounced for African American women who remain in subordinate roles. Black feminists emphasize "the knowledge gained at intersecting oppressions of race, class and gender" in order to describe the knowledge held by Black women (Collins, 2000, p. 11). Other researchers have taken the ideas of Black feminists further to include various aspects of being Black into the consideration. Dillard and Okpalaoka (2011) used the term *endarkened feminist epistemology* to distinguish "from mainstream (White) feminism in that it is located in the intersection or overlap of the culturally constructed notions of race, gender, class, and national other identities" (p. 148). In this sense, the endarkened feminist ideals use a transnational view by considering various national contexts (e.g., U.S. and African National) to portray the wisdom and spirituality of Black women's ways of knowing.

Queer Theory

Influenced by CRT and feminist theories, Queer Theory "considers identity to be a social construction and critiques the power structures in the social environment that construct identity" (Jones & Abes, 2013). This questioning is heavily influenced by post-structural theory and focused on how society constructs normative behaviors (or a grand narrative) around sexual orientation and the concepts of gender and biological sex (Broido & Manning, 2002; Gamson, 2000). Gamson (2000) posited that "Queer theory undercuts earlier notions of an autonomous, coherent self" (p. 358) by making identity the center of research yet incorporating multiplicity, partial identities, and instability in the analysis of data.

The central tenets of Queer Theory are as follows:

•   Heteronormativity—the social norm being defined by heterosexuality. This norm is then used to understand relationships and power. Queer Theory objects to this social norm (Jones & Abes, 2013);
•   Performativity—the manner in which individuals create social identities within their daily lives—the performance of gender. This provides the illusion of having one gender as normal and more static than it actually is. Queer theorists use this idea to illustrate that identity is "an ongoing process of expression and enactment, rather than an end product of development" (Jones & Abes, 2013, p. 199). Identity, then, is seen as more fluid;
•   Desire—this tenet attempts to separate desire from the dichotomous view of superior or inferior norms, or social binaries. Rather, desire, in this case, is about the incompleteness that can be felt when socially acceptable definitions of desire are placed on someone who does not meet the heteronormative norms society expects (Jones & Abes, 2013); and
•   Becoming—refers to the unfolding of identity without an endpoint (Abes & Kasch, 2007; Jones & Abes, 2013).

Within the higher education literature are a growing number of examples of research using Queer Theory as a theoretical perspective. Abes and Kasch (2007) used Queer Theory to consider the multiple identities of lesbian college students and stated that this perspective allowed for the critical analysis of "the meaning of identity, focusing on intersections of identity and resisting oppressive social construction of sexual orientation and gender" (p. 620). Renn (2010) suggested that "Elisa Abes is perhaps the best example of a scholar applying queer theory to understanding college student identities. . . . Abes embraces the complexity and inherent contradictions of studying the unstable concept of identity without further reifying identity categories and the construction of normal-against-queer" (p. 135). Others have used Queer Theory to study faculty work, developmental theory, campus climate, and the status of research within higher education (Renn, 2010).

Intersectionality

The very notion of intersectionality prevents it from being placed within one specific philosophical tradition. The tenets undergirding intersectionality place an individual within larger structures of inequality and advance an analytic framework for understanding how privilege and oppression influences that individual (Dill & Zambrana, 2009; Jones & Abes, 2013). Intersectionality attempts to look at the intersections of identities, such as gender and race (Crenshaw, 1991). This perspective purports that identity is difficult to capture theoretically and methodologically, and therefore consideration of multiple identities simultaneously embraces aspects of post-structural, postmodern, and queer theory all together (Abes, Jones, & McEwen, 2007).

A growing number of higher education researchers are utilizing intersectionality as a theoretical perspective (Museus & Griffin, 2011). Intersectional research is characterized by (a) a primary emphasis and centering on the lived experiences of individuals; (b) an exploration of identity salience as influenced by systems of power and privilege and the interacting nature of such systems; and (c) a larger purpose and goal of contributing to a more socially just society (Dill & Zambrana, 2009; Jones, 2009). However, even with clearly outlined criteria for intersectional research, it is difficult to implement (McCall, 2005). Intersectionality has been used as a theoretical perspective to view the development of students through multiple lenses. Most widely recognized is the Model of Multiple Dimensions of Identity (Abes, Jones, & McEwen, 2007; Jones & Abes, 2013), which acknowledges that salience of social identities varies according to how individuals organize their experiences, choices, and decisions and the influence of larger contextual influences that represent structures of inequality. Intersectionality is misused when the focus is only on the individual or on multiple identities. As Bowleg (2008) pointed out, "The interpretive task for the intersectionality analyst is to make explicit the often implicit experiences of intersectionality, even when participants do not express the connections.... Making these connections through our interpretations, is the key goal of intersectionality research" (p. 322). This comment suggests that when using intersectionality as a theoretical perspective, researchers must pay careful attention to the analysis and interpretation of data.

Emerging Tensions

Several tensions emerge that one must consider when using a theoretical perspective. First is the commensurability of the perspective with the epistemology and methodology selected. The picking and choosing of various epistemologies and perspectives should be done with care and with knowledge of the elements necessary for each aspect of research (Lincoln, Lynham, & Guba, 2011). The earlier example of using positivist paradigm with a postmodern or post-structural perspective illustrates that the axiomatic (beliefs and assumptions) elements would not be commensurate and therefore these two choices would not likely be appropriate. Other tensions to consider can include the a priori use of a perspective when the methodology calls for findings to emerge from the data (e.g., grounded theory). In her study on political activism, Hernandez (2012) discussed her own tension between constructivist epistemology, used by researchers in student development research, and the use of CRT. As a result of this tension, she wrote that her choice was to use constructionist, rather than constructivist, epistemology because it emphasizes the role of culture on lives and the influence on how the researcher views the world. Therefore, she found that constructionism allowed for "a stronger influence of one's social world (e.g., one's culture, experiences with racism and privilege) on one's perspectives" (Hernandez, 2012, p. 685). These decisions also prompted her to use narrative inquiry as the methodology, which provided congruence between epistemology, theoretical perspective, and methodology.

Another tension is the blending of approaches, which is recommended only when researchers have experience with multiple studies and can visualize the tensions that can arise during the research process. Abes (2012) adopted the phrase "theoretical borderland" (p. 189) from Gloria Anzaldúa, a Latina feminist, and framed her study by blending perspectives. In this study, Abes explained that, because different theories alone were incomplete, she sought to "straddle multiple theories, using ideas from each to portray a more complete picture of identity" (p. 190). In her study of lesbian college students she used constructivism, queer theory, and intersectionality to manage "multiple viewpoints" (p. 209) that emerged from her participants.

Finally, one of the more common tensions that emerges within higher education research is the use of a theoretical perspective as a methodology. Although blurring or blending of the elements within a qualitative study can be skillfully done by an experienced researcher, it may be more difficult to manage for an early career researcher. Because academic disciplines use different terminology, there may be some confusion about what blurring or blending is actually occurring. An example of blending is the use of critical race theory (CRT) as a methodology within the higher education literature. As you read earlier, CRT emerged from legal studies and therefore a researcher must understand that the use of the term "methodology" within legal research is very different than what would be considered methodology within social science research. Russo (2006) described legal research as "a form of historical-legal research that is neither qualitative nor quantitative . . . it is a systematic investigation involving the interpretation and explanation of the law" (p. 6). This statement should be taken within the context that it was made—in a book that contained several chapters attempting to describe "methods" of doing legal research; it does illustrate that the elements required within social science research are not the same as legal research. Later on in the book on legal methods, Lee and Adler (2006) described what would be considered methodologies in education (such as ethnography and case study) as "qualitative genres" (p. 34). Even when authors attempt to provide guidance as to what elements are needed in the various types of research, the ideals of epistemology, methodology, and perspective are not clearly considered. Often these elements are reconciled in a simplistic view as the role of the researcher "is often explicitly analyzed and documented" (Kromrey, Onwuegbuzie, & Hogarty, 2006, p. 96) to illustrate the subjectivity involved in how the researcher's involvement "flavored" (p. 97) data analysis. This explanation is not meant to critique legal research but to explain how educational research requires a much more detailed explanation of researcher epistemology, methodological tenets, and theoretical perspective. Inevitably, methodology is "interwoven and emerges from the nature of particular disciplines" (Lincoln, Lynham, & Guba, 2011, p. 97), yet researchers should understand how one discipline's use of CRT as a methodology may be seen by a different discipline as a perspective. For this reason, what might be called a methodology in legal research may not have the necessary elements of a methodology in education research.

Summary

This chapter provided potential perspectives to consider and recognized that not every qualitative study has to have a theoretical perspective. The choice to include this element into a study is dependent on the questions of interest, the researcher's personal worldview, and what societal issues influence the phenomenon. Depending on these aspects, a theoretical perspective can be used to further highlight the issues and richness that emerge within the data. The advantages of using a theoretical perspective include the ability to see research as a transformative process that considers social issues of privilege and oppression in the analysis of data. Without a theoretical perspective, the findings provided may oversimplify the interpretation of the societal and cultural issues highlighted within the tenets of various theoretical perspectives. On the other hand, the disadvantage of using a theoretical perspective is that the researcher may forego the use of a known methodological approach for one that is commensurate with a theoretical perspective. The example of Hernandez's (2012) careful consideration of CRT not being commensurate with constructivist epistemology illustrates the careful reflection that needs to occur.

The key issue to remember is that researchers should consider all elements of a good research study. A high quality study explicitly explains how these elements come together in a commensurate manner to enhance the understanding of the phenomenon at hand. First and foremost, the descriptions in this chapter are meant to introduce concepts and should not be seen as the only or final source on these theoretical perspectives. The references should be used to find and read primary sources in order to form ideas and interpretations. This is an essential element of becoming a good researcher and conducting a good qualitative study.

Exercises

Chapter-related

These questions are meant to be reflective, rather than suggesting "right or wrong" answers, as well as helpful as you consider whether using a theoretical perspective is appropriate for your study.

1. From your own viewpoint ask yourself these questions:
    a. What power and privilege do I possess? (Even people of color can have privilege.)
    b. When and how do I recognize those privileges?
    c. Do I experience forms of oppression?
    d. When and how do I recognize those oppressive moments?
    e. Do these views infiltrate how I view the details of my daily living?
2. Using the responses to the previous questions, consider what theoretical perspectives are congruent with these ways of viewing the world. What are the benefits of incorporating a specific theoretical perspective? What are the potential drawbacks?

Research Process

1. Using one of the specific questions you identified in the first chapter, brainstorm a phenomenon of interest (e.g., experiences of student veterans, access to college for first generation students, or campus climate for Muslim women) and consider these questions:
    a. How do historical attitudes influence how this phenomenon is viewed today?
    b. What are the issues of power and oppression that influence how individuals may view this phenomenon?
2. Are your responses to the previous questions reflected in one or more of the perspectives described in this chapter? If so, how would using a theoretical perspective add richness and nuance to your study?

4   Designing Research

The temptation is great, we have found, for qualitative researchers to begin the research process with an idea of methods firmly entrenched in their minds. Comments such as "I am going to interview some Latino students on campus about their experiences," "We are observing classroom discussion patterns in engineering classes for our study on gender differences," or "I am analyzing all the statements about internationalizing at land grant institutions" are illustrative of a primary focus on methods. This focus on methods leads a researcher with a compelling interest (e.g., "What is life like for Latino students on this campus?") that is then quickly connected to a particular method (e.g., "Well, I'll find out by interviewing some Latino students"). Although the researcher might learn something from this approach, as the preceding chapters emphasize, such a strategy does not constitute good practice in qualitative research because it leaves out the important connection to epistemological views and theoretical perspectives that inform how one might investigate a particular phenomenon. As Glesne (2011) noted:

> Every research study is, therefore, informed by higher-level theory, even though researchers sometimes are not aware of these theories because they are embedded in their assumptions about the nature of reality and knowledge. Part of your duty as a researcher is to figure out what philosophical and theoretical perspectives inform the kind of work you choose to do. (p. 5)

Because preceding chapters focused extensively on philosophical, epistemological, and theoretical considerations, particular attention will be given in this chapter to methodology and methods. We begin with an overview of the elements of a research design and then follow with discussion of specific methodological approaches most commonly used in higher education and student affairs research. We provide examples from published research to illustrate the central and defining characteristics of each approach.

Developing a Research Design

The overarching framework for a study includes articulation of all aspects of the research (e.g., epistemological and theoretical perspectives and methodological approach and methods) and how they are interrelated. This framework provides scaffolding called the *research design*. In this section, elements of a research design are presented and connections between the elements are explored.

Elements of a Research Design

The elements of a research design most typically include:

- *epistemology*, which conveys philosophical assumptions about what constitutes knowledge;
- *theoretical perspective*, which is also philosophical in nature and informs methodological choices;
- *methodology*, which describes general strategies of inquiry and influences the choice of methods; and
- *methods*, which refer to the actual and detailed procedures of and techniques for participant selection, data collection, data analysis, and reporting (Creswell, 2013; Crotty, 1998).

Although these terms are frequently used interchangeably in the literature, they are conceptually distinct and integrally related to one another and imply important decision points to be made in the research process (Jones, 2002). Crotty (1998) articulated well the nature of these questions and research decisions: (a) What epistemology informs the theoretical perspective of the area of inquiry? (b) What theoretical perspective lies behind the methodology in question? (c) What methodology governs our choice and use of methods? and (d) What methods do we propose to use? It is important to point out that, although these elements are presented as though they form a step-by-step process, they are more interactive and iterative than lockstep. That is, each step is informed by another, and, as a researcher moves into a new step, there is often reason to return to a previous step. For example, data collection may be informed by initial data analysis, or analysis of results may be interpreted using multiple theoretical perspectives.

As introduced in Chapter One, the research process begins by identifying and understanding the assumptions a researcher holds about the phenomenon under investigation, how the researcher will come to know more about this phenomenon, and what might become known through the inquiry. This is central to the research design because how the researcher responds to these questions will then provide the guidance and direction for every other decision to be made. For researchers working within the qualitative research tradition, regardless of methodological choice, certain characteristics of the design will most often be present. These include the following: understanding emerges from an emic or insider's perspective, the researcher functions as the instrument of research, research occurs in natural settings and is context dependent, research is inductive in nature and emphasizes in-depth understanding, and researcher findings emphasize rich description of the phenomenon under investigation

(Merriam, 2009). Because of these characteristics, qualitative inquiry is often situated as an interpretivist approach to research with an emphasis on the socially constructed nature of reality and the importance of context (Glesne, 2011). However, as discussed in Chapter Three, other theoretical perspectives exist that influence the research design. Erickson (2005) highlighted the distinctions made by theoretical perspectives:

> The interpretive qualitative researcher would say that the question "what is happening" is always accompanied by another question: "and what do those happenings mean to those who are engaged in them?" And a critical qualitative researcher would add a third question, "and are these happenings just and in the best interest of people generally?" (p. 7)

How these more general characteristics are enacted and realized through the research process varies considerably depending upon one's epistemological and theoretical perspective, which then informs the choice of methodology and method. For example, if one is interested in exploring the experiences of White students engaged in service-learning, which route one takes depends upon one's worldview or beliefs about how one comes to know (refer back to the worldview exercise in Chapter One). In Table 4.1 we provide some examples of the relationships between epistemology, methodology, and method.

The important point here is that attention and thoughtfulness must be given to these questions in order to develop a good research design. Furthermore, evidence of researcher decisions regarding epistemology and theoretical perspective must be present in all elements of the research design. For example,

Table 4.1 Relationships Between Elements of the Research Design

Epistemological Grounding	Primary Focus of Research	Methodological Implications
Post-positivist	Development of White racial identity	Survey that includes specific items that measure White racial identity on a scale
Constructivist	Students' understanding and meaning-making about their lived experiences as racial beings	Semi-structured interview guide using phenomenological approach to get at how students come to see themselves as White in the service-learning context
Critical/subjectivist	Interrogation of power relationships that maintain the privileges of being White in a service-learning context	Participant observation and interviewing using critical ethnography that places the researcher in the setting alongside study participants to examine the oppressive structures and cultural norms in the setting

as will be described in greater detail in this chapter, interviews function as a qualitative data collection method in a variety of theoretical perspectives and for a diverse array of methodologies. However, interview questions in a critical inquiry should be worded differently than questions in a phenomenological study, for example.

Statements regarding the purpose of the study and the corresponding research questions should also reflect the philosophical underpinnings (e.g., epistemology and theoretical perspective as both are philosophical in nature) of a study and show congruence between the elements of the research design. In other words, readers of your work should never lose sight of your epistemological and theoretical perspective because it should be evident in all aspects of the research design. Table 4.2 provides a diverse array of examples from published research that illustrate the connections between various elements of the research design. Incidentally, Table 4.2 also demonstrates the different terms that researchers use to describe elements of the research design and the discerning reader will note that some researchers are more explicit about this than others.

Table 4.2 Elements of Research Design and Examples

Research Study Focus	Purpose of the Study	Philosophical Underpinnings
College Men's Gender Identity	"The purpose of this constructivist grounded theory study was to understand the process of college men's gender identity development" (Edwards & Jones, 2009, p. 212).	Constructivist: "This study on college men's gender identity development was approached through a social justice theoretical framework using grounded theory methodology" (Edwards & Jones, 2009, p. 212).
University Diversity Policies	"... I use critical race theory (CRT) as an analytic framework through which to examine the relative subordination of people of color in university settings and how racial inequality may be reproduced through educational policies" (Iverson, 2007, p. 587).	Post-structural: "This investigation used the method of policy discourse analysis to investigate university diversity policies to understand how these documents frame diversity and what reality is produced by diversity action plans" (Iverson, 2007, p. 592).
Lesbian College Student's Multiple Social Identities	"The purpose of this research is to apply constructivism and intersectionality to explore multiple interpretations of relationships among one lesbian college student's social identities" (Abes, 2012, p. 187).	Hybrid-Constructivist and Critical: "Data came from three phases of a constructivist longitudinal study of lesbian identity in which I used narrative inquiry methodology" (Abes, 2012, p. 191).

(continued)

Table 4.2 (continued)

Research Study Focus	Purpose of the Study	Philosophical Underpinnings
Racial Consciousness Among White Male Students Attending an HBCU	"The purpose of this study was to explore the White racial consciousness (WRC) among full-time, White male undergraduates attending a public, predominantly Black HBCU" (Peterson & Hamrick, 2009, p. 35).	Constructivist: "In terms of research framework, phenomenology was the primary theoretical perspective that guided this qualitative, interpretive study focusing on human development, racial consciousness, and educational environments. (Peterson & Hamrick, 2009, p. 36).
Short-term Immersion Programs	"...little is known about the meaning students make of their experience and the nature of the immersion that shapes such potentially transformative learning outcomes, which serves as the purpose of this study" (Jones, Rowan-Kenyon, Ireland, Niehaus, & Skendall, 2012, pp. 201–202).	Constructivist: "To investigate the meaning students made of their experiences as participants on a short-term immersion program, we utilized a multisite case study approach in naturalistic settings. This methodological approach is anchored in a constructivist theoretical framework; thus, highlighting the central role of context and presuming multiple social realities and participant interpretations of these constructions of the social world" (Jones et al., 2012, pp. 204–205).
Recognizing Racist Thoughts	"This study investigated the process individual students go through to recognize racist thoughts in their own lives and within their environment" (Torres, 2009, p. 504).	Constructivist: "The gap that emerges within this theoretical framework [literature review] on racism and racist idea is the possibility of understanding racist ideas as a developmental task within the individual. . . . The study used a constructivist, grounded theory methodology" (Torres, 2009, p. 508).
Black Women College Students	"My study explores the complexities of Black female college students' positive attitudes regarding gender equality and negative attitudes towards the word feminist" (Winkle-Wagner, 2009, p. 183).	Critical: "Data for my study are part of a larger critical ethnographic study of women's college experiences and identity" (Winkle-Wagner, 2009, p. 183).

(continued)

Table 4.2 (continued)

Research Study Focus	Purpose of the Study	Philosophical Underpinnings
Student Veterans	"The purpose of this study was to explore the transition experiences of college student veterans who had returned from war zone deployments and subsequently re-enrolled in college" (Rumann & Hamrick, 2010, p. 436).	Constructivist: "We adopted an interpretive theoretical perspective grounded in constructionist epistemology. . . . phenomenology served as the guiding methodological framework because of the aim to understand respondents' experiences from their perspectives" (Rumann & Hamrick, 2010, p. 436).
Collegiate Evangelical Student Organization	An ethnographic examination of evangelical students and "how students' participation in a homogeneous evangelical student organization enhances their satisfaction with their collegiate experience and helps them develop important life lessons and skills" (Magolda & Ebben Gross, 2009, p. 14).	Critical constructivist: "In addition to interpretivism, we also acknowledge our critical social science (i.e., critical theory) leanings. The critical influence in this Students Serving Christ (SSC) study is evident in three distinct ways. First, we infused the issue of power into the interpretive tapestry. . . . Second, we clearly acknowledge our own presence, position, politic, and subjectivity. . . . Third, we use difference and conflict, rather than similarities and consensus, as organizing concepts in our analysis" (Magolda & Ebben Gross, 2009, p. 25).

Connecting Epistemological and Theoretical Perspectives With Methodological Approaches

As the examples in Table 4.2 demonstrate, the relationship between the philosophical underpinnings or epistemological and theoretical perspectives to methodological approaches is an important one because it conveys *how* the researcher is grounding an investigation of a particular phenomenon and *what* the researcher is interested in exploring. These decisions never begin with an articulation of methods because nearly every method is appropriate within any methodological approach. That is, interviews may be used in a constructivist-grounded theory or a critical narrative inquiry and observations are appropriate in both ethnography and case study designs. However, methodologies vary considerably in terms of their philosophical and disciplinary origins and thus their fit within certain traditions.

Most qualitative methodological approaches are designed within constructivist/interpretive (with an emphasis on understanding and the lived experience), critical/subjectivist (with an emphasis on emancipation and social change), or post-structural (with an emphasis on deconstruction and power) epistemological and theoretical perspectives (Glesne, 2011; Lather, 2007). For example, a researcher may utilize critical theory as a theoretical perspective but engage this perspective with either ethnography or narrative inquiry. Although the choice of a theoretical perspective gives shape to the selection of appropriate methodological approaches, the decision about a particular methodology then provides the direction for decision making regarding methods. In the example just provided, a critical ethnography would most likely rely on extensive fieldwork and participant observation; whereas a critical narrative study would more typically engage participants in in-depth, unstructured interviews that elicit stories.

Methodological Approaches

Methodology is best described as a *strategy* that guides the actual research plan and represents "a theory of how inquiry should proceed. It involves analysis of the assumptions, principles, and procedures in a particular approach to inquiry (that, in turn, governs the use of particular methods)" (Schwandt, 2007a, p. 193). Once a study is situated in a particular philosophical tradition, which informs the methodology, the methodological approach becomes the rudder for all additional research decisions. A number of methodological approaches from which to choose exists in qualitative inquiry. Although it is not possible here to provide a comprehensive description of each, what follows is an introduction to several methodological approaches most prevalent in the higher education scholarly literature, which are

- grounded theory,
- narrative inquiry,
- phenomenology,
- case study, and
- ethnography;

as well as a discussion of several of the elements that distinguish one approach from another. In addition, we will include a brief mention of several other approaches that are gaining traction in higher education, including autoethnography, digital storytelling, and photoethnography. Examples from the studies referenced in Table 4.2 and others will be provided to illuminate the particularities and characteristics of each approach. In some cases, this may mean that certain characteristics will appear in this chapter and in another chapter because they are both a central feature of a particular methodological approach and a more general element of qualitative inquiry (e.g., sampling in grounded theory). Lastly, the connections between methodology and methods will also be explored. Methodological texts and primary sources for these methodologies must be consulted and studied before embarking upon designing research. However, the descriptions that follow should provide the reader with a beginning understanding of each methodological approach, key terminology and characteristics that should be present in the design of a study using each approach, and ample citations that point in the direction of the important methodological literature with which a researcher would want to be familiar.

Grounded Theory

Grounded theory methodology is succinctly described as "a systematic, inductive, and comparative approach for conducting inquiry for the purpose of constructing theory" and is characterized by "researchers' persistent interaction with their data, while remaining constantly involved with their emerging analyses . . . . The iterative process of moving back and forth between empirical data and emerging analysis makes the collected data progressively more focused and the analysis successively more theoretical" (Bryant & Charmaz, 2007, p. 1). Charmaz (2006) identified the defining characteristics of ground theory as follows:

- Simultaneous involvement in data collection and analysis;
- Constructing analytic codes and categories from data, not from preconceived logically deduced hypotheses;
- Using the constant comparative method, which involves making comparisons during each stage of the analysis;
- Advancing theory development during each step of data collection and analysis;
- Memo-writing to elaborate categories, specify their properties, define relationships between categories, and identify gaps; and
- Sampling aimed toward theory construction, not for population representativeness (pp. 5–6)

Many novice researchers are drawn to grounded theory because of what appears to be a structured blueprint for conducting research, which may be perceived as missing in other methodological approaches. However, a closer review of the historical origins, epistemological evolution, and defining characteristics presents a more sophisticated understanding of grounded theory methodology.

Historical Origins and Epistemological Evolution

Grounded theory methodology was developed by two sociologists, Barney Glaser and Anselm Strauss, and is explained in their pioneering book, *The Discovery of Grounded Theory* (1967). Each was socialized and trained in a different research paradigm (e.g., quantitative and interpretive) that, when brought together, incorporated both the flexibility and structure characteristic of grounded theory. Representing two traditions in sociology at the time, their conceptualization of grounded theory integrated Glaser's quantitative training at Columbia University with Strauss' foundation in symbolic interactionism and pragmatism (Charmaz, 2006). The merging of these two disciplinary traditions resulted in what is now viewed as an objectivist-grounded theory and, as conceived by Glaser and Strauss, employs a systematic and structured set of procedures to build an inductively derived theory grounded in the actual data and informed by the phenomenon under study. Although now sometimes criticized for their entrenchment in positivist assumptions, in their time, Glaser and Strauss were perceived as critics in their own right of the prevailing one right way (Lather, 1986) to conduct research; instead, they were seeking "freedom from the sterile methods that permeated social science research at the time" (Star, 2007, p. 77). In fact, many would argue that Glaser and Strauss' work did much to advance the legitimacy of qualitative inquiry (Charmaz, 2006).

The emphasis on the development of theory in grounded theory is often misunderstood and oversimplified as reflected in " 'the grounded theory mantra,' which, in its minimal form, comprises the claim 'theory emerged from the data'" (Bryant & Charmaz, 2007, p. 32) and implies "theory almost mystically emerging from the data" (p. 46). Instead, the implication is that theory is developed through an interactive process that involves the creation and refinement of abstract conceptualizations of particular phenomena. As Charmaz (2006) explained:

> Most grounded theories are substantive theories because they address delimited problems in specific substantive areas such as a study of how newly disabled young people reconstruct their identities. The logic of grounded theory can reach across substantive areas and into the realm of formal theory, which means generating abstract concepts and specifying relationships between them to understand problems in multiple substantive areas. (p. 8)

The generation of theory in grounded theory is accomplished through the use of specific strategies, as will be explained more fully in what follows in this chapter.

As noted, the original conception of grounded theory as described by Glaser and Strauss (1967) is firmly rooted in positivist and objectivist views of reality and a prescribed set of procedures. The credibility, utility, and efficacy of grounded theory were further advanced with the publication of Strauss and Corbin's text, *The Basics of Qualitative Research: Grounded Theory Procedures and Techniques* (first published in 1990 and now in its third edition, which was published in 2008). Strauss and Corbin's mark on the development of grounded theory research was to preserve its objectivist roots and emphasize technical procedures (Charmaz, 2006). They introduced specific analytic strategies and vocabulary, such as open, axial, and selective coding; the conditional matrix; properties and dimensions; causal and intervening conditions; and theoretical saturation. In relation to the epistemological evolution of grounded theory, Juliet

Corbin reflected in the preface of the third edition of *The Basics of Qualitative Research*, "But one day I looked about and found that I had been labeled a 'post-positivist.' 'Oh dear,' I thought, 'I've been classified and labeled just like we do in qualitative research!' " (Corbin & Strauss, 2008, p. vii). Quipping that while she was busy at work a "Qualitative Revolution" (p. vii) was going on signaled her awareness of the move to more constructivist approaches to grounded theory.

Kathy Charmaz (2000, 2006) is the scholar who has advanced a constructivist approach to grounded theory, which she suggests, "places priority on the phenomena of study and sees both data and analysis as created from shared experiences and relationships with participants and other sources of data (Charmaz, 2006, p. 130). Because constructivists place a primacy on meaning-making and interpretation of participants and researchers alike, constructivist-grounded theory not only "theorizes the interpretive work that research participants do, but also acknowledges that the resulting theory is an interpretation" (Charmaz, 2006, p. 130). This characteristic of constructivist-grounded theory necessarily foregrounds the importance of researcher reflexivity related to interpretations. Charmaz (2005) also discussed constructivist-grounded theory as a methodology by which to advance social justice research by "combining critical inquiry and grounded theory in novel and productive ways" (p. 529). Social justice issues, such as power, hegemony, privilege, and inequality, become sensitizing concepts in grounded theory research and then lead the researcher to investigate "if, when, how, to what extent, and under what conditions these concepts become relevant to the study" (Charmaz, 2005, p. 512). This is an important contribution to grounded theory because Charmaz paves the way for researchers to use constructivist and critical perspectives as both an epistemological framework but also as a methodological approach (Robbins, 2012).

Although a preponderance of grounded theory research in higher education contexts employs constructivist approaches, other approaches exist that incorporate theoretical perspectives, such as postmodernism or feminist theory with specific methodological strategies. For example, Adele Clarke (2005) developed an approach called situational analysis, which "allows researchers to draw together studies of discourse and agency, action and structure, image, text and context, history and the present moment—to analyze complex situations of inquiry broadly conceived" (p. xxii). Drawing upon postmodern thought and emphasizing the contingent and unstable nature of the social worlds in which individuals move, Clarke (2005) described three mapping approaches that preserve the complexities of empirical realities:

1.   Situational maps that lay out the major human, nonhuman, discursive, and other elements in the research situation of inquiry and provoke analysis of relations among them;
2.   Social worlds/arena maps that lay out the collective actors, key nonhuman elements, and the arena(s) of commitment and discourse within which they are engaged in ongoing negotiations—meso-level interpretations of the situations; and

3. Positional maps that lay out the major positions taken, and *not* taken, in the data vis-à-vis particular axes of difference, concerns, and controversy around issues in the situation of inquiry. (p. xxii)

Her approach provides a visual image for the relationships and processes in the data as well as for capturing micro, meso, and macro elements of analysis.

By way of an example of how researchers illuminate the distinctions between approaches to grounded theory research, Edwards and Jones (2009) made explicit their approach:

> By examining college men's identity development from a social justice theoretical perspective, this study was conducted to gain a better understanding of how internalized patriarchy is learned, reinforced, and perhaps transcended by individual men . . . . Grounded theory conducted from a constructivist epistemological paradigm is particularly suited for examining processes, structure, and context, all of which are key tools in broadening rather than narrowing the inquiry and exploring identity as socially constructed phenomenon in the context of hierarchical social structures such as patriarchy. (p. 212)

This is a good example of the important connection between epistemology and methodology. The decision to locate a study within a constructivist, critical, or objectivist framework brings consequences for how research questions are framed and for strategies of inquiry and particular methods. What follows is a description of some of the most important defining characteristics and strategies of grounded theory methodology.

Constant Comparative Method of Data Analysis and Coding

Making constant comparisons is at the heart of data analysis and coding in grounded theory. Charmaz (2006) defined the constant comparative method as:

> A method of analysis that generates successively more abstract concepts and theories through inductive processes of comparing data with data, data with category, category with category, and category with concept. Comparisons then constitute each stage of analytic development. (p. 187)

Constant comparisons are made at every stage of the analytic process, which is typically referred to as coding. Corbin and Strauss (2008) laid out a very structured and complex coding schema that reflects the foundational work of Glaser and Strauss. We are going to present the more flexible process of coding and analysis presented by Charmaz (2006) because her framework is more widely used in higher education research. She identified two main phases of coding: initial and focused coding, which are then followed by theoretical coding.

Initial coding.   The initial stage of coding involves close reads of transcripts and the data through line-by-line coding. As the researcher reads through every transcript, the questions to ask include, "What are these data a study of?" and "What do the data suggest?" (Charmaz, 2006, p. 47). The responses to these questions result in the naming through codes of specific chunks of data. Charmaz (2006) recommended that initial coding be characterized by "speed and spontaneity" (p. 48) and that words used as codes should reflect action. So, for example, rather than coding using the word "speed," a more active code would be "read quickly," which conveys the data as action. In this phase of coding, the researcher "fractures" the data, which results in many codes that typically cover a wide variety of topics (Charmaz, 2006). Charmaz (2000) cautioned against "pasting catching concepts on our data" (p. 515) at this stage of the analysis and instead recommended staying very close to the participants' words. The number of codes generated will depend in part on the number of participants and amount of data collected. Initial coding in the Edwards and Jones (2009) study resulted in more than 1,100 individual line-by-line codes.

Focused coding.   Codes developed through focused coding "are more directed, selective, and conceptual" (Charmaz, 2006, p. 57) than initial codes and means using "the most significant and/or frequent earlier codes" (p. 57) to make analytic sense of large amounts of data. Focused coding enables the researcher to make an analytic turn as focused codes become more integrative and theoretically rich categories. As Dey (2007) explained, "Categories are not simply generated by data, but through judgment in terms of some cognitive frame of reference by which we make sense of experience" (p. 170). An example of the analytic move from initial coding to focused coding from the Edwards and Jones (2009) study is represented by an initial code titled "proving manhood" which then became, as a focused code, "proving masculinity as insecurity."

Theoretical codes are integrative and "specify possible relationships between categories you have developed in your focused coding" (Charmaz, 2006, p. 63). Theoretical coding results in "an analytic storyline that has coherence" (Charmaz, 2006, p. 63) and may be aided by the incorporation of concepts and theories from the literature. However, Charmaz (2006) cautioned that "each preconceived idea [e.g., from the literature] should *earn* its way into your analysis" (p. 68). Theoretical codes form the foundation for the emerging grounded theory. In Edwards and Jones's (2009) study, theoretical coding resulted in the use of the metaphor of a mask and "putting my man face on." The strategies of the constant comparative method of data analysis and theoretical sampling make the relationships among sampling, data collection, and data analysis explicit. We now turn to the important role of theoretical sampling in grounded theory.

Theoretical Sampling

As will be discussed in the next chapter, sampling is an integral element to conducting any study. As Morse (2007) parsimoniously stated, "Excellent data are obtained through careful sampling" (p. 235). She goes on to elaborate:

> An excellent participant for grounded theory is one who has been through, or observed, the experience under investigation. Participants must therefore be experts in the experience or the phenomenon under investigation, they must be willing to participate, and have the time to share the necessary information; and they must be reflective, willing, and able to speak articulately about the experience. Not all of those people who volunteer to participate in your study will have all of the characteristics of an excellent participant. (p. 231)

Like other methodological approaches, grounded theory studies begin with convenience sampling during which participants are selected because they have experienced the phenomenon of interest. This early sampling process helps to define the scope of the phenomenon, boundaries, and the trajectory of the process (Morse, 2007). Next, purposeful sampling is utilized after initial data analysis and to locate participants who are going through some dimension or particular stage of the trajectory. Then, at the later stages of the study, theoretical sampling, a defining characteristic of grounded theory, is utilized. As should be clear, in grounded theory research, data collection, sampling, and analysis are integrally related and occur in an iterative process.

Theoretical sampling is often misunderstood, most typically because researchers place the emphasis on sampling by adding additional participants, rather than on the theoretical dimension of this strategy. As data analysis moves from description to more abstract conceptualization, theoretical sampling is a strategy used, "which means seeking and collecting pertinent data to elaborate and refine categories in your emerging theory" (Charmaz, 2006, p. 96). What is important to note is that the emphasis is on developing analytic categories and themes, saturating them so no new properties emerge, thus refining categories enough that they form an emerging theory (Charmaz, 2006; Corbin & Strauss, 2008). "Sampling" in theoretical sampling can sometimes mean adding new participants, returning to existing participants, or going back to existing data to theorize more deeply. Thus, theoretical sampling is concept driven, not person driven. As Charmaz (2006) stated, "Initial sampling in grounded theory is where you start whereas theoretical sampling directs you where to go . . . . In short, theoretical sampling pertains only to conceptual and theoretical development" (pp. 100–101). One of the best ways to get into theoretical sampling is through memo-writing (Charmaz, 2006).

Memo-Writing

Memo-writing is essential to the analytic process in grounded theory. In fact, Lempert (2007) suggested "It is *the* fundamental process of researcher/data engagement that results in a 'grounded' theory. Memo writing is the methodological link, the distillation process, through which the researcher transforms data into theory" (p. 245). Similarly, Charmaz (2006) wrote that "memo-writing is the pivotal intermediate stop between data collection and writing drafts of papers" (p. 72). Researchers should start writing memos early in the analytic process—essentially, whenever something comes to mind that relates to what is happening in the data. Memos should be more spontaneous than mechanical and written as a conversation with oneself, but they should always serve analytical purposes rather than descriptive (Charmaz, 2006). Lempert (2007) suggested that later memos may incorporate literature to use "the ideas and theoretical insights of other researchers to inform and to sensitize myself to potential patterns in the data" (p. 255). They may also include participants' quotations so as to provide "an immediate illustration of the analytical topic" (Lempert, 2007, p. 256). Taken together, memos then become integral to the analysis and writing process, to the emerging theory, and to the final written product in a grounded theory study.

Narrative Inquiry

Narrative inquiry is a broad term and may include various approaches, such as life history, oral history, biography, or autoethnography (Creswell, 2013; Glesne, 2011). It is also important to distinguish between narrative inquiry and narrative analysis. Many different qualitative approaches rely on narrative texts for analysis, as does narrative inquiry. However, narrative inquiry as a methodological approach relies on "life experiences as narrative by those who live them" (Chase, 2011, p. 421) or "the study of stories or narratives or descriptions of a series of events" (Pinnegar & Daynes, 2007, p. 4). Creswell (2013) clearly articulated the distinction:

> "Narrative" might be the *phenomenon* being studied, such as a narrative of illness, or it might be the *method* used in a study, such as the procedures of analyzing stories told (Chase, 2005; Clandinin & Connelly, 2000; Pinnegar & Daynes, 2007). As a method, it begins with the experiences as expressed in the lived and told stories of individuals. (p. 70)

Although often described as an interdisciplinary methodology, narrative inquiry enjoys a long history in psychology and increasingly in student development research. This is primarily because of the relationship between stories, identities, and meaning making. As Chase (2011) explained, "Narrative theorists define narrative as a distinct form of discourse: as meaning making through the shaping or ordering of experience, a way of understanding one's own or others' actions, of organizing events and objects into a meaningful whole, of connecting and seeing the consequences of actions and events over time . . . by maintaining a focus on narrated lives" (p. 421).

Clandinin and Rosiek (2007) echoed this focus in what they called a "shared commitment" among narrative researchers, to "the study of experience" (p. 69). They drew upon Clandinin and Connelly's (2000) discussion of defining features of narrative inquiry and emphasize the importance of attention to temporality, sociality, and place. Temporality refers to the continuity of experience as situated in time. That is, experience is grounded in the past and present, which are carried into future experiences. Clandinin and Rosiek (2007) elaborated that "Events, people, and objects under study are in temporal transition and narrative inquirers describe them with a past, present, and a future" (p. 69). Sociality captures the integral relationship between the individual and social context. Narrative researchers then focus on the individual (e.g., feelings, hopes, values, and dispositions) and the individual's interaction with the larger social context (e.g., environment, external forces, and other people) (Clandinin & Rosiek, 2007). Sociality also includes the relationship between the researcher and participant and the importance of recognizing the researcher as someone who brings social context into this relationship. Finally, place "draws attention to the centrality of place, that is, to the specific concrete, physical, and topological boundaries of place where the inquiry and events take place" (Clandinin & Rosiek, 2007, p. 70).

Chase (2011) offered a helpful discussion of several different approaches to narrative inquiry that explicate different areas of emphasis that may be taken by researchers. Summarized, these include focus on the following:

- The relationship between people's life stories and the quality of their life experiences. These researchers usually emphasize *what* people's stories are about—their plot, characters, and sometimes the structure or sequencing of their content.
- Narrative *as* lived experience, as social action. The researchers are as interested in *how* people narrate their experiences, as in what their stories are about.
- The relationship between people's narrative practices and their local narrative environments . . . . These researchers are more interested in understanding *narrative reality* in any local context—what does and doesn't get said, about what, why, how, and to whom—than they are in understanding individuals' stories per se.
- Researchers treat[ing] *their* stories about life experience (including research itself as a life experience) as a significant and necessary focus of narrative inquiry. (pp. 421–423)

In an example from published research Jones, Segar, and Gasiorski (2008) used a narrative methodological approach to explore students' constructions of meaning of their high school service-learning graduation requirement. They explained, "To access these experiences and perceptions, narrative inquiry was utilized as an approach that illuminates human experiences as lived and told as stories" (Chase, 2005; Clandinin & Connelly, 2000) (p. 7). In this statement the researchers not only provide a rationale for the use of narrative inquiry, but they also provide methodological citations to demonstrate their knowledge of this specific approach.

We have gone to some length to introduce narrative inquiry so as to provide a glimpse into the complexities of narrative approaches. Novice researchers are sometimes drawn to narrative inquiry because of the emphasis on story telling.

However, as this introduction hopefully makes clear, stories are central to narrative inquiry, but this is not simply about telling stories and studying people's lives. As Clandinin and Rosiek (2007) summarized:

> Beginning with a respect for ordinary lived experiences, the focus of narrative inquiry is not only a valorizing of individual experiences but also an exploration of the social, cultural, and institutional narratives within which individuals' experiences were constituted, shaped, expressed, and enacted—but in a way that begins and ends that inquiry in the storied lives of the people involved. (p. 42)

In these next sections, we highlight several other central characteristics of narrative inquiry and provide examples from published research to illustrate these characteristics in practice.

Analysis of Narratives

What distinguishes the analysis of narratives in narrative inquiry from other approaches in which narratives are collected? At the most basic level, it is the emphasis on stories and understanding lived experiences through the stories told by those narrating them. Analysis of narratives involves both developing an understanding of the individual life stories as well as a more holistic narrative. Or as Josselson (2011) explained, narrative analysis "involves gaining an overall sense of meaning and then examining the parts in relation to it—which involves changing our understanding of the whole until we arrive at a holistic understanding that best encompasses the meanings of the parts" (p. 228). Josselson further broke down this process into four activities: (a) an overall reading of each interview to begin to ascertain general themes and then returning to specific parts of each transcript to develop meaning while also keeping an eye on how the meaning of each part contributes to an understanding of the whole; (b) multiple readings of each transcript to track different narratives at play within each and how these relate to one another; (c) with multiple readings, a story that captures both the whole and the patterns in the parts begins to emerge; and (d) dialogue the themes with the theoretical literature to deepen the researcher's understandings of the meanings and emerging stories (p. 228). In these iterative readings, the researcher pays attention to the structure of the narratives, the content, the larger contexts and the ways in which these overlap. In the end, the outcome of a narrative analysis is "to illuminate human experience as it is presented in textual form in order to reveal layered meanings people assign to aspects of their lives" (Josselson, 2011, p. 240).

In returning to the study conducted on a service-learning high school graduation requirement, Jones, Segar, and Gasiorski (2008) described an analytic process that moved from description to more analytical and interpretive themes to re-story the narratives of their participants. Interested in the meaning that participants made of this requirement, particularly in light of the intended outcomes of such a requirement, the researchers were first struck by what appeared to be a "non-story." That is, few participants offered "transformative" or "life-changing" narratives so often found in the service-learning literature. This led the researchers to create three narratives that told the story of these participants which they titled: "A (Dis) Serving Narrative: The Connection between the High School Service-learning Requirement and College Involvement"; "An Acquiescent Narrative: High School Experiences with the Requirement"; and "A Tenuous Narrative of Required Service and Participation: A Double-Edged Sword." Each narrative theme was accompanied by quotations from participants to warrant the interpretive claims made by the researchers. This example also suggests the important relationship between narrative analysis and representation by the researcher, an issue to which we next turn.

Researcher as Narrator

Although the researcher collects individual narratives in the form of stories in narrative inquiry, the researcher also "re-storys" these narratives through analysis and interpretation. This places the researcher in the role of narrator of others' stories and experiences and requires great trust between the researcher and participant (Marshall & Rossman, 2011). Further, as Josselson (2011) suggested, "The construction of the story reflects the current internal world of the narrator as well as aspects of the social world in which he or she lives" (p. 227). How the researcher/narrator brings his or her own story into the narratives of participants depends in part on the theoretical perspective grounding the study (as will be discussed more fully later in this chapter and as discussed in Chapter Three); yet, regardless, the researcher must be attuned to both the role being played as narrator and the responsibility this carries.

Because of the emphasis in narrative inquiry on hearing the stories within each narrative, on listening across the narratives of all participants, as well as on tuning into what is not said or the implicit narratives (Chase, 2005; Josselson, 2011), the researcher must understand "what is storyworthy" (Chase, 2005, p. 661). This involves both the ability of the researcher to develop interview questions that evoke stories from participants and then to tell the story in such a way that interprets and conveys the content and the meaning of the stories in a more holistic way (Chase, 2005; Josselson, 2011). As poignantly described by Weis and Fine (2000), researchers often embark upon a "voyeuristic search for a good story" (p. 48), which raises the question of what constitutes a *good* story (and what would be a *bad* story). In discussing their research on urban poor and dropouts, they went on to write that, "By looking for great stories, we potentially walk into the field with constructions of the 'other,' however benevolent or benign they seem, feeding the politics of representation and becoming part of the negative figuration of poor women and men" (pp. 48–49). This dynamic results in what Weis and Fine (2000) referred to as a "triple-representational problem" (p. 53). That is, researchers must consider how we present ourselves, the narrators, and "others."

Researchers then must make decisions about their voices and how to represent the voices of their participants. Chase (2005) suggested that narrative researchers may utilize different (and potentially overlapping) narrative strategies or voices in telling the stories of participants. She refers to these as the authoritative voice, the supportive voice, and the interactive voice. An *authoritative voice* both connects and separates the researcher's and participants' voices by providing long excerpts from participants' stories and interspersing the researcher throughout. However, the researcher also "assert[s] an authoritative interpretive voice on the grounds that they have a different interest from the narrators in the narrators' stories" (Chase, 2005, p. 664). A possible critique of this narrative strategy is that the researcher's interpretations are given more weight. When using a *supportive voice*, the narrative researcher foregrounds the participants' voices. Although still needing to make decisions about how to tell a participant's story, "the goal of this narrative strategy is to bring the narrator's story to the public—to get the narrator's story heard—researchers do not usually dwell on how they engaged in these interpretive processes" (Chase, 2005, p. 665). A critique of this strategy is that the researcher may "romanticize the narrator's voice" (p. 665). The *interactive voice* is a narrative strategy that "displays the complex interaction—the intersubjectivity—between researchers' and narrators' voices. These researchers examine *their* voices—their subject positions, social locations, interpretations, and personal experiences—through the refracted medium of narrators' voices" (Chase, 2005, p. 666). Because the researchers using this narrative strategy make themselves known in the text, they "are vulnerable to the criticism that they are self-indulgent and that they air dirty laundry that nobody wants to see" (p. 666).

Connecting Theoretical Perspectives With Narrative Inquiry

As has been discussed throughout this book, the theoretical perspective employed by a researcher influences other elements of the research design. Although by definition, narrative inquiry seems consonant with constructivist and interpretive perspectives, narratives may also be designed using critical approaches or utilizing ethnographic or case study strategies, for example. Adopting one of these approaches should shift the way in which narratives are constructed and presented, what is deemed "storyworthy," and the narrative voice used by the researcher. A few examples from published research illustrate this point. Patton and Catching (2009) used critical race theory (CRT) to explore the counternarratives (a core tenet of CRT) of African American faculty in higher education and student affairs programs. The authors describe CRT as both the conceptual and methodological framework for their study and counterstorytelling as a method for analyzing and telling the stories of those on the margins of educational discourse. Their critical race counternarrative is a composite story "that explicate[s] the hegemonic and overlapping nature of race, racism, and power" (Patton & Catching, 2009, p. 717).

Another example of the influence of theoretical perspective is found in the work of Jones, Robbins, and LePeau (2011) and Jones, LePeau, and Robbins (2013) who conducted a narrative case study exploring the meaning students made on an alternative break trip focused on HIV/AIDS. The researchers analyzed the data in this narrative study using both a constructivist approach and then one informed by critical theory. When situated within a constructivist framework, the results were presented as a contextual narrative (focused on the setting of the trip), individual narratives (which described the story for each participant), and shared narratives (which addressed the storylines shared by all participants). This narrative analysis highlighted the constructions of meaning and stories as told by the participants themselves, not straying too far from their narratives and without overlaying a strong theoretical perspective. Because the researchers noticed the presence of implicit narratives and silences surrounding issues of power, privilege, HIV/AIDS, and reciprocity, they employed critical theory to analyze the data again in order to listen "*through* [emphasis added] the person's story to hear the operation of broader social discourses shaping that person's story of their experience" (Clandinin & Rosiek, 2007, p. 55). The result of this narrative analysis using a critical perspective produced narratives (represented by the themes that follow in quotations) that focused on the students ("Modifying my schema about living with HIV and dying of AIDS"), the residents with AIDS in the health center where students worked ("You're lucky you get to do service"), and friends and family ("She would cry if I went to Africa"). As a result of a critical analysis of narratives, the researchers were able to interrogate some of the taken-for-granted outcomes often associated with service-learning and thus tell a different story from the one using a constructivist approach.

Further, emerging approaches to narrative are gaining interest such as the blurring of epistemological boundaries to produce a "borderlands of narrative inquiry" (Clandinin & Rosiek, 2007, p. 57). This approach recognizes that "in the practice of research . . . philosophical exactness is often a luxury" (p. 58) and advances the promise of multiple and overlapping philosophical contributions in understanding individuals' storied lives. Another newer approach is that of digital storytelling, an approach "that draws on the power of digitized images to support the contents of the story" (Marshall & Rossman, 2011, p. 154). This approach is characterized as emancipatory because of the emphasis on participant driven use of voice, image, and sound to tell a story. Rolón-Dow (2011) incorporated digital storytelling in a study framed by critical race theory that explored how students in high school constructed their identities and racialized educational contexts. Even with new approaches to the study of narratives, what remains is a belief "that stories matter and that, increasingly, we are interested in knowing the stories that all people live and tell" (Clandinin & Rosiek, 2007, p. 71).

Phenomenology

The primary focus of phenomenology is the essence of a particular phenomenon or lived experience. Phenomenology is both a school of philosophy associated with the works of Hans-Georg Gadamer, Edmund Husserl, Martin Heidegger, and Maurice Merleau-Ponty and a methodology (Arminio, 2001; Merriam, 2009). Each of these philosophers created a slightly different school of phenomenological thought (e.g., Gadamer's work focused on the philosophical and historical, Husserl's on transcendental psychology, Heidegger's on hermeneutic phenomenology, and Merleau-Ponty's on existential phenomenology), but all share important constituent elements (Crotty, 1998). Because most research in education represents hermeneutic phenomenology, the focus here is on this approach. Hermeneutics refers to the interpretation of an object for the purpose of understanding. Martin Heidegger's (1962) focus was on a phenomenological analysis of *Dasein* or being-in-the world. Schwandt (2001) suggested that "phenomenologists insist on careful description of ordinary conscious experience of everyday life (the *life-world*)—a description of 'things' (the essential structures of consciousness) as one experiences them" (p. 191).

The philosophical foundation of hermeneutic phenomenology provides direction for phenomenological research, which focuses on the uniqueness of the lived experience or *essence* of a particular phenomenon. As such, phenomenology is always anchored in the *lifeworld* of the individual and the meaning making associated with being-in-the-world. According to van Manen (1990),

> From a phenomenological point of view, to do research is always to question the way we experience the world, to want to know the world in which we live as human beings. And since to *know* the world is profoundly to *be* in the world in a certain way, the act of researching—questioning—theorizing is the intentional act of attaching ourselves to the world, to become more fully part of it, or better, to *become,* the world. Phenomenology calls this inseparable connection to the world the principle of "intentionality." (p. 5)

An important, yet challenging, principle to grasp in phenomenological research is that this lifeworld is prereflective. That is, uncovering the essence of experience means surfacing the meaning or the structure of the experience itself, rather than providing a conceptualization of the experience. This requires great thoughtfulness and caring (Heidegger, 1926/1962). van Manen (1990) explained this distinction: "Phenomenology . . . differs from almost every other science in that it attempts to gain insightful descriptions of the way we experience the world prereflectively, without taxonomizing, classifying, or abstracting it," and it "offers us the possibility of plausible insights that bring us in more direct contact with the world" (p. 9).

What does the research process look like in a hermeneutic phenomenological study? What does it mean to illuminate an aspect of the lifeworld *as we find it?* Before turning to several important components of phenomenological research, it is important to acknowledge a central tension to this approach. In addition to the central assumption that there is an essence to shared experience (Patton, 2002), van Manen (1990) wrote,

> To *do* hermeneutic phenomenology is to attempt to accomplish the impossible: To construct a full interpretive description of some aspect of the lifeworld, yet to remain aware that life is always more complex than any explication or meaning can reveal. (p. 18)

In an example from published research, Rockenbach, Walker, and Luzader (2012) stated the purpose of their phenomenological study as "to uncover the meaning, dimensions, and processes of spiritual struggles in college students' lives" (p. 55) in order to understand the phenomenon of spiritual struggle. In this statement, they emphasized an uncovering process to get at an in-depth understanding of spiritual struggle. What is important to note here is that the focus in phenomenology is on a particular phenomenon (e.g., spiritual struggle), not on the meaning students make of spiritual struggle (which would be more appropriate in a narrative inquiry), although such meaning making might constitute part of the essence.

Doing Phenomenological Research

Phenomenology, on the surface, holds initial appeal to novice researchers because of the emphasis on "lived experience," despite the reality that much qualitative inquiry focuses on lived experience. However, as Patton (2002) pointed out, because of this appeal, the meaning of phenomenology is diluted through the absence of an in-depth understanding of what it requires. To *do* phenomenological research means to get at the essence of a particular phenomenon among a typically small group of individuals who have experienced the phenomenon (Creswell, 2013). Patton (2002) identified the central question of phenomenologists as "What is the meaning, structure, and essence of the lived experience of this phenomenon for this person or group of people" (p. 104). And this meaning is not simple description but instead "the very nature of a phenomenon, for that which makes a some-'thing' what it is—and without which it could not be what it is" (van Manen, 1990, p. 10). This is referred to as the *qualis* in phenomenology, that what-is or essence of a particular, everyday phenomenon.

van Manen (1990), in his book entitled *Researching Lived Experience*, provided one explication, often cited, of the methodological approach to conducting hermeneutic phenomenology. He identified six critical research activities that are not intended to outline a series of steps, but rather are themes central to this approach that exist in dynamic interplay with one another. Taken together, however, they do provide the researcher with a guide for conducting phenomenological research. These six activities and a brief descriptor are as follows:

- *Turning to the question*—Establishes the connection between the researcher and the phenomenon of interest as an "abiding concern" to the researcher, including the "preunderstandings" the researcher brings to the study;
- *Investigating experience as we live it*—Guides the data collection process with an emphasis on getting at the core and structure of an experience, rather than a conceptualization of it. Phenomenologists ask, "What is it like to experience [phenomenon of interest, which typically represents everyday and ordinary occurrences]?" Creswell (2013) added a second open-ended question, which is "What contexts or situations have typically influenced or affected your experiences of the phenomenon?" (p. 81);
- *Reflecting on essential themes*—Describes data analysis through the process of reflection and writing, which exposes the structure and essence of the lived experience. In reading and reflecting on the data collected, phenomenologists identify significant statements that "provide an understanding of how the participants experienced the phenomenon" (Creswell, 2013, p. 82) and then move into developing clusters of meaning, which, together, are used to write a textural description of what participants experienced and a structural description of the contexts or settings that influenced how participants experienced the phenomenon. Finally, a composite description is written of the essence of the phenomenon of interest and gets at the underlying structure of the phenomenon (Creswell, 2013);
- *The art of writing and rewriting*—Moves the researcher closer to the composite description and involves thoughtfulness, attentiveness to language, and a constant back-and-forth between thinking, reflecting, writing, formulating, reformulating, and rethinking;
- *Maintaining a strong and oriented relation*—Assists the researcher in staying focused on the phenomenon of interest and developing the deeper understanding required to get to the essence. van Manen (1990) wrote, "To be oriented to an object means that we are animated by the object in a full and human sense" (p. 33) and represents what matters to the researcher and thus represents a philosophy of action;
- *Balancing the research context by considering parts and whole*—Represents the tension identified earlier between the assumed essence of a phenomenon and the complexities of lived experience and the "overall design of the study/text against the significance that the parts must play in the total textual structure" (van Manen, 1990, p. 33).

Phenomenological Interviewing and Analysis

Because of the emphasis on in-depth understanding and underlying structure of a particular everyday phenomenon, phenomenological interviewing is the typical means of data collection (Merriam, 2009). However, it is important to point out that phenomenological interviewing may be appropriate across methodological approaches but is not the same as conducting phenomenological research, which is distinguished by more than the nature of interviewing. Interviews must be conducted with individuals who have directly experienced the phenomenon of interest (Patton, 2002) and interview questions must be constructed to access the structure and meaning of the particular phenomenon. For example, a phenomenologist interested in student experiences with intercultural learning would not ask *how* students learn about intercultural differences, but instead, *what is the nature or essence* of the experience of intercultural learning. Open-ended questions are most often utilized by the researcher so as to enable participants to describe their experiences of the phenomenon and the meanings they make. For example, in the study referenced earlier on the nature of spiritual struggle, Rockenbach et al. (2012) explained that "The first interview focused on the meaning of spiritual struggle for participants, the nature and experience of their particular struggle, and the ways in which spiritual struggle had shaped them" (p. 61). In another study on the nature of race-related guilt, Arminio (2001) conducted five to six interviews with each participant with the first interview guided by very open-ended questions to begin to get at the essence of race-related guilt, such as "tell me your story," "tell me what is important to you," and "tell me your thoughts on race" (Arminio, 2001, p. 242).

Seidman (1989) suggested that phenomenological researchers utilize a "three in-depth interviews" approach to data collection. The three interviews enable participants to reflect on past and present experiences with the particular phenomenon of interest. More specifically, the first interview focuses on past experiences and the second interview on present experiences. The third interview "joins these two narratives to describe the individual's essential experience with the phenomenon" (Marshall & Rossman, 2011, p. 148). Because of the in-depth nature of the interview questions and the focus of some phenomenological studies on topics that may be emotional (e.g., the essence of spiritual struggle and the essence of guilt, loneliness, caring, or helping), the researcher must work hard at establishing rapport and trust with participants.

As noted, getting to the essence and structure of a particular phenomenon, which represents the focus of both data collection and analysis, is not easy. Unlike other methodological approaches, the outcome of phenomenological research is less about portraying individuals' unique experiences and meaning-making and more so about uncovering an essential structure of a particular phenomenon that resonates with many individuals. This is accomplished when readers give a "phenomenological nod" to findings. That is, they read the written account of the essence of a particular phenomenon and nod, thinking, "yes, I see myself in this depiction." van Manen (1990) noted that "the essence or nature of an experience has been adequately described in language if the description reawakens or shows us the lived quality and significance of the experience in a fuller and deeper manner" (p. 10). According to Giorgi, to accomplish this result through phenomenological analysis requires (a) reading for a sense of the whole; (b) differentiating the description into meaning units; (c) reflecting on the significance of each meaning unit; and (d) clarifying the structure of the phenomenon (as cited in Wertz, 2011. p. 131). Creswell's discussion of phenomenological analysis embraces similar analytic activities but is described as follows: (a) develop a list of significant statements; (b) group the significant statements into larger units of information or meaning units; (c) write a description of the "what" the participants in the study experienced with the phenomenon; (d) write a description of "how" the experience happened; and (e) write a composite description of the phenomenon incorporating the what and the how (Creswell, 2013, pp. 193–194). The important point here is that many are drawn to phenomenology because of a perceived focus on the "lived experience." However, phenomenological analysis is much more than this.

Epoché and Bracketing

Phenomenology demands great reflexivity on the part of the researcher. This is not uncommon in other methodological approaches; however, in phenomenology, it is specifically described as *epoché* and is treated as a first step in phenomenological analysis. Epoché and bracketing are often treated as synonymous in the literature, but in fact they represent two distinct, yet related, steps in phenomenological research. Epoché was described by Moustakas (1994) as when "the everyday understandings, judgments, and knowings are set aside, and the phenomena are revisiting, visually, naively, in a wide-open sense, from the vantage point of a pure or transcendental ego" (p. 33). This process of internal reflection and setting aside personal assumptions results in a "phenomenological attitude shift" (Patton, 2002, p. 485) and enables the researcher to become clear about one's pre-understandings. Although epoché is an ongoing process throughout analysis, bracketing follows epoché in an analytic process referred to as phenomenological reduction. Once the researcher's pre-understandings are identified during epoché, then these pre-understandings are put aside through bracketing. Patton (2002) noted that bracketing comes from Husserl's work and requires that "the researcher holds the phenomenon up for serious inspection. It is taken out of the world where it occurs. It is taken apart and dissected. Its elements and essential structures are uncovered, defined, and analyzed" (p. 485).

Despite Husserl's claim that "bracketing out" is important to phenomenological work, others acknowledge that this is impossible. Instead, as van Manen (1990) suggested, "It is better to make explicit our understandings, beliefs, biases, assumptions, presuppositions, and theories" (p. 47), thereby exposing the pre-understandings that influence our interest in a particular phenomenon. Rockenbach, Walker, and Luzader (2012) commented directly on this challenge and wrote:

> We wrestled with the tension between the phenomenological tradition of epoché and our collective position that the realities described in qualitative research are a reflection of the intertwining subjectivities of researchers and participants. For us, existing within this tension involved revealing our

subjectivities through epoché and approaching the study with a heightened consciousness of the potential implications of our identities and experiences for the interpretation we constructed together with our participants. (p. 58)

In another example from published research, Bergerson and Huftalin (2011) investigated the phenomenon of openness to social identity-based difference. They explicitly addressed their use of bracketing throughout their research process "to examine, chronicle, and become more aware of our assumptions" (p. 383). Despite these two examples, reference to epoché and bracketing is often left out of published reports of phenomenological research. This may be due to page restrictions of many journals, but as a core component and process of phenomenological research, it is critical to engage in the practice of thinking through what epoché and bracketing represent to the research process.

Case Study

Case study methodology is frequently used in higher education and student affairs research because many of our work environments and the situations we encounter represent "cases." The temptation becomes great, then, to simply identify a known group on campus (e.g., student organization, residential community, or service-learning class) and design a "case study." However, the term is often used incorrectly because researchers new to case study often refer to it only as a unit of analysis rather than as a methodological approach. In fact, Flyvbjerg (2011) organized his chapter on case study in the fourth edition of *The Sage Handbook of Qualitative Research* around five misunderstandings about case study research. Both perceptions are correct but appropriate in different contexts and serve different purposes. For example, Stake (2005) suggested, "Case study is not a methodological choice but a choice of what is to be studied" (p. 443), whereas Merriam (2009) defined case study as "an in-depth description and analysis of a bounded system" (p. 40). Although Flyvbjerg (2011) stated that "if you choose to do a case study, you are therefore not so much making a methodological choice as a choice of what is to be studied" (p. 301), he goes on to provide additional characteristics and defining qualities that are very helpful to a more nuanced understanding of case study. In particular, Flyvbjerg (2011) emphasized that case studies are:

- Defined by the demarcation of the unit's boundaries;
- Intensive; that is, include more detail, richness, completeness, and depth;
- Influenced by developmental factors in that they evolve over time and in specific time and place; and
- Focused on the relation to environment or context. (p. 301)

What distinguishes case study methodology from other qualitative approaches is the intensive focus on a *bounded system,* which can be an individual, a specific program, a process, an institution, or a relationship. Implicit in the selection of case study methodology is the assumption that there is something significant that can be learned from a single case (Stake, 2000). The bounded system provides lines around what is to be studied, and what is not and must be clearly explicated. Merriam (2009) further explained that the phenomenon of interest must be "intrinsically bounded" (p. 41) to represent a case and in which "the unit of analysis, *not* the topic of investigation, characterizes a case" (p. 41). She offered the following helpful example:

> … a study of how older adults learn to use computers would probably be a qualitative study but not a case study, the unit of analysis would be the learners' experiences, and an indefinite number of older adult learners and their experiences using computers could be selected for the study. For it to be a case study, *one* particular program or *one* particular classroom of learners (a bounded system), or *one* particular older learner selected on the basis of typicality, uniqueness, success, and so forth, would be the unit of analysis. (p. 41)

Despite the seeming confusion about case studies, or what Flyvbjerg (2011) called a "definitional morass" (p. 302), next we elaborate on several defining characteristics that do exist along with illustrations from published research.

Connecting Case Study to Theoretical Perspective

Because case study is both a unit of analysis and a methodology without a presumed philosophical tradition attached to it, case studies are very conducive to being combined with a theoretical perspective. For example, referring back to one of the examples of published research (Jones, Robbins, & LePeau, 2011), this case study is described as a narrative case study and "the analysis of narratives is embedded within the single case of the New York City ASB [alternative spring break] program" (p. 29). Similarly, a case study might be designed as a critical case study because the inquiry "keeps the spotlight on power relationships within society so as to expose the forces of hegemony and injustice" (Crotty, 1998, p. 157), such as the example of Jones and Abes (2003) in their case study of a service-learning context focused on student understanding of HIV/AIDS. This connection to a theoretical perspective both adds philosophical richness and depth to a case study and provides direction for the design of the case study research project. The case study methodology then becomes emblematic of the philosophical tradition and the particular unit of analysis.

Setting the Context

Although all qualitative research is naturalistic, or occurs in natural, real-world settings (Patton, 2002), setting the context in some studies is more crucial than in others (e.g., case study and ethnography) because the context is an integral part of the "case." Because cases are situated within a bounded system, understanding the relationship of the case to the bounded system is crucial. This process begins by situating the specific phenomenon of interest (the case) in a larger context by describing what that context looks like. This has implications for both the design of the case study research and how the results are presented.

In the example of the case study investigating the influences of social identity on service-learning outcomes, the context of the ASB trip to work with people with AIDS was fully described (Jones, Robbins, & LePeau, 2011) and was written in a way to draw the reader into the setting:

God of love, we confess our day to day failure to be human . . .

We confess that we cut ourselves off from each other and we erect barriers of division.

We confess that by silence and ill-considered word we have built up walls of prejudice.

We confess that by selfishness and lack of sympathy we have stifled generosity and left little time for others . . . . (from the Riverside Church bulletin, March 16, 2008)

And so began the service at Riverside Church on our Sunday in New York City, the first full day on what would become the students' moniker for their experience, "ASB-New York." Little did we know that this reading would foreshadow the week to come. (Jones, Robbins, & LePeau, 2011, p. 27)

Great care is usually given in presenting this context in written form so that readers have a way of understanding both the boundaries of the particular case and the relationship of the case to a larger context. This typically occurs as the researcher introduces the case study methodology in a section entitled "setting the context," "description of the setting," or "context for the study." This section should be richly descriptive to draw the reader into the setting and provide the reader with enough details to create a picture of the larger context within which the case is nested.

Types of Case Studies

Case studies are also distinguished from one another depending on the purpose of the research, and a researcher must provide a rationale for why studying a particular case is important and appropriate. Different reasons for studying a case call for different levels of focus. Merriam (2009) described particularistic, descriptive, and heuristic case studies. A particularistic case study focuses on a very specific phenomenon, which can be a situation, individual, program, or event, and, as such, is most useful in solving problems that emerge from daily life (Merriam, 2009). The emphasis of a descriptive case study is on the outcome of the investigation, which should produce rich description of a particular phenomenon, typically in narrative form. Heuristic case studies focus on understandings and insights gleaned from the case study investigation and lead to new meaning and rethinking about the phenomenon (Merriam, 2009).

Stake (2000) further delineated types of case studies, identifying intrinsic, instrumental, and collective case studies. An intrinsic case study is used when the researcher is interested in understanding the particulars of one case—that is, "because, in all its particularity *and* ordinariness, this case itself is of interest" (Stake, 2000, p. 437). An instrumental case study is less about the case itself and more directed toward understanding of an issue. As Stake (2000) defined it, "The case is of secondary interest, it plays a supportive role, and it facilitates our understanding of something else" (p. 437). A collective case study focuses on several instrumental cases in order to draw some conclusions or theorize about a general condition or phenomenon (Stake, 2000). In their study of student understanding of HIV/AIDS in the context of a service-learning class, Jones and Abes (2003) defined their approach to case study as a hybrid between an intrinsic and instrumental case study because of the focus of the partnership (intrinsic) and issues related to student understanding of HIV/AIDS (instrumental).

Sampling

Because the single most defining characteristic of case study methodology is the emphasis on the bounded system or case, sampling, or identifying and selecting, the case is very important. A case is bounded if, and only if, it is clearly identifiable and limited in scope. Merriam (2009) suggested:

> One technique for assessing the boundedness of the topic is to ask how finite the data collection would be, that is, whether there is a limit to the number of people involved who could be interviewed or a finite time for observations. If there is no end, actually or theoretically . . . then the phenomenon is not bounded enough to qualify as a case. (p. 41)

Because of the focus on a single case, the selection of the case, or unit of analysis, is purposeful. That is, it represents a phenomenon of interest to the researcher and can be "unique or typical, representative of a common practice, or never before encountered" (Merriam, 2002, p. 179). Identification of the particular case is both theoretically driven and then practically executed through the determination of specific sampling criteria. As with other methodologies, the selection of the case emerges from the theoretical framework because this provides the foundation for the particular investigation and leads to the purpose of a study. Once the purpose is clear, sampling criteria are identified that will most likely enable the researcher to get closest to the phenomenon under investigation (see Chapter Five for greater discussion of sampling).

What is unique about case study methodology is that multiple levels of a bounded system may exist, which then impact the sampling strategies required.

Thus, sampling occurs on at least two levels: selection of the case and selection of the participants within the case. Criteria for sampling in case studies are usually purposeful, with an emphasis on information-rich participants (Patton, 2002). In the example from the study on student understanding of HIV/ AIDS in the context of a service-learning class, the case, or unit of analysis, was identified as the university-community partnership, studied through the perspectives of student and community participants (Jones & Abes, 2003). The case was bounded by the AIDS service organization affiliated with the service-learning class. In this study, all the students who had been enrolled in the class and involved with the AIDS service organization were invited to participate, as were all staff members and instructors. This sampling strategy and the subsequent data collection procedures provided the researchers with insight into all aspects of the case.

Analysis in Case Study

Data analysis in case study research is influenced by the theoretical perspective, if relevant. That is, if a researcher identifies a study as a narrative case study, an ethnographic case study, or a critical case study, for example, then analysis of data collected will reflect these perspectives. Further, oftentimes researchers draw upon the constant comparative method characteristic of grounded theory for data analysis in case study research. However, several data analysis procedures exist that are germane to case study. The first point to keep in mind when conducting data analysis in case study research is the purpose of case studies; that is, to investigate a bounded system. Therefore, data analysis should lead the researcher to a clear explication and understanding of the case (Merriam, 2009). Second, because of the focus on a case, typically multiple forms of data are collected to fully investigate the case (e.g., interviews, documents, and observations) which yields a lot of data that the researcher must manage. This becomes what Yin (2008) referred to as the case *study database*, distinguished from the case *study report*, which is what is produced by the researcher as a result of data analysis.

Data analysis is also influenced by whether a researcher is conducting a single case study or multiple case study (which involves collecting data from multiple cases). If the emphasis is on a single case, then that case must be richly described, integrating multiple sources of data and setting the case within its particular context or setting. In a multiple case study, data must be analyzed by looking at each case individually (often referred to as within-case analysis) and across cases (e.g., comparative case analysis or cross-case analysis) to provide a holistic picture and understanding of the case when multiple sites or cases are considered (Merriam, 2009).

Specific procedures for conducting data analysis in case study are described by Stake (1995) and include what he referred to as categorical aggregation, direct interpretation, correspondence and patterns, and naturalistic generalizations. Categorical aggregation refers to "the collection of individual instances from the data" (Creswell, 2013, p. 199) until something can be said of the data as a group. Direct interpretation emphasizes individual participants in each case as a meaning unit in and of itself. As Creswell (2013) notes, this is "a process of pulling the data apart and putting them back together in meaningful ways" (p. 199). Correspondence and patterns emphasize the themes and relationships among the categories that are emerging in the data and "consistency within certain conditions" (Stake, 1995, p. 78). Correspondence and patterns emerge from both categorical aggregation and direct interpretation in an effort "To understand behavior, issues, and contexts with regard to our particular case" (Stake, 1995, p. 78). Finally, naturalistic generalizations "are conclusions arrived at through personal engagement in life's affairs or by vicarious experience so well constructed that the person feels as if it happened to themselves" (Stake, 1995, p. 85). This requires the researcher to provide enough rich and narrative description of the details of the case to engage the reader in the case in such a way that the reader vicariously experiences the case.

Ethnography

The disciplinary roots of ethnography come from the field of anthropology and have at their core an interest in cultural phenomena, cultural contexts, or cultural interpretations of a particular group of people and their behaviors, norms, rituals, and values. Both Merriam (2002) and Schwandt (2001) emphasized that ethnography integrates both process (e.g., how data are collected) and product (e.g., written text that reflects a cultural interpretation). Merriam (2002) elaborated on this distinction:

> Historically associated with the field of anthropology, ethnography has come to refer to both the method (how the researcher conducts the study) and the product (a cultural description of human social life). This dual use of the term had led to some confusion in what is called ethnography; that is, the mere use of data gathering techniques associated with ethnography does not result in an ethnography unless there is a cultural interpretation of those data. (p. 236)

Because of the primary emphasis on cultural understanding and interpretation, ethnographic research is characterized by extensive fieldwork, immersion in a particular setting, prolonged engagement and relationship building, and the generation of thick description to describe the people, processes, relationships, and space in that setting. Ethnographers approach these settings with the questions of "What do people in this setting have to know and do to make the system work?" and "If culture, sometimes defined simply as shared knowledge, is mostly caught rather than taught, how do those being inducted into the group find their 'way in' so that an adequate level of sharing is achieved?" (Wolcott, 2010, p. 74). The outcome of this research is to produce "an ethnography," which, as Van Maanen (2011) defined it, is a "written representation of a culture (or selected aspects of a culture). It carries quite serious intellectual and moral responsibilities, for the images of others inscribed in writing are most assuredly not neutral" (p. 1)

Ethnography, like other methodological approaches, may also be connected with other approaches, such as an ethnographic case study, or with theoretical perspectives, such as a critical ethnography or feminist ethnography. In addition, specific forms of ethnography exist, such as autoethnography, performance ethnography, and photoethnography. These forms of ethnography are distinctive in some regards given the use of methods of autobiographical writing, cultural expression, and digital images. In autoethnography, researchers maintain a focus on cultural analysis but connect personal narratives or biography to culture. Autoethnographies are first-person accounts and "showcase concrete action, dialogue, emotion, embodiment, spirituality, and self-consciousness. These features appear as relational and institutional stories affected by history and social structure" (Ellis, 2004, p. 38). Performance ethnography, relatively unexplored in higher education research, is a distinct form of ethnography that emphasizes performance as both the subject of research and method (Hamera, 2011) and addresses every day rituals and patterns of behavior. As Hamera (2011) summarized:

> Performance ethnography offers the researcher a vocabulary for exploring the expressive elements of culture, a focus on embodiment as a crucial component of cultural analysis and a tool for representing scholarly engagement, and a critical, interventionist commitment to theory in/as practice. (p. 318)

Photoethnography also maintains the commitment to cultural analysis but through visual representations that augment ethnographic narrative detail. Photoethnography may be related to digital storytelling when the camera is in the hands of the participants in a study who document their own stories through the use of self-selected images. Regardless of these distinctions and various approaches, all ethnographic research is characterized by an interest in understanding in a holistic way the complex dynamics of a particular group or human society to "produce historically, politically, and personally situated accounts, descriptions, interpretations, and representations of human lives" (Tedlock, 2000, p. 455).

In an example from published research, Magolda and Ebben Gross (2009) conducted an ethnographic study of an evangelical student organization at a public university. Magolda and Ebben Gross anchored their study in what they described as "an interpretive worldview with critical theory leanings" (p. 25). They clearly explained their approach:

> In short, by adopting an interpretive lens, we sought to fully engage with participants in the SSC [Students Serving Christ] setting in order to capture various members' understanding of themselves, their organizations,

their values, and the world around them . . . . The critical influence in this SSC study is evident in three distinct ways. First, we infused the issue of power into the interpretive tapestry; specifically, the book focuses on sub-culture power relations on campus and reveals how power operates within the SSC context. Second, we clearly acknowledge our own presence, posi-tion, politics, and subjectivity—acknowledging we are intimately involved with the research context and with SSC participants in the creation of knowledge. Third, we use difference and conflict, rather than similarities and consensus as organizing concepts in our analysis. (p. 25)

Their critical approach is reflected in all aspects of the research design and particularly in the analysis and interpretation of data. Several defining char-acteristics of ethnography are highlighted next with examples from published research.

Access and "Getting In"

The dynamics of gaining access is also addressed in Chapter Six, but we include it here because of its particular importance to ethnographic research. In order to effectively conduct ethnographic research, the researcher must become an "insider" in the community of interest. This means that the process of gaining access is very important. Although some may see gaining access as purely a logistical issue, Hammersley and Atkinson (1983) pointed out:

The process of gaining access is not *merely* a practical matter. Not only does its achievement depend upon theoretical understanding, often disguised as "native wit," but the discovery of obstacles to access, and perhaps of effec-tive means of overcoming them, themselves provide insights into the social organization of the setting. (p. 54)

Gaining access then is not merely, nor only, a matter of gaining permission to conduct a study in a particular setting. Instead, the process involves self-reflection about the researcher's role as a member (either new or not) of this group, one's own identity in relation to the community under study, as well as knowledge of the norms, values, beliefs, and behaviors of the group.

In their study of an evangelical student organization, Students Serving Christ (SSC), Magolda and Ebben Gross (2009) discussed the issues associated with gaining access to this group. They wrote

Our greatest barrier to gaining access to the SCC was that we were non-believers in the eyes of SSC evangelicals. As outsiders desiring to study a student subculture that has historically been maligned by educational researchers and journalists, we needed to take extra care to explain the goal of our study and possible consequences for the group. (pp. 26–27)

Similarly, in her critical ethnography of Black women in college, Winkle-Wagner (2009) discussed the challenges she experienced as a White researcher in gaining access to potential participants. She reflected

> ...I realized that as a White woman attempting to gain the trust and partici-pation of African American women, I couldn't simply attend a meeting here and there and beg for participants. I couldn't only be interested in doing research *about* African American women. I had to do research *with* them, in *their* way if I were to gain insight into their experiences or if I wanted to begin to encourage them to remain involved in the project. (p. 50)

In both of these examples, significant relationship building was required in order to gain access to the setting and the people in these settings and ulti-mately, to gain credibility for their research projects.

Immersion and Participant Observation

The characteristic method of data collection in ethnography is participant observation, which necessarily involves extensive work in the field or, as it is referred to in ethnography, *fieldwork*. Van Maanen (2011) suggested that

> Fieldwork usually means living with and living like those who are studied. In the broadest, most conventional sense, fieldwork demands the full-time involvement of a researcher over a lengthy period of time (typically unspecified) and consists mostly of ongoing interaction with the human targets of study on their home ground. (p. 2)

Thus, becoming immersed in the field and engaging as a participant observer is a time consuming process and not easily accomplished with a few observations or interviews. The role of the researcher in the field is also one that requires great thoughtfulness and raises complex issues involving ethics in the field, appear-ance, deception, and authenticity. Although this may be self-evident, an impor-tant distinguishing characteristic of ethnography is the primary emphasis on observation and listening, rather than asking questions through interviewing. Nonetheless, variation exists in the degree to which a researcher may participate and become immersed in the research setting. Glesne (2011) referred to this as the "participant-observation continuum" (p. 64). She further elaborated on the inherent contradiction in a term that suggests one is both participant and observer and put forth a continuum "from mostly observation to mostly partici-pation" (p. 64). Spradley (1980) outlined five different modes of observation for ethnographers: complete, active, moderate, passive, and nonparticipation (which are not mutually exclusive as the example provided below will demonstrate). Where researchers situate themselves on this continuum is influenced by the focus of the study and theoretical perspective. For example, a study grounded in a post-positivist worldview would most likely find the researcher as an observer, whereas a study framed by critical theory would require the researcher to be more actively involved as a participant in the setting.

In the study of evangelical students involved in the student organization Students Serving Christ (SSC), Magolda and Ebben Gross (2009) described their approach to participant observations:

> Our fieldwork observations included attending more than 50 events and programs, such as public and private ministry services, evangelical training sessions, Servant Leadership meetings, and Bible study gatherings. We began with generic and unfocused observations, which allowed us to gain preliminary impressions and the "lie of the land." Over time, we sharpened our observations' focus by keying in on specific domains of interest (e.g., marginalization) and events (e.g., Bible study). (p. 27)

Thus, using Spradley's modes of observation and participation, Magolda and Ebben Gross (2009) began their fieldwork as passive participants and then moved toward a more participatory stance. However, because of their lack of content expertise with the Bible, for example, and the practices of SSC, they never moved into a role as full participants.

In order to gain the full benefits of immersion in a setting and observations, the ethnographer must carefully record these observations. Glesne (2011) recommended that ethnographers begin by paying attention to everything in the *setting* and "make notes and jot down thoughts without narrow, specific regard for your research problem. Study the setting and describe it in words and in sketches, using all your senses" (p. 69). Using a field notebook, or some means by which to record all observations and thoughts, Glesne (2011) advocated for a detailed focus on the participants in the setting, events happening in the setting, how people are interacting in the setting (affective and behavioral dimensions), and verbal and nonverbal communications. She further distinguished between the kinds of notes to be made: descriptive, analytic, and subjective. Descriptive notes are very concrete, non-judgmental, and detailed. Analytic notes are more reflective in nature and capture the researcher's impressions, feelings, and initial analytic hunches related to observations. Subjective notes, or a researcher journal, add to the descriptive and analytic notes by inserting the researchers' recordings related to their own identities and the setting, feelings, and issues that come up. As Glesne (2011) described:

> Writing in your research diary becomes a means for thinking about how the research is co-created among you and research participants; how actions and interactions shape what follows, and where power dynamics lie. It is a location for reflecting on ethical issues that trouble you. (p. 77)

Because ethnographers are immersed in a particular setting over an extended period of time, this kind of reflexivity is very important, especially as the researcher navigates the transition from outsider to insider through participant observation and in a specific cultural context.

Generating "Thick Description"

Good ethnographic research must generate "thick description" (Denzin, 2001; Geertz, 1973), which offers the reader entry into the culture as it exists and is interpreted by the researcher. Thick description is defined as "description that goes beyond the mere or bare reporting of an act (thin description), but describes and probes the intentions, motives, meaning, contexts, situations and circumstances of action" (Denzin, 1989, p. 39). This is an important point as many beginning researchers stop analysis with description and fail to make an analytic turn to theorize and interpret their descriptions. Glesne (2011) elaborated on this point suggesting, "The goal of theorizing, then, becomes that of providing an understanding of direct lived experience instead of abstract generalizations" (p. 35). As a result of thick description, a reader is drawn into the setting and able to understand through rich, detailed description of that setting, the cultural nuances and patterns present. For example, using this brief excerpt from Magolda and Ebben Gross (2009), we see the power of thick description in providing a vivid account of a particular setting that integrates both description and interpretation:

Let Us Pray

"Everyone says 'hello.' " We are going to pray now. I've got to go. Bye." Aaron clicks shut his cellular phone to conclude the conversation with his fiancée. That act signals the start of this week's Students Serving Christ (SSC) Beacon prayer meeting, during which students devote an hour of their time to communicate with God about ways to reach non-Christians .... The SSC director asks Rebecca to lead the group in prayer. Rebecca complies as her 15 peers (8 women and 7 men) bow their heads. "Lord, thank You for gathering us together .... Help us open our hearts to all those who are on campus. Lord, we will be faithful. We will follow what You want us to do." ... The solemn tone of these opening prayers is a stark contrast to the lighthearted banter that preceded the service, as students joked about their not-so-coordinated attire, their favorite sports teams, and the ministry road trip they cancelled because of inclement weather. Participants appear unfazed by the program's usual starting time of 5:30 pm—a time when most of their peers are unwinding after a long day of classes or eating dinner. For these students, prayer takes precedence. (pp. 57–58)

As a reader of this text, one begins to imagine the setting, to understand the dynamics of the setting, and to gain a glimpse into the interpretations of the setting constructed by the researchers, all characteristics of thick description. In order to write such rich description, a researcher must spend a significant amount of time immersed in the setting, getting to know the people, dynamics, cultural nuances, and rituals characteristic of the particular setting.

Cultural Interpretation and Representation

Immersion in the field produces thick description, which is then analyzed and interpreted through a cultural lens. One of the primary interests in the researcher's interpretations is that participants' perspectives are accurately and fully represented. This is referred to as an *emic*, or insider (Patton, 2002), perspective. There is no one analytic strategy associated with ethnography; however, what is central to analysis is a cultural lens and interpretation. Geertz (1973) suggested that this emphasis on cultural analysis "is guessing at meanings, assessing the guesses, and drawing explanatory conclusions from the better guesses, not discovering the Continent of Meaning and mapping out its bodiless landscape" (p. 20). Magolda and Ebben Gross (2009) adopted Geertz's cultural framework to analyze all their data and noted that "through this process of establishing relationships between data and 'playing with ideas,' theory inductively emerges from the field experience" (p. 31). Decisions are also made by the ethnographer about how to present and represent findings. Described by Van Maanen (1988, 2011) as realist, confessional, and impressionist tales, each conveys a different approach to the presentation of findings. Realist tales, the more traditional approach of cultural anthropologists, "provide a rather direct, matter-of-fact portrait of a studied culture, unclouded by much concern for how the fieldworker produced such a portrait" (Van Maanen, 2011, p. 7). The representation produced is presumed "to be *true* to life" (Glesne, 2011, p. 244). Confessional tales foreground the perspectives of the researcher and include "Stories of infiltration, fables of fieldwork rapport, minimelodramas of hardships endured (and overcome), and accounts of what fieldwork did to the fieldworker" (Van Maanen, 2011, p. 73). By contrast, Impressionist Tales may include elements of both realist and confessional tales as they

> are bundled together in such a way that they alter, in the end, whatever state or situation was said to obtain at the beginning of the tale . . . . Impressionist tales are not about what usually happens but about what rarely happens." (Van Maanen, 2011, p. 102)

Few good examples of ethnographic research exist in higher education and student affairs literature. Most likely this is due both to the intensive immersion in the field and the extensive time required to complete an ethnographic study. Although many researchers may utilize methods characteristic of ethnography, such as participant observation, it is the prolonged engagement and cultural interpretations that distinguish ethnography from other methodologies. However, cultural understandings of many aspects of higher education, such as the student experience, campus environments, and policies, are important to higher education and student affairs practice.

Summary

This chapter connected epistemological foundations with methodological approaches, emphasizing the important characteristics that distinguish one methodology from another. Researchers must take care in situating each study in an epistemological tradition that serves as an anchor for other elements of the research design. One such element is sampling or participant selection, which is the focus of the next chapter. Sampling is much more than simply a technique for finding and interacting with participants. It, too, is reflective of methodological approaches.

Exercises

Chapter-related

1. In your own words, write a few sentences about the role that methodological approach plays in a qualitative study. As opposed to studies that are discussed solely in terms of methods employed, what contribution does a methodological approach make to the elements of research?

2. Review each methodological approach presented in this chapter and jot down two to three strengths and limitations of each. Also jot down two to three elements that distinguish one approach from another.

Research Process

1. Consider your compelling interest and emerging questions in relation to different methodological approaches. Develop two to three research questions for each methodological approach. How does the methodological approach shift the emphasis and focus on the purpose of the study?

2. Write several statements that flow from your compelling interest that begin with "The purpose of this study is . . ." Continue to work at this statement until you believe you have clearly communicated a focus for a study.

3. Identify the methodological approach best suited for a study with this focus and three to five characteristics that define this methodological approach. What are the strengths and limitations of this particular approach?

4. Pair your methodological approach with two to three different theoretical perspectives and consider how each pairing shifts elements of your research design. For example, how would your research questions differ using a constructivist narrative approach compared with a critical narrative?

5   Perspectives on Sampling

Participant selection, or *sampling*, as it has been called historically, is perhaps the most understudied and least understood dimension of the qualitative research process. Many researchers treat sampling as simply a procedural strategy that yields a pool of participants for a particular study. However, this approach fails to consider the relationship between sampling and other elements of the research design. In particular, the quality of the data collected by the researcher is largely dependent upon the participants in a study, which requires locating "excellent participant[s]" (Morse, 2007, p. 229). Hence, the importance of sampling cannot be overemphasized. The purpose of this chapter is to make explicit the decisions involved in sampling in qualitative research and to explore the complexities of issues that emerge when considering these decision points. Particular attention will be given to sampling strategies, sampling criteria, coverage, and issues related to establishing diverse samples and researcher positionality. Intentional focus on these issues is important in any research project because poor sampling decisions directly impact data quality, credibility, and trustworthiness of findings (Marshall & Rossman, 2011).

More specifically, Morse (2007) identified three principles upon which all sampling in qualitative inquiry is dependent: excellent research skills, the relationship between "excellent" participants and excellent data, and targeted and "biased" approaches. The first principle, "excellent research skills are essential for obtaining good data" (Morse, 2007, p. 230), emphasizes the skill of the researcher in collecting good data, which relates directly to the number of participants needed to obtain good data. Morse (2007) explained by suggesting:

> These attributes of an excellent interviewer influence the quality of the data and ultimately the size of the sample: the better the data quality, the fewer the number of interviews and participants required in a study. In other words, the more targeted the content of the interviews, the better the data, the fewer interviews will be necessary, and the lower the number of participants recruited into the study. (p. 230)

This principle emphasizes the integral connection between sampling and thoughtfully considered data collection, such as developing effective interview questions. The second principle, "it is necessary to locate 'excellent' participants to obtain excellent data" (Morse, 2007, p. 231), specifies that not all people interested in participating in a study will make "excellent" participants. That is, excellent participants "must therefore be experts in the experience or the phenomena under investigation. . . . In other words, the qualitative researcher must select participants to observe or interview who know the information (or have had or are having the experience) in which you are interested" (pp. 231–232). This is the crux of what is referred to as *purposeful* sampling (Patton, 2002). The third principle, "sampling techniques must be targeted and efficient" (Morse, 2007, p. 233), also emphasizes the importance of and prevailing strategy of purposeful sampling. Morse (2007) discussed this principle in relation to "bias," which the uninformed often wage as a critique of qualitative inquiry. Instead, Morse (2007) suggested that "excellent qualitative inquiry is inherently biased" because participants are "deliberately sought and selected" (p. 234). Purposeful samples, then, are guided by elements of the research design, such as the purpose of the study and research questions, about which the researcher must be very clear in order to move forward with sampling.

As noted, sampling in qualitative inquiry is characterized as *purposeful,* that is, sampling for *information-rich* cases holds the greatest potential for generating insight about the phenomenon of interest. As Patton (2002) defined, "Information-rich cases are those from which one can learn a great deal about issues of central importance to the purpose of the research, thus the term *purposeful* sampling" (p. 46). This definition returns the researcher to the purpose of the study and research questions. Stated differently, in every study, what constitutes information-rich cases will depend upon the phenomenon under investigation, the methodological approach, and the questions designed to illuminate understanding of this phenomenon. The researcher then must "seek out groups, settings, and individuals where (and for whom) the processes being studied are most likely to occur" (Denzin & Lincoln, 2011, p. 245).

We begin to see how these three principles may be reflected in examples from published research. The following statements about sampling strategies and participants demonstrate the importance of sampling to the overall research design:

- Potential respondents were identified through purposeful and referral sampling. Selection criteria included respondents' withdrawals from college upon activation, re-enrollment in college upon their return, and full-time undergraduate status at the time of data collection. (Rumann & Hamrick, 2010, p. 437)
- Participants were recruited for the study using purposeful sampling techniques that involved establishing specific criteria for participation and, within those criteria, sought maximum variation. Only undergraduates who had experienced a spiritual struggle in their life were eligible to participate in the study, but we strove to include students who exhibited different types of struggles as well as students of diverse worldviews, sexualities, and races/ethnicities. (Rockenbach, Walker, & Luzader, 2012, pp. 58–59)

- I conducted a search of the Web for each "1862 land-grant" institution in each of the 50 states; I used the search function and keywords *diversity* and *diversity plan....* I sought those universities that had a diversity committee, charged by a senior administrator (president, provost), that had at least one diversity action plan generated within the past 5 years. (Iverson, 2007, pp. 590–592)
- Using purposeful sampling, I selected three groups (an early-intervention need-based aid program, a merit-based aid program, a peer mentoring program, and a living-learning community in the residence halls) from which to select African American women (ages 18–22) for voluntary participation in the project. To recruit the women, I sent emails to all of the women in the four groups. (Winkle-Wagner, 2009, p. 53)

As the statements above suggest, decisions regarding sampling strategies are instrumental to a study, not only because they result in participants for a particular study, but also because they serve as further reflection of the researcher's theoretical perspective, methodological approach, and interpretive stance (Jones, 2002). These connections will be discussed in greater detail later in this chapter. On the face of it, sampling appears as a pretty straightforward process: identifying and inviting individuals to participate in research. In actuality, the process is of utmost importance to qualitative research designs because "The strategy of participant selection in qualitative inquiry rests on the multiple purposes of illuminating, interpreting, and understanding—and on your own imagination and judgment" (Glesne, 2011, p. 46).

Language and Coverage

The notion of sampling, regardless of paradigmatic orientation, suggests the identification of a subset of a larger phenomenon. However,

> Nowhere is the difference between quantitative and qualitative methods better captured than in the different strategies, logics, and purposes that distinguish statistical probability sampling from qualitative purposeful sampling.... Not only are the techniques for sample selection different, but the very logic of each approach is distinct because the purpose of each strategy is different. (Patton, 2002, p. 46)

The random-sampling characteristic of quantitative research is intended to produce results that may be generalized to a larger population. By contrast, in qualitative inquiry, a sample is purposefully drawn with an emphasis on information-rich cases that elicit an in-depth understanding of a particular phenomenon. Morse (2007) made this distinction between the different sampling logics very explicit:

> If we select a sample randomly, the factors that we are interested in for our study would be normally distributed in our data, and be represented by

some sort of a curve, normal or skewed. Regardless of the type of curve, we would have lots of data about common events, and inadequate data about less common events. Given that a qualitative data set requires a more rectangular distribution to achieve saturation, with randomization we would have too much data around the mean (and be swamped with the excess), and not enough data to saturate our categories in the tails of the distribution. (p. 234)

Although using the prevailing language of post-positivist research, Morse (2007) clearly illuminates the underlying differences between samples randomly and purposefully created.

A common and persistent question asked by those not as familiar with qualitative inquiry is "How can you say anything about this topic if your sample is so small?" Qualitative researchers must have a good answer to this question (suggestions for responses are offered later in this chapter). To respond, however, a researcher must understand the logic and purpose of qualitative sampling and then convey the rationale behind sampling decisions. Some qualitative researchers avoid any pretense of quantitative language in describing sampling strategies (e.g., the concept of "N," referring to participants as subjects or respondents, or identifying a "small" sample as a limitation of the study). Instead, these qualitative researchers may use terms such as *participant selection, conversation partners, narrators,* and *co-investigators*—all of which reflect a different conceptualization and purpose of the research design and approach. Even the word *sampling* is grounded in a post-positivist perspective; however, it does remain most prevalent in the qualitative research scholarship.

Although sampling in qualitative research focuses on information-rich cases, appropriate *coverage* of the phenomenon is critical. Coverage refers to more than sheer numbers of participants (e.g., sample size, which will be discussed later in this chapter) and also relates to the relationship between one's methodological approach, research questions, data collection, and participant selection strategies. Morse and Richards (2002) referred to this as the "scope of a study" and suggested, "The scope of a study is never just a question of how many, but always includes who, where, and which settings will be studied; in what ways, by whom, and for how long they will be studied; and what can be asked and answered" (p. 68). The implication is that participant selection must be intentional with consideration given to the relationships between how well participants are able to illuminate the phenomenon under investigation, the nature of the questions asked of participants, and the contextual influences on participant selection, data collection, and analysis. Too many qualitative researchers err on the side of convenience when considering these factors, deciding to limit participation based on time and resources. However, as Patton (2002) implored, "While convenience and cost are real considerations, they should be the last factors taken into account . . . convenience sampling is neither purposeful nor strategic" (p. 242). In other words, much stronger rationales for sampling decisions must be used than simply convenience.

Determining when a researcher reaches appropriate coverage is fraught with ambiguity when considered in the context of sampling. In fact, complete coverage of a particular phenomenon may be an elusive, rarely achievable goal. How, then, might the qualitative researcher address the tensions inherent in coverage? First, researchers need to take special care in framing the purpose of the study. Because there is a direct relationship between the purpose of the study, sampling criteria, and participant selection, if the purpose statement is too broad, then coverage will be more difficult (if not impossible) to approximate. *Stated differently, if the purpose statement is not clear, then researchers won't know who they are looking for as "excellent" participants* (italics added for emphasis). A clear and succinct statement of purpose should give the reader some indication of who (or what) the researcher is interested in investigating and, hence, who would and would not be included as participants.

Second, once the research is conducted, it is important for researchers to be very explicit about the kind of coverage achieved. This is preferred to the sometimes subtle (or not) suggestions that coverage was accomplished in an interview with five individuals (which, again, may be possible given the scope of the study and methodological approach) because the researcher interviewed them more than once. In fully describing the sample, researchers make clear who is in the sample and why. Last, although Patton (2002) cautioned against using convenience as a leading criterion for sampling, the reality is that most researchers have some limitations of time and resources. Thus, coverage may nearly always be compromised by some dimension of convenience. This, then, becomes a limitation of a study and should be noted. However, this reality does not diminish the researcher's responsibility to achieve coverage because many of these research decisions depend upon the good judgment of researchers as they weigh the options available in light of the most efficacious scholarship.

Participant selection and coverage, then, in qualitative research is guided by the purpose of the study, methodological approach, and research questions, with particular attention to the selection of "cases" most likely to provide in-depth coverage and insight into the phenomenon under investigation. A variety of sampling strategies is available to accomplish this research goal (discussed later in this chapter). However, before a researcher makes decisions about *how* to create a sample or group of participants for a study, the criteria upon which the sample will be selected, or *who* the researcher is looking for and *why*, must be determined.

Sampling Criteria

The identification of sampling criteria is central to participant selection. *Sampling criteria* refer to those variables, characteristics, qualities, experiences, and demographics most directly linked to the purpose of the study and, thus, important to the construction of the sample. In other words, given the purpose of the study and primary research questions, certain characteristics must be present in the sample that are most likely going to elicit insight and greater depth of understanding about the phenomenon of interest. Sampling criteria, then, serve as the foundation for sampling decision making and must be made explicit as the guide for selecting a sample. Although we focus most directly in this section on selection of participants (individuals) it is important to note that research contexts are also selected. That is, a researcher must be able to explain and defend why a specific research context is chosen (e.g., institutions, organizations, and settings) and then introduce this research context to the reader beyond simple demographic descriptors.

Related to the description of the research context, researchers must be able to defend why certain characteristics are important as selection criteria. For example, what is the rationale for a sample composed of only women? Who are all African American? Attend one institution? Are between the ages of 18 and 22? Represent a diverse array of academic majors? And live on campus? Each of these categories represents a criterion of interest to the researcher and must be defended with a rationale as to why each is important to the study. Each reflects a specific and intentional decision by the researcher. In examples from published research, we learn something about the criteria utilized in constructing the sample by reading how the sample is described:

- Seven individuals who met the selection criteria were invited to participate; six accepted the invitation, and the seventh was interested but declined due to limited availability. . . . Six student veterans, five men and one woman were the respondents for this study. Five respondents re-enrolled at the university as full-time students following their return from duty; Karen transferred to the university from a small private college. (Rumann & Hamrick, 2010, pp. 437–438)

- Twenty-six students indicated interest in participating in the study, but we limited the sample to 12 "information-rich" cases with diverse identities and struggles. Two participants withdrew before completion of the study (for unspecified reasons), leaving a total of 10 participants who comprised the sample for the study (Rockenbach et al., 2012, p. 59). The researchers then also included a table which provided further information about the participants, such as a sample comprised of seven women and three men, seven White and three participants of color, year in college, academic major, religious affiliation, and type of spiritual struggle.

- Iverson (2007) reviewed the websites for the land grant institutions in each of 50 states to assess the meeting of criteria related to a senior administrator appointed diversity committee and a diversity action plan. She wrote, "My Web search was complemented with numerous e-mail exchanges and phone conversations with academic and administrative personnel to discern which universities had policies that met the sampling criteria and to collect any documents not accessible via the Web. The search yielded a data sample of 21 reports from 20 institutions." (Iverson, 2007, p. 592)

- To recruit participants for a study of gospel choir participation among African American undergraduates, Strayhorn (2011) attended three weekly meetings of the gospel choir, with the last meeting including an announcement made by the choir's president about the study. Strayhorn (2011) wrote, "This approach yielded 21 participants, representing 36% of the choir's total membership at the time of the study. The sample included 13 women and 8 men; 5 first-year students, 4 sophomores, 7 juniors, and 5 seniors, which represented a wide range of academic majors (ranging from highly technical to performing arts fields), hailed from diverse family environments (e.g., single-parent, guardian-led), identified as 'Christian,' despite differences in denomination (e.g., Catholic, Baptist, Pentecostal), and most (76%) were in-state students." (pp. 140–141)
- In a phenomenological study of queer students of color in activist roles, Vaccaro and Mena (2011) developed the following criteria for participation: (a) self-identification as a person of color; (b) self-identification as a gay, lesbian, bisexual, transgender, or queer individual; (c) member of the Queer Student Group (QSG) or self-identified LGBTQ student activist; and (d) not enrolled in class or in a counseling relationship with either researcher (p. 345). Six queer student activists of color indicated interest in participating, met the criteria, and were selected.

Some of these characteristics contribute toward an effort in describing the sample and also imply what is important to the researcher and presumably central to an understanding of the study. Sampling criteria might include demographic detail (e.g., race, ethnicity, gender, social class, or age); membership in an organization or community (e.g., gospel choir, residence hall, or fraternity); relationship to phenomenon under investigation (e.g., veterans in transition, perspective of a parent, advocate, or recipient of a service); particular status (e.g., first-generation African American woman, honors student, award recipient, or new professional); or level of involvement (e.g., leader in a group, participant in an alternative break program, someone required to complete community service, senior student affairs administrator, or social justice educator), to name a few of the many possibilities. Often, in a study, the researcher is interested in participants who possess several sampling criteria simultaneously, such as African American fraternity men or White students involved in an anti-racism training program. What is critical in all studies is to make the sampling criteria explicit, with appropriate rationale that can be traced back to the purpose of the study, in part, because the makeup of the sample influences all other dimensions of the researcher design.

Clearly identifying sampling criteria is important because, if the researcher is not explicit, then questions may remain about the scope of the sample. For example, a researcher may frame a study as one on "women's identity development," and yet a closer read of the study indicates that the study includes all White women. Or similarly, a study on "drinking in fraternities" excludes historically Black fraternities. In addition to providing a rationale for why certain criteria are central to the study and utilized to guide sampling decisions, it is also important to define criteria when/if there might be any doubt. For example, if the criterion of *new professional* is identified, the researcher should make explicit whether this is defined by length of time in the profession (first five years of work) or in relation to receipt of a degree (within five years from completion of a master's degree). In their study exploring the dynamics of lesbian identity, Abes and Jones (2004) discussed their sampling decision to use the word lesbian instead of queer, recognizing that this may not be the identity label used by some participants. Had the researchers chosen to use the word queer, for example, a different group of interested participants might have emerged. Terminology and defining terms and criteria are critical to the sampling process. So, too, is the decision making in relation to sample size.

Sample Size

The oft-quoted passage from Patton (2002) that "[t]here are no rules for sample size in qualitative inquiry" (p. 244) is typically offered as the strongest rationale for a small sample size. However, Patton (2002) went on to write, "Sample size depends on what you want to know, the purpose of the inquiry, what's at stake, what will be useful, what will have credibility, and what can be done with available time and resources" (p. 244). Patton's (2002) intent was not to give blanket permission to qualitative researchers to feel good about a small sample size. Instead, he directed the researcher back to the purpose and significance of the study, as well as the methodological approach, and suggested these must all be connected to decisions about sample size. For example, phenomenological investigations, with an in-depth emphasis on the essence of a particular phenomenon, tend toward smaller numbers of participants, whereas an ethnographic study, by definition, must include multiple perspectives from multiple sources in order to accomplish the cultural analysis and interpretation characteristic of this approach. Creswell (2013), in his summary of five approaches to qualitative inquiry, provides guidance about sample sizes that are reflective of these different traditions. Thus, the methodological approach, coupled with the purpose of the study, provide both guidance and a rationale for sample size decisions.

It is important to point out again that the language of sample size is grounded in a positivist perspective. As noted earlier in this chapter, the quantitative paradigm utilizes sampling procedures and criteria regarding sample size that are anchored in randomization and generalizability. In quantitative investigations, typically the researcher identifies the population and sample at the onset of the investigation and then implements procedures to create this particular sample. The notion of sample size takes on different meaning in qualitative research. In thinking about the decision making surrounding sample size in qualitative investigations, the concept of *theoretical sampling*, taken from the literature on grounded theory, is instructive. Bryant and Charmaz (2007) defined theoretical sampling as follows:

> When engaging in theoretical sampling, the researcher seeks people, events, or information to illuminate and define the boundaries and relevance of

the categories. Because the purpose of theoretical sampling is to sample to develop the theoretical categories, conducting it can take the researcher across substantive areas. (p. 611)

Although some of this language is specific to grounded theory, the transferable ideas are that data gathering and sampling are guided by the goal of maximizing opportunities to uncover data relevant to the purpose of the study and that the sampling process interacts with data analysis. That is, as themes or categories begin to emerge through analysis of data, the researcher identifies additional sites or individuals who hold the potential of yielding theoretically relevant data. Thus, sampling continuously evolves throughout the research process, and the researcher continues to sample (and collect data) until these opportunities are maximized or until patterns in the data continuously emerge. This is a different approach from selecting your sample at the beginning of a study and declaring it final.

This concept related to maximizing data and sample size is called *saturation*. When themes or categories are saturated, then the decision to stop sampling is justified. Saturation occurs when the researcher begins to hear (or observe, or read) the same or similar kinds of information related to categories of analysis. Lincoln and Guba (1985) referred to this as *sampling to the point of redundancy*. They elaborated:

> In purposeful sampling the size of the sample is determined by informational considerations. If the purpose is to maximize information, the sampling is terminated when no new information is forthcoming from new sampled units; thus *redundancy* is the primary criterion. (p. 202)

Sampling to redundancy may not always be feasible or realistic given the constraints of time and resources. To navigate this tension, Patton (2002) suggested, "The solution is judgment and negotiation. I recommend that qualitative sampling designs specify *minimum samples* based on expected reasonable coverage of the phenomenon given the purpose of the study and stakeholder interests" (p. 246). For example, Marshall and Rossman (2011) offered this helpful guidance:

> While funding and time constraints affect sample size, the weightier concerns center on the question of research purpose. An unknown culture or profession studied in-depth over time may be composed of one case study or ethnography. A study of new mothers' receptivity to training for breast-feeding could have a huge sample, in a vast array of settings, with good funding and a large research team. A small sample would be useful as thick cultural description. A large sample in disparate and varied settings with diverse participants would also be seen as very useful since the ease of transferability would be enhanced. (p. 103)

Regardless of sample size, the researcher must take care to explain sampling decisions and to justify the sample size in relation to the focus of the study.

Once sampling criteria are identified and sample size given consideration, then the researcher must determine *how* to locate participants who meet the criteria. This is referred to as the *sampling strategy*.

Sampling Strategies

A sampling *strategy* is the way to identify and secure the individuals, organizations, documents, or research settings that reflect the sampling criteria developed. A sampling strategy is a method that implies a plan for identifying those who may shed light on a phenomenon of interest to the researcher. This plan is linked to the purpose of the study and methodological approach. A variety of strategies is available to the researcher, each serving a different purpose. Several texts provide excellent descriptions of these strategies and the purposes each serves (e.g., Creswell, 2013, p. 158; Marshall & Rossman, 2011, p. 111; Patton, 2002, pp. 230–244).

It is important to note that utilizing more than one strategy may be appropriate. Participant selection in qualitative research, regardless of methodological approach, is usually a fluid, flexible, and ongoing process. Different from quantitative methods, the sample in qualitative approaches is rarely set and static before a study commences. Relating to the discussion of coverage, the researcher presumably continues to sample until appropriate coverage is achieved. Furthermore, as data are collected and initial analysis is conducted, new insights about how the participant group should be bounded may emerge as the research process evolves. The issue of flexibility needed in sampling is related to sample size and will be discussed later in this chapter.

In thinking about sampling strategies for a particular study, the researcher must focus on both selecting a strategy and then providing a rationale for why the strategy is most appropriate. Although no fixed rules exist for which sampling strategies attach to particular methodological approaches, there are clear differences among strategies so that some align more closely with certain methodologies than others. For example, in case study methodology, the selection of a case suggests a focus on the specificity of a particular case (e.g., critical case sampling strategy); and in phenomenology, with the appropriate emphasis on the lived experience of a particular phenomenon, participants must clearly reflect this phenomenon (e.g., intensity sampling). In an ethnographic study with emphasis on understanding cultural nuances and influence, the researcher must gain access to a diverse group of participants to provide in-depth perspectives on cultural dynamics (e.g., snowball sampling). However, the selection of the individuals within the case, or ethnography, may be selected by utilizing a number of strategies depending on the purpose of the study (e.g., maximum variation, negative case, or typical case).

To illustrate several of the strategies most typically utilized in higher education and student affairs research, we provide several examples from published research in Table 5.1.

Table 5.1 Sampling Strategies

Purpose of Study	Sample	Sampling Strategies
The purpose of this study was "to investigate the meaning students made of their experiences as participants on a short-term immersion program" (Jones, Rowan-Kenyon, Ireland, Niehaus, & Skendall, 2012, p. 204).	Consistent with case study methodology, sampling occurred on two levels: selection of cases and participants within each case. This resulted in four trips (cases in a multi-site case study) and 37 students.	Sought maximum variation among the trips and used purposeful sampling to select the cases (4 trips). Participants selected using criterion sampling (e.g., all participants on each trip were invited to participate in the study).
"To investigate how racial microaggressions in White environments can produce psychological conditions of racial battle fatigue, this study examined African American male students' social and academic experiences at elite, historically White campuses" (Smith, Allen, & Danley, 2007, p. 559).	Using purposeful sampling identified 36 African American male students attending one of six universities around the country.	Criterion sampling to identify the institutions and intensity sampling to identify the individuals.
"Collectively, constructionist epistemology and the aforementioned theoretical perspective on masculinity led me to inquire into the meanings the participants ascribed to masculinity, contextual factors that influenced those meaning, and behavioral norms that emerged as a consequence of privileged and marginalized social constructions of masculinity in the research site" (Harris, 2008, p. 459).	Twelve undergraduates selected using the assumptions of the social construction of masculinity—that is, men are not a homogenous group and that gender identity is intersected by other identity dimensions (theory driven sampling); participants included five who were White, four African American, two Latino, one Asian American; eleven heterosexual and one gay; four were student-athletes; two were fraternity members; ten were raised in two-parent homes.	Used purposeful sampling by inviting nominations from key informants and gatekeepers; resulted in 12 participants.
"The purpose of this descriptive and interpretive qualitative study is to understand and describe the experiences of 22 women at one university who moved from classified (clerical) roles into professional positions" (Iverson, 2009, p. 142).	Twenty-two women who were employed at the university from 7–45 years; ages from early 30s to mid-60s; all were White; holding a variety of professional positions with the university.	Criterion sampling required that each woman had advanced from classified to professional ranks and identified using key informants and snowball sampling whereby initial participants identified others.

(continued)

Table 5.1 (continued)

Purpose of Study	Sample	Sampling Strategies
"The purpose of this study was to understand the essence or common experiences of queer students of color in activist roles at a predominately white, mid-sized university" (Vaccaro & Mena, 2011, p. 343)	Six queer student activists of color who met 4 clearly defined criteria volunteered to participate and all were selected. All were undergraduate students; 2 female, 3 male, 1 genderqueer; and 2 Latino, 2 African American, 1 Chinese American, and 1 biracial.	As a phenomenological study, participants must have experience with the particular phenomenon being studied. For the purpose of this study, student activist was defined as an individual who worked for social change and equality for LGBTQ people on campus (p. 345). Students of color in the Queer Student Group (QSG) were recruited to participate.
"This study seeks to investigate the processes involved in adult life beyond the early 20s that could influence how Latino ethnic identity evolves . . . . This study highlights the life events that can influence how adult Latinos view their ethnic identity at various points through their adulthood" (Torres, Martinez, Wallace, Medrano, Robledo, & Hernandez, 2012, p. 4).	To address adult identity issues among Latinos, a pragmatic approach was used which included an electronic survey of open-ended questions and sampling via listservs. This resulted in 80 useable responses with the majority women (79%) and born in the U.S. of foreign-born parents (49%).	Purposeful sampling was used to distribute the electronic survey, followed by snowball sampling to increase responses.

What is most critical when considering sampling strategies is making the connection between the strategies utilized to generate a purposefully drawn sample and what it is the researcher wants to learn more about (e.g., the purpose of the study and research questions). This enables the researcher to identify the most appropriate sampling strategies for a particular study. For example, depending on the questions addressed in a study, a sample may be identified through the process of *maximum variation* in order to cast a wide net on the phenomenon of interest or through *intensity* sampling that suggests that the phenomenon of interest is intensely present (Patton, 2002).

Gaining Access

A related process, and one integral to sampling, is that of gaining access to participants for research and developing rapport. Simply identifying sampling criteria and strategies for creating a sample does not at all assure the actuality of a group of individuals who agree to participate. As Glesne (2011) discussed:

> Gaining access is a process. It involves acquisition of consent to go where you want, observe what you want, talk to whomever you want, obtain

and read whatever documents you require, and do all of this for whatever period of time is necessary to satisfy your research purposes. (p. 57)

Gaining access to participants or a particular field site is sometimes an easy process and sometimes fraught with difficulty—what makes the difference is the nature of the research project, existing relationships the researcher has with those who can provide access, and the care the researcher has taken to know the context of the site and the participants within it (Glesne, 2011). The process of gaining access may be more challenging when the researcher is using a critical perspective and thus perhaps held suspect by those granting access or when the researcher is requesting full immersion in a particular setting, as would be more typical in ethnographic research. For example, Magolda and Ebben Gross (2009) wrote about the ideological differences between themselves and the director of Students Serving Christ (SSC). They elaborated:

> Our status as nonbelievers was an initial barrier that we predicted would result in the SSC, as well as other evangelical campus groups, declining our invitation to participate in the study. Fortunately, we were incorrect. Ironically, it was the evangelical mission of the SSC—to spread the Word of God to nonbelievers—that influenced the director's decision to permit us to study the SSC. . . . Ultimately, we forged a respectful partnership with Matthew and his congregation that we sustained throughout the study. (p. 27)

Attention to several relationship-oriented processes will aid the researcher in facilitating access to participants.

Gatekeepers and Key Informants

One of the primary strategies for gaining access is through negotiation with gatekeepers and key informants. These are the individuals who know individuals and/or settings that meet the sampling criteria determined by the researcher. Gatekeepers and key informants typically hold some kind of formal or informal authority such that they may grant consent to enter a research setting (Glesne, 2011). Key informants may differ from gatekeepers because they are less likely to have authority to grant access, but as an insider, may be able to influence gatekeepers. And once access is gained, key informants are integral to identifying the most suitable participants for a study because of their insider status. Key informants may also help researchers understand the politics at a particular setting, cultural considerations, or other dynamics that might impact the researcher's request for access. Patton (2002) described key informants as "people who are particularly knowledgeable about the inquiry setting and articulate about their knowledge—people whose insights can prove particularly useful in helping an observer understand what is happening and why" (p. 321). Although key informants are crucial to providing access to participants to whom the researcher needs introduction, Patton (2002) cautioned against an overreliance on their perceptions of what is going on as "truth" rather than as "necessarily limited, selective, and biased" (p. 321).

Gatekeepers may be approached through someone else who knows these individuals or through a request for communication from the researcher to the gatekeeper. Although the first strategy is advantageous because the researcher's credibility can be established by someone already known to the gatekeeper, in either case, the importance of preparation cannot be underestimated. This means that the researcher must provide a compelling case for the request for access that includes presenting a clearly thought out plan for research, illustrating evidence of knowledge of the research site and contexts as well as the participants in that context, establishing credentials as a researcher, providing assurance of anonymity and confidentiality, and responding to the questions and concerns the gatekeeper might raise (Glesne, 2011). Patton (2002) captured the challenge in strategically negotiating access from gatekeepers as:

> … figuring out how to gain entry while preserving the integrity of the study and the investigator's interests. The degree of difficulty involved varies depending on the purpose of fieldwork and the expected or real degree of resistance to the study. Where the field researcher expects cooperation, gaining entry may be largely a matter of establishing trust and rapport. At the other end of the continuum are those research settings where considerable resistance, even hostility, is expected, in which case the entry becomes a matter of "infiltrating the setting." And sometimes entry is simply denied. (p. 310)

In fact, in a follow up study to one on high school service-learning graduation requirements, Susan was interested in interviewing high school teachers, high school students, and others in the high school impacted by such a requirement. Entry into the high schools in the state with the requirement involved a formal letter of request to the individuals in each county responsible for the oversight of research initiatives, which had to include a clear statement of deliverables and how the research would contribute to academic achievement (e.g., testing related to No Child Left Behind). Ultimately, the request was turned down in every school district.

One of the best ways to provide assurance of integrity as a researcher and to demonstrate commitment to the project and potential participants is by spending time at the site, developing relationships, and gaining insider knowledge. Glesne (2011) referred to this as "logging time" (p. 58) and explained this as:

> Just being around, participating in activities, and talking informally with people gives them time to get used to you and learn that you are okay. This approach leads to better data than one in which a superior [state superintendent of schools] requests a subordinate [principal] to cooperate with you. (p. 58)

In an example of published research focused on student understanding of HIV/AIDS in the context of a university-community partnership conducted by Jones and Abes (2003), both researchers were very familiar with the site for the research (an AIDS service organization) because each was a regular volunteer with the organization. As a result, access to the site was easily granted because of the relationships researchers developed with the staff and clients and their insider knowledge of the context of the research site. The ability to develop insider knowledge and to become visible and known at the site is closely connected with another important sampling-related issue, that of developing rapport and trust with participants.

Establishing Rapport and Developing Trust

The presence of rapport and trust is integral not only to securing participants for a study, but also to sustaining participation over time. In fact, the relationship between researcher and participants is one of the hallmarks of qualitative inquiry; however, this relationship can be neither presumed nor taken for granted. Establishing rapport and developing trust take time, care, and persistent attention throughout the research process. The presence of rapport suggests the development of a relationship characterized by reciprocity and mutuality. However, what makes rapport in the context of qualitative inquiry potentially problematic is that rapport is needed primarily so that the researcher can accomplish certain results. Rapport is not enough in a research relationship as it is more typically the presence of trust that facilitates a reciprocal relationship. As Glesne (2011) suggested, ". . . qualitative research should move in a direction in which trust is needed for working together on the issue under inquiry. Rapport, however, is often a precursor to building trust and part of gaining access and 'fitting in'" (p. 141).

The foundation upon which rapport sits is "the ability to convey empathy and understanding without judgment" (Patton, 2002, p. 366). This suggests the importance of trust and respect in a researcher-participant relationship, which must be present in all aspects of the research process, such as initial contacts with participants, active listening during interviews, and showing appreciation for their time and expertise. Although not writing specifically about qualitative research, Noddings's (1984) foundational work on caring is particularly instructive in thinking about trust and respect in the context of the research process. Noddings suggested that when we care or are in a caring relationship with another, then we are *feeling with* that person:

> I do not "put myself in the other's shoes," so to speak, by analyzing his [sic] reality as objective data and then asking, "How would I feel in such a situation?" On the contrary, I set aside my temptation to analyze and to plan. I do not project; I receive the other into myself, and I see and feel with the other. (p. 30)

A researcher's ability to care, to receive the other, is the backbone of trust and respect. Such a relationship communicates to one's participants a genuine regard for them as individuals and a deep commitment to understanding their experiences. Noddings's notions about caring in relation to the research process dovetail with Patton's (2002) suggestions about the importance of both rapport and *neutrality* in qualitative research. He explained this helpful distinction as follows:

> Rapport is a stance vis-á-vis the person being interviewed. Neutrality is a stance vis-á-vis the content of what that person says. . . . Rapport means that I respect the people being interviewed, so what they say is important because of who is saying it. . . . Neutrality means that the person being interviewed can tell me anything without engendering either my favor or disfavor with regard to the content of her or his response. I cannot be shocked; I cannot be angered; I cannot be embarrassed; I cannot be saddened. Nothing the person tells me will make me think more or less of the person. (p. 365)

Although there are no recipes for the creation of trust and respect in the context of qualitative research, what follows are a number of specific strategies and qualities that may contribute to facilitating and maintaining trust and respect:

- Convey your interest in the project with your initial invitation to participate as well as your knowledge of the phenomenon under investigation.
- Be clear in the expectations you have of participants, and consider the question of why someone would want to participate in such a study—are there meaningful incentives you might offer?
- In addition to incentives, consider the question of how you might develop reciprocity in the context of the research process—what might participants get out of their involvement in your research?
- Recognize that methodological approach influences the processes of gaining access and building rapport. For example, in a feminist inquiry, participants should play a more active role in conceptualizing all aspects of the study design.
- Tune in—and adjust accordingly—to the culturally relevant norms, behaviors, appearances, language, and values of participants. This means learning about and developing an insider's view of the context and culture you are investigating and exploring. This may mean researchers will adjust their own behavior, language, or expression of beliefs.
- Be sensitive to the impact of your presence in the research setting. However unobtrusive you might feel, the mere presence of a researcher may be cause for anxiety, attention, or scrutiny.
- Consider the relationship between your own socially constructed identities (e.g., race, ethnicity, age, gender, sexual orientation, and social class) and

those of your participants, and consider what differences these might make in your ability to establish rapport and trust (this will be discussed further in this chapter and in Chapter Seven).

• Pay attention to the physical environment when interviewing or observing participants. Are they in a natural setting or a place of their choosing? Eliminate any potential distractions that may influence your ability to be with the participant.

• Make sure that your active listening and observation skills are strong. Effective interviewing is crucial to good research and depends upon very strong listening skills.

• Rapport and trust are also built by the ability to ask good questions. This requires practicing (typically through pilot studies), then following up with appropriate probes that demonstrate that you heard the initial response and stimulate further reflection or insight about the phenomenon.

• Rapport and trust must be sustained throughout the research process. One way to navigate this is through involving participants in member checking of data and, most importantly, your interpretations of the data. In other words, have you told their story in a way they recognize and find meaningful?

Issues Related to an Interest in a "Diverse" Sample and Researcher Positionality

Related to decisions about sampling and criteria used to identify participants for a study is the interest in a "diverse" sample. This interest has necessarily evolved out of a commitment to inclusion in research designs by representing in samples those whose life experiences and stories have previously been excluded or marginalized through the research process (Jones, 2002). However well-intentioned and important these efforts are, creating a "diverse" sample requires careful and thoughtful attention to the issues of researcher positionality and to the potential of unwittingly further marginalizing particular voices through a tokenism inherent in the sampling process. Stating an interest in securing a "diverse sample" has become a researcher mantra, yet often without the critically necessary reflection on issues of power, privilege, and representation that are inherent in the sampling process. The issue of researcher positionality was discussed in greater detail in Chapter Two. However, researcher positionality is also connected to sampling in important ways that are rarely addressed in the literature, particularly related to the creation of a diverse sample and to researching within, or outside, the researcher's own community or social identities. These two specific considerations, as they connect to sampling and participant selection, will be addressed in this chapter.

The question of researcher positionality, or the connection between the researcher's socially constructed identities and those of participants and how this connection plays out in relation to power dynamics and representation, is a complicated one because it necessarily illuminates issues associated with what constitutes a "diverse sample" and researching within—or outside—the researcher's own community. In a foundational work on this subject, Fine (1994) referred to this negotiation as "working the hyphen" of *self-other*, with "the hyphen that both separates and merges personal identities with our inventions of Others" (p. 70). Fine (1994) elaborated:

> By *working the hyphen*, I mean to suggest that researchers probe how we are in relation with the contexts we study and with our informants, understanding that we are all multiple in those relations. . . . Working the hyphen means creating occasions for researchers and informants to discuss what is, and is not, "happening between," within the negotiated relations of whose story is being told, why, to whom, [and] with what interpretation, and whose story is being shadowed, why, for whom, and with what consequence. (p. 72)

The importance of working the hyphen by qualitative researchers is apparent when examining what constitutes diverse samples. Far too often, this diverse sample is created by including one of this and one of that, as if to suggest that the voice of disability, for example, is heard by the presence of one individual with a disability. This issue is exacerbated in many qualitative studies because of a relatively small sample size, so the question becomes what can a researcher say about what in a "diverse sample" of 10 participants?

In an article exploring an approach that suggests that only gays and lesbians can speak to sexuality or that race is only salient for African Americans, Maynard (2000) wrote that such an approach not only encourages "benign description" but also misses the critical point that "these things structure *all* our lives, no matter how invisible they might be in experiential terms, [and] we are not excused from confronting them because we are not members of a particular oppressed group" (p. 99). Morse (2007) further suggested that when qualitative researchers focus their sampling criteria on demographic diversity rather than "the conceptual/informational needs of the study . . . the most common outcome . . . is that the researcher pools data from all cultural groups. This means that all cultural variation is lost in the analysis, which is probably the reverse of the researcher's intent in selecting a multicultural sample in the first place" (p. 232).

These cautions are not meant to be interpreted as an endorsement of homogenous samples. Instead, these complexities must be carefully considered by the researcher and addressed in providing a rationale for sampling. Researchers need to position themselves in relation to the phenomenon under investigation (why do I care about this topic?), the methodological approach (what assumptions do I carry about how knowledge is constructed?), and participants in the study (how does who I am and where I come from influence what I know and what I hear and observe?). Robbins (2012), in her research on racial consciousness among White women in student affairs graduate programs, provided an exemplary rationale for the diversity of her sample. Grounding her rationale in the scholarship of student development theory and an intersectional approach to identity, she wrote:

> Seeking "information-rich cases that manifest the phenomenon intensely but not extremely" (Creswell, 2007, p. 127), I selected 11 participants whom I deemed to have the potential to offer rich stories about their experiences with White identity. Additionally, consistent with maximum variation sampling (Creswell, 2007) and building on lessons learned from previous studies of White women (Frankenberg, 1993), these participants reflected diversity across multiple dimensions of social identity, geographic regions, age and life experiences, and other educational and professional experiences.... In taking an intersectional approach, my goal was not to "represent" categories of difference.... This kind of cross-cultural analysis was not my intention, nor did I wish to essentialize any individual or identity by making assumptions about representativeness. Rather, I sought to construct a sample, and, thus, the emergent grounded theory in an inclusive manner (Jones, et al., 2006; Morse, 2007). Thus, I attended carefully to categories of difference that were salient in the lives of participants and relevant to the purpose of the study. (pp. 96–97)

Researcher positionality not only influences assumptions about the importance of diverse samples but also what is noticed when constructing samples. Again, Fine (1994) framed this issue well: "The social sciences have been, and still are, long on texts that inscribe some Others, preserve other Others from scrutiny, and seek to hide the researcher/writer under a veil of neutrality or objectivity" (p. 73). Applying this to higher education research, a White researcher, for example, interested in the experiences of female students participating in the STEM program, which is specifically designed for women, might miss the fact that this "special program" consists of 99% White women. Because she is not conscious of her own White racial identity, she fails to see how this potentially influences both her research decisions and outcomes. Similarly, many examples exist where researchers claim to investigate the experiences of men or women but fail to explicate any racial, ethnic, or cultural information that may make a significant difference to what might be said about the experiences of particular individuals in the findings. Duster (2000) framed a question that relates to diverse samples this way: "What [does] it mean to be conscious of 'race' when one is doing research?" (p. xii). He goes on to suggest that this question is related to two additional questions: "who has *access* to what scene, and with what outcome? ... And *whose questions get raised* for investigation?" (p. xii). These examples suggest the important relationship between researcher positionality and the creation of a "diverse" sample, as well as the intersection of race, and other social identities, with all elements of a research design.

Because many researchers are interested in creating diverse samples, researcher positionality is connected to the issue of researching within and/or outside one's own community. Researchers may embark upon a project that takes them out of their own identities or communities with a naïve assumption that this should not or would not make a difference. We do not want to suggest here that sampling outside of one's own community is not possible, but, more so, that great attentiveness and discernment be given about the implications of such work. Furthermore, attentiveness is also required when a researcher's participants are similar in identities and/or communities. A similarity or commonality may be presumed when that is not the case. Even when a researcher has given thoughtful consideration to who is included in a sample, issues still arise. In a refreshing example of transparency, Winkle-Wagner (2009) included a chapter in her book titled *Research Across the Color Line* and candidly addressed the challenges she had as a White woman constructing a sample of African American women. She conveyed:

> I remember feeling a knot in the pit of my stomach as this research project began. Weeks had passed, and I had been waiting in dorm lounges, coffee shops, pizza places, conference rooms, and the campus union alone with stacks of pizzas, over and over again—waiting for the women to come. I had worried about how, as a White woman, I would gain trust with African American women, and these solitary meetings enlightened me that perhaps the customary way of recruiting participants into my research project would not work in this case. (p. 49)

Interestingly, the way in which Winkle-Wagner tackled this issue was to more intentionally connect her sampling process with her critical approach to the study. In her words, "I got real" (Winkle-Wagner, 2009, p. 49), which meant she engaged differently with her participants, focusing on getting to know them and their lives (not just as research participants) and on the issue of the relationship between her research and social change. Participants were involved in the research design as well as data collection and analysis. Because the eradication of discrimination and oppression in higher education was an issue the participants also cared about, they became engaged in the research process.

Another poignant example of the relationship between sampling, researcher positionality, and the communities within which research is conducted is offered by two researchers who engaged in a collaborative project investigating the school experiences of Mexican children (Merchant, 2001; Zurita, 2001). Zurita, a Mexican American woman, connected with her participants in a way that Merchant, a White woman, could not. Researching within Zurita's community elicited great anguish about her role as a researcher, how school officials constructed her role [which was very different from the way they constructed the role of Merchant and included "(a) the 'other;' (b) a tutor and hired hand; (c) 'Mexican expert;' and problem solver; and (d) a radical militant"] (p. 23), and what she perceived as her unwitting perpetuation of social inequality by simply documenting unjust conditions rather than working for change. Merchant (2001) described her intellectual awareness of the influence of her racial identity and White researchers' tendency to speak for the other but noted that this "was not enough to prevent me from lapsing into culturally biased patterns of research" (p. 15). Negotiating these relationships in the research context requires careful attention to positionality, power, and privilege.

Summary

What these examples from research suggest is the importance of examining the complex dynamics at work when participants in a study mirror, or do not mirror, the social identities of the researcher. The realities of researching within and/or outside the researcher's own community influence criteria identified for sampling, sampling strategies and approaches, access to participants, and the rapport and trust developed between researcher and participant. Most typically, when sampling and participant selection are discussed, the processes are situated as though they exist outside of any kind of sociocultural or theoretical context. In fact, each dimension of sampling discussed in this chapter is patterned and influenced by this context as well as the researcher's positionality within a sociocultural reality. Not to acknowledge the role these dynamics play in all aspects of the research design, including sampling and participant selection, is to perpetuate an "Othering" that results in a distancing between self and other, researcher and participant.

Connecting sampling to the outcome of qualitative studies, Patton (2002) offered helpful guidance:

> Thus, when selecting a small sample of great diversity, the data collection and analysis will yield two kinds of findings: (1) high-quality, detailed descriptions of each case, which are useful for documenting uniqueness, and (2) important shared patterns that cut across cases and derive their significance from having emerged out of heterogeneity. Both are important findings in qualitative inquiry. (p. 235)

Careful attention to the dynamics of sampling and participant selection works to connect sampling criteria and strategies to all elements of the research design, the purpose of the study, and to the development of relationships that are the anchor of good qualitative research.

Exercises

Chapter-related

1. How are you thinking differently about sampling after having read this chapter? What considerations had not occurred to you before?

2. What are the potential influences of your own positionality and social identities in relation to sampling? Revisit your responses to the questions at the end of Chapter Three regarding the power and privileges you possess.

3. How will you appropriately "work the self-other hyphen"?

4. What complexities involved in claiming a "diverse sample" are important?

Research Process

1. Look again at your statement of purpose.
   - Identify what the statement of purpose tells you about your sample.
   - What does your methodological approach tell you about your sample?

2. Now think about your sample in relation to your methodological approach.
   - List who should be in your sample—what are you trying to understand about this group as they experience your phenomenon of interest (purpose)?
   - Identify 3–4 sampling criteria for your study. How can you defend the selection of these criteria?
   - Are there any other sampling considerations that flow from your statement of purpose and methodological approach?
   - What constitutes saturation given your topic and your sample? How will you know you have accomplished saturation?

6   Challenges in Collecting Data

It would take an entire tome to thoroughly discuss data collection; that is not our intent here. Rather, we want to explore some of the challenges and complexities that often occur during the data collection process. Data collection involves a number of processes that must be managed, including negotiating issues of power. Furthermore, there are numerous data collection methods beyond the one-on-one interview, especially methods made possible by digital technologies. We begin our exploration by uncovering the challenges and complexities in more traditional data collection methods and then move to discuss challenges and complexities in more recent avenues of data collection made possible by technological advances. We follow that with a cursory discussion of researcher power in data collection and conclude by summarizing some of the challenges in conducting a mixed methods study. Yet, before data can be collected, a data collection management plan is necessary.

Challenge of Creating a Data Management Plan

Managing qualitative data is a job in and of itself (Hays & Singh, 2012). Devising a system of data management before data are collected will prevent confusion during analysis (Marshall & Rossman, 2011; Merriam, 2009). One reason for the enormity of managing qualitative data is due to the vast array of data sources, which can include diaries, journals, recordings, photographs, films, observations, maps, blogs (Gibbs, 2007) as well as numerous files, folders, and reams of transcripts and field notes. Furthermore, because the data analysis process blends with the data collection process, there is no clear distinction between where one process ends and the other begins. Remember that one of the goals of research in the qualitative paradigm is to increase complex understanding about the data (Gibbs, 2007). Producing complex findings entails managing data units that are labeled, sorted into categories, and then revealed as themes (Charmaz, 2006). Such complexity necessitates a sophisticated data management system.

Marshall and Rossman (2011) suggested that a data management plan should include attention to how to systematically record data in a way that is appropriate for the methodology and aids in the analysis. For example, though some researchers suggest taking notes during interviews (Creswell, 2013), and that may be appropriate for some methodologies, "in some situations taking notes interferes with, inhibits, or, in some way acts on the setting and the participants" (Marshall & Rossman, p. 205). How also might recording equipment influence data collection? For example, because in more participatory forms of research the role of the researcher is integrated in the setting, note taking and recording may be intrusive. Additionally, when conducting field work in an ethnographic study, note taking would be expected. But, when utilizing methodologies such as phenomenology or grounded theory, note taking during an interview would be less appropriate.

Hays and Singh (2012) recommended the use of a "case display" (p. 317) to assist in data management. A "within-case display" is a "snapshot" or a reduction of the data such as information of an individual participant (p. 317). Snapshots might include prominent characteristics, whereas a "cross-case display" is a snapshot of patterns across all of the cases (participants), such as participants' majors (p. 317). These strategies allow researchers to "absorb large amounts of information quickly" (Hays & Singh, 2012, p. 317). Consequently, data management must involve substantial storage space.

A challenge for all researchers is to maintain the confidentiality of participants' identities. The real names and locations of participants should be kept in a separate file from the pseudonyms in the data files. All electronic documents must be password protected (Gibbs, 2007).

Organizing data often includes color coding of text, files, or even index cards as well as sections of three ringed binders. Line numbering, wide margins, and double spacing will be of particular assistance (Gibbs, 2007). Tapes, thumb drives, and files must be thoroughly labeled. Having not only sufficient but also extra supplies, including confidential interviewing space, batteries, and tapes, is all part of managing data collection (Marshall & Rossman, 2011). Many qualitative researchers find computer software programs necessary in managing data (Creswell, 2013; Gibbs, 2007) and several word processing programs are sufficiently sophisticated to assist in data management (Merriam, 2009). We do not discuss qualitative software programs in any depth here as other texts do, although we do agree that these programs are helpful in managing voluminous amounts of data. The point of all of these suggestions is to make data "easily retrievable and manipulatable" (Marshall & Rossman, 2011, p. 206). van Manen (1990) believed that over reliance on poorly managed data leads to either "despair and confusion" or "a chaotic quest for meaning" (p. 67).

Besides data, researchers will also need to manage the analysis process. As the analysis begins, researchers may want to organize their notes and memos by the categories as concretely and detailed as possible about what was seen, heard, and felt. Methodological notes are memos researchers send to themselves about how data were collected, impressions about the context and environment, and beginning theoretical hunches or interpretations. Personal notes refer to feelings, including fears, concerns, and commitments (Gibbs, 2007, p. 31; also

Merriam, 2009). These notes too must be managed as they help address obligations researchers have for ensuring trustworthy inquiry, as discussed in Chapter Two. Hays and Singh (2012) recommended keeping data five to seven years after completion of a study.

Creating a plan for managing data supports researchers in the collection and analysis process and prevents possible misperceptions of the data and general disorder. We turn now to a discussion of the vast array of data collection methods and some of the nuances of various approaches.

Challenge of Selecting the Most Appropriate Types of Methods

Data collection methods include far more opportunities than one-to-one interviews and surveys. Document reviews, observations, and participant journaling are additional traditional methods of data collection. Advancements in technology, however, have even broadened the notion of what data are and can be. Verbal storytelling is a traditional method of collecting data in studies grounded in constructivism, constructionism, interpretivism, critical theory, and post-structuralism, but other forms of storytelling allow greater flexibility in storying that includes the "words as well as the worlds of participants" (Finley, 2008, p. 98). These methods include forms of art (dance, film, photography, poetry, and drama) but also blogs, counterstories, testimonials, and mystories. As Finley (2008) observed, one challenge to the broader notion of data is whether others (particularly journal editorial boards and grant funding agencies) will view the study as research once it is completed. Another challenge is to make clear how "boundary-crossing approaches" (such as art forms) "are responsive to social dilemmas" (Finley, 2008, p. 101). Yet, overcoming these challenges is beneficial in that these forms open up the imagination for new ways of viewing problems and possibilities (Finley, 2008; Talburt, 2004). An example of this is performance ethnography (also discussed in Chapter Four), which creates opportunities to unveil oppression, to show how oppression is experienced, and to transform practice (Finley, 2008). In a study of digital storytelling, Rolón-Dow (2011) illustrated the unveiling of oppression as experienced when one participant conveyed her loneliness of being the only person of color in a classroom by including in her digital story two photographs of empty classrooms. In one, the student circled a desk and wrote "My desk: I am the only Black student" (p. 168). This photo appeared in her digital story while the song "Hey there Lonely Girl" was played. Rolón-Dow (2011) expressed that this "communicated a message that being the lone minority student in a mostly white space felt like an aggression on [the participant's] spirit and mind" (p. 168).

As described in Chapter One, decisions about data collection are guided by research questions formed from a compelling interest, the methodology chosen as the map to explore the research question, and the methods that are aligned with that methodology. Table 6.1 presents data collection methods most associated with particular methodologies (Crotty, 1998; Denzin & Lincoln, 2008).

Table 6.1 Methodology and Preferred Methods

Methodology	Preferred Methods
Ethnography	Group and individual interviews, field observations, internet-mediated discourse, content analysis
Grounded Theory	Group and individual interviews, observations, content analysis
Phenomenology	Individual interviews, written reflections, diaries
Case Study	Group and individual interviews, content analysis, observations
Narrative	Storying through interviewing, collective testimonies, digital story telling

Sources: Fontana & Frey (2008), Gadamer (1992), Hays & Singh (2012), Merriam (2009)

As discussed in Chapter One, another consideration in creating the data collection plan is its do-ability (Marshall & Rossman, 2011). Considerations about time, money, access to participants, feasibility, and researcher knowledge and skill are factors that play into what data will be collected. For example, a researcher conducting a case study exploring students' judgments and experiences with alcohol may find it difficult to recruit willing participants (particularly at small institutions or at community colleges). Instead, the researcher may choose to review documents such as incident reports and observe behaviors in public spaces.

Often, the method chosen to collect data is the interview. Below, we discuss the challenges of interviewing, including individual and group interviews, phone interviews, and methodological considerations in interviewing.

Challenges in Interviewing

Though most people are familiar with interviews due to our culture's fascination with them (Fontana & Frey, 2008), there are a number of challenges and complexities to be negotiated in interviewing for data collection purposes. Because interviews have become common place on television, radio, and podcasts, novices may believe that interviewing is easy, when instead it requires complex skills such as active listening.

> "The interview" for an ethnographer may mean something quite different than a therapist, or for an investigative journalist. In each case the concept of interview is charged with the reality assumptions, truth criteria and the general goals of the disciplined methodology within which the interview functions. (van Manen, 1990, p. 28)

More Than Simply Asking Questions

Perhaps unlike what is necessary in other types of interviews, Fontana and Frey (2008) emphasized the importance of good listening skills for qualitative researchers during interviews. Similarly, in listing the characteristics of skilled interviewing, Kvale and Brinkman (2009) described active listening as having "an ear for . . . subjects' linguistic style" (p. 166), hearing "with an evenly hovering attention" the "nuances of meaning in an answer, and seeking to get the nuances of meaning described more fully" (p. 167). Too, according to Kvale and Brinkman, the effective interviewer listens to the emotion embedded in what is said and knows when a topic is too difficult to pursue. Listening also requires interviewers to remember enough of what was said previously in the same interview to ask for clarification or elaboration of subsequent connected statements. Charmaz (2006) encouraged researchers to rephrase important concepts back to participants, stating for example "Let's see if I have grasped these events correctly" (p. 26). Glesne (2011), too, stressed the critical nature of listening in interviewing. She wrote,

> At no time do you stop listening, because without the data your listening furnishes, you cannot make any of the decisions inherent in interviewing: Are you listening with your research purposes and eventual write-up fully in mind, so that you are attuned to whether your questions are delivering on your intentions for them? . . . . You listen and you look, aware that feedback can be both nonverbal and verbal. You observe the respondent's body language to determine what effects your questions, probes, and comments are having. (pp. 118–119)

Furthermore, in commenting on narrative research, Chase (2008) suggested that "*during interviews* the narrative researcher needs to orient to the particularity of the narrator's story and voice" (p. 70) (emphasis in original).

Being a constant active listener can be exhausting, requires skill and preparation, and is only one of the challenges in interviewing. Another challenge is understanding the influence of methodology on interviewing.

One Interview Style Does Not Fit All: The Influence of Methodology on Interviews

Methodology influences and provides guidance to the purpose and type of interview. The challenge is using this methodological guidance in selecting the appropriate type of interview from the variety possible, some of which are described below. For example, ethnographers want to know about the particularities of culture and its influence (Merriam, 2009; van Manen, 1990). According to van Manen (1990), the hermeneutic phenomenological interview has two purposes. One is to explore "experiential narrative material that may serve as a resource for developing a richer and deeper understanding of a human phenomenon" and the other serves "as a vehicle to develop a conversational relation with a partner (interviewee) about the meaning of an experience" (p. 66). Always, phenomenologists "stay close to an experience as it is immediately lived" (p. 66). According to van Manen, phenomenologists ask participants to be concrete by being specific and "exploring the whole experience to the fullest" (p. 67). If a participant seems to be experiencing a "block" (p. 68) van Manen suggested that researchers pause and be silent, then ask a question from the last statement the participant made.

According to Clandinin and Connelly (2000) oral history interviews are common in narrative inquiry. They are "autobiographical and contain stories" (p. 112). Too, annals and chronicles are often part of narrative oral history interviews. Annals include a "list of dates of memories, events, and stories" whereas chronicles are "sequences of events in and around a particular topic" (p. 112). Timelines and family stories passed down through generations can also be informative in narrative inquiry.

As Table 6.1 indicates, numerous sources of data collection are appropriate in a case study. Determined by the focus of the study, one source in each study is predominant and sometimes that is the interview (Merriam, 2009). Yin (2009) explained that researchers have two obligations in interviewing. One is to follow the line of inquiry determined in the case study protocol and the other is to ask the questions in an unbiased way. The case study researcher is interested in "facts as well as opinions about events" (p. 107); hence, case study interviews tend to be semi-structured and in-depth. Yin differentiated informants from respondents. Informants not only offer insights about the topic being studied but also "initiate access to corroboratory or contrary sources of evidence" (p. 107). Because of the nature of in-depth interviews, the actual interview may take place over several meetings. But, case study interviews can also be focused, when particular information is needed. Even in the focused interview, the case study interviewer should act naïve about the topic (Yin, 2009).

In her description of grounded theory inquiry, Charmaz (2006) differentiated interviews that promote in-depth exploration (also called intensive interviews) from informational interviewing that have an "objective cast" (p. 25). More common is the in-depth interview that "elicits each participant's interpretation of his or her experience" (p. 25). In-depth interviews are particularly appropriate in grounded theory because they "are open-ended yet directed, shaped yet emergent, and paced yet unrestricted" (Charmaz, 2006, p. 28). This is because, in grounded theory, researchers begin learning from data collection at the beginning of the inquiry, explore initial ideas, then return to the field asking questions that focus on missing pieces. About intensive interviews, Charmaz (2006) suggested,

> Devise a few broad, open-ended questions [questions that cannot be answered by yes or no]. Then you can focus your interview questions to invite detailed discussion of [the] topic. By creating open-ended, non-judgmental questions, you encourage unanticipated statements and stories to emerge . . . . The structure of the intensive interview may range from a loosely guided exploration of topics to semi-structured focused questions. Although the intensive interview may be conversational, it follows a different etiquette. The researcher

should express interest and want to know more . . . . As the interview proceeds, you may request clarifying details to obtain accurate information and to learn about the research participant's experiences and reflections. Unlike ordinary conversation, an interviewer can shift the conversation and follow hunches. An interview goes beneath the surface of ordinary conversations and examines earlier events, views, and feelings afresh. (p. 26)

Charmaz (2006) reminded researchers that "Research participants appraise the interviewer, assess the situation, and act on their present assessments and prior knowledge in taken for granted ways" (p. 27). Because of this the researcher "chooses questions carefully and asks them slowly" (p. 29). She begins an interview with a very open question such as "Tell me what a good day is like for you" (p. 33).

In-depth exploration and informational interviewing are just two types of interviews. Below we investigate others.

Selecting the Appropriate Type of Interview

Interviews in qualitative research are often described as structured, semi-structured, unstructured, and conversations (see Table 6.2).

Table 6.2 Types of Interviews

Structured	Semi-structured	Unstructured	Conversation
Little flexibility	Flexible	Flexible	Flexible
Questions are pre-established	Broad, open questions are pre-established	Begin with broad open questions then move to more specific questions based on previous answers	Topic is pre-established
Each participant asked same question	Broad data wanted from all participants with pre-established probes	Interview context and participant taken into account	Each conversation takes its own path
Purpose is preciseness	No set phrasing or order	Purpose is to uncover complexity	Purpose is for participants to come to an understanding
Little follow up or clarification	Some follow up or clarification	Follow up and clarification encouraged	Follow up and clarification imperative
Participants answer questions	Participants answer questions and clarify answers	Participants help shape the interview	Participants are equals in shaping the discussion

Sources: Fontana & Frey (2008); Gadamer (1992); Hays & Singh, (2012); Merriam (2009)

Structured interviews reflect positivist and postpositivist stances where there is little flexibility for the interviewer as each participant is asked the same "pre-established questions with a limited set of response categories" (Fontana & Frey, 2008, p. 124). Also in structured interviews, the pace of the questions is pre-established (Hays & Singh, 2012). Because the purpose is to "capture precise data" (Fontana & Frey, 2008, p. 129), there is little follow up or clarification. Unstructured interviews, on the other hand, are open-ended and flexible, the purpose of which is to "understand the complex behavior of members of society without imposing any a priori categorization that may limit the field of inquiry" (Fontana & Frey, p. 129). Unstructured interviews are often associated with ethnography and oral history (Clandinin & Connelly, 2000; Hays & Singh, 2012; Kvale & Brinkman, 2009) and are used to inquire about a phenomenon about which little is known (Merriam, 2009). They also focus on the context of the time and environment of the interview (Hays & Singh, 2012). However, according to Clandinin and Connelly (2000), published studies using oral history interviews have been structured, semi-structured, and unstructured. In semi-structured interviews, researchers devise a loose interview protocol and several open ended questions utilizing a few clarifying questions, such as asking about feelings, what happened next, or the topic's significance (Morse & Richards, 2002). In semi-structured and unstructured interviews, questions are worded in a way that gives participants leeway in responding. Often, the order of the questions to be asked and exact wording to the questions are not determined prior to the interview (Merriam, 2009). Typically in unstructured and semi-structured interviews, participants are involved in constructing the "structure and process" of the interview (Hays & Singh, 2012, p. 239). Grounded theory researchers often utilize unstructured interviews. Chase (2011) advocated for using in-depth interviews for narrative studies. She also promoted the notion of "framing the interview as a whole with a broad question . . . . This requires knowing what is "storyworthy" in the narrator's social setting" (Chase, 2008, p. 71).

Conversations were promoted by Gadamer (1960/1992) during which the researcher and participant are led by the topic, not by the questions. He wrote, "The way one word follows another, the conversation taking its own twists and reaching its own conclusion, may well be conducted in some way, but the partners conversing are far less the leaders of it than the led" (p. 385). He also thought that, in a true conversation, the goal is understanding. For that to occur, participants engaged in conversation must open "into the other . . . truly accepting the other's point of view as valid . . . so that we can be one with each other on the subject" (p. 385). Philosophical phenomenology is consistent with conversational interviews. This is the case as well in action research. McNiff, Lomax, and Whitehead (2003) offered the importance of what they called dialogical conversations where "all parties attempt to respond to others in ways that will enable the conversation to continue" (pp. 26–27). These conversations with informed others allow action researchers to create their own theory of practice. By their nature, both unstructured interviews and conversations are in-depth and intensive.

The point here is that topic, methodology, and type of participant all influence the decision of what type of interview to conduct and what questions and topics to pose and pursue. In addition, epistemology and theoretical perspective also influence what is asked in an interview. For example, critical theorists expose issues of power, privilege, and oppression, so questions are created with that purpose in mind.

Once a researcher has determined the type of interview (most likely semi-structured, unstructured, or conversational), and methodology and theoretical perspective has been considered, the researcher can begin to contemplate interview questions.

Creating Questions That Lead to Increased Insight

Novice researchers often consider too narrowly or too broadly the variety of questions that can be asked in an interview. Though interview questions are influenced by methodology, researchers should consider a comprehensive interview protocol. According to Kvale and Brinkman (2009), an interview typically involves questions of the following categories: introductory (e.g., Can you tell me what it is like for transfer students here . . . ?), follow-up (pause or tell the interviewee to go on), probing (e.g., Can you say something more about that?), specifying (e.g., How did your body react to . . . ?), direct (e.g., Have you ever . . . ?), indirect (e.g., How do you believe others feel about the needs of transfer students . . . ?), structuring (e.g., Now turning to a different topic about transfer students, . . . ?), and interpretive (e.g., You mean then that . . . ?) (pp. 135–136). They also indicated the importance of allowing for pauses of silence during the interview to encourage participants to take further time to contemplate the topic. Pauses also allow participants to feel as if they are not being cross examined. Hays and Singh (2012) added the following types of interview questions: background (e.g, What class year are you?), behavior or experience (e.g., Tell me about the services you provide as a peer advisor?), opinion or value (e.g., How do you perceive the ways transfer students are treated here?), knowledge (e.g., What percentage of the student body here are transfer students?), feelings (e.g., What feelings come up for you when you work with transfer students?), sensory (e.g., Describe for me the sights and sounds of the transfer student orientation), and probing (e.g., Can you give me an example? What happened next? What was that like for you? How so? Help me understand). Table 6.3 depicts these types of questions in a phenomenological study exploring the experiences of transfer students.

Other types of questions were suggested by Merriam (2009). These included hypothetical (e.g., If you were president of this institution, what would you do about transfer students becoming more engaged in the institution?), devil's advocate (e.g., How might a contrarian view the transfer student experience? Some people claim that transfer students are less loyal to the institution, how would you address that?), and ideal position (e.g., What do you think is the ideal transfer student experience?), and interpretive (e.g., clarify tentative impressions). Moreover, Merriam (2009) suggested avoiding asking leading questions,

Table 6.3 Types of Interview Questions

Type of Question	Phenomenology Example
Background	What class year are you? When did you transfer to this institution? What were the substantive reasons for your transfer?
Behavior or Experience	Tell me about your experiences as a transfer student peer advisor.
Opinion or Value	Of your experiences here as a transfer student, which have you most valued?
Knowledge	What percentage of the student body here are transfer students? How does that influence your experiences?
Feeling	What feelings come up for you when discussing your experiences as a transfer student?
Sensory	Describe for me the sights and sounds of the transfer student orientation as you experienced it.
Probing	Can you give me an example? What happened next? What was that like for you? How so? Help me understand . . .

(discussed in more detail later), closed questions, and multiple questions simultaneously, but urged "a ruthless review of your questions to weed out poor ones" as well as evaluating questions during a pilot test (p. 79).

The purpose of the research also influences interviewing. Baxter Magolda and King (2007) wrote about interviews that assess development. In those studies, researchers utilize responsive interviewing or interviews that are "*in situ* (situated in one's natural position), meaning that researchers respond to what is heard and probe for additional insight rather than create pre-established interview questions. Subsequent interview questions are based on a participant's previous response. This requires skilled active listening because researchers "locate the boundaries of the interviewee's assumption" (Baxter Magolda & King, p. 496). A sympathetic and supportive researcher builds rapport "that assists interviewers in substantive self-reflection" (p. 496). These interviews not only assess development but also promote development by "model[ing] the dynamics of practice that promote self-authorship" (p. 506).

Avoiding Leading Questions

Responsive interviewing is the antithesis of asking leading questions. Leading questions can have both explicit and implicit motives. Often, participants may desire to be led, wanting to assure that what they say is of interest to researchers or even "the right answer." To counter this concern, Baxter Magolda and King (2007) reminded researchers to not finish interviewees' sentences even when participants appear to be struggling to find language that communicates what they are thinking. This means that researchers need to allow for pauses and moments of silence while participants reflect and gather their thoughts.

Table 6.4 Differentiating Appropriate From Leading Questions

Type of Question	Appropriate Question	Leading Question
Behavior or Experience	How do you experience safety?	Tell me about how you feel unsafe because of your social identities.
Opinion or Value	What is safety? Who is responsible for safety?	What do you think the institution should do about you feeling unsafe?
Knowledge	What do you know of the incidents on campus regarding safety?	Describe the campus crime report.
Feeling	What are the feelings you experience as you speak about these issues?	Tell me the negative feelings you experience as you speak about these issues.
Sensory	What are the sights and sounds you experience at a recent rally about safety?	What are the sights and sounds of student anger you experienced at a recent rally about safety?

Explicitly asking leading questions is a common challenge for novice researchers. In Table 6.4, we provide a list of types of interview questions and differentiate appropriate questions from leading questions in a fictitious study in which the compelling interest is to study student safety on campus.

Leading questions communicate that the researcher has already made some assumptions instead of the researcher and participant constructing or making meaning of a topic.

"Bad Data"

Can there be "bad qualitative data?" We have heard some researchers refer to "bad data" meaning that no insight could be gleaned from the data collected. If bad data exist, it is because researchers asked bad questions to inappropriate participants. As mentioned above, appropriate questions are open. Yin (2009) also emphasized posing "how" questions rather than "why" questions as why questions tend to prompt defensiveness. It is important to solicit the same information without asking why and to avoid multiple questions asked simultaneously; instead, pose clear, succinct questions. Pilot testing interview questions with non-participants is a useful way to obtain feedback about interview protocol and questions. Piloting interview questions provides information about the clarity of questions, whether or not responses lead to greater insight about the phenomenon of interest, and the sequencing of questions to promote rapport and trust.

Unfortunately, participants can move off topic and discuss tangential issues. The researcher should not assume that the topic is unrelated, but rather ask

"Please excuse my interruption, but help me understand the connection to [research topic]." If participants are not bringing the researcher closer toward the researcher's compelling interest then,

> Is the problem in the question, in the respondent, or in the way you are listening? Has your question been answered and is it time to move on? If so, move on to what question? Should you probe now or later? What form should the probe take? (Glesne, 2011, p. 119)

Glesne's questions illustrate the complexities involved in interviewing.

Though participants typically experience an interview as valuable, Kvale and Brinkman (2009) recommended a debriefing after interviews. Discussing personal reflections with a stranger can elicit anxiety. Therefore, debriefing after the interview can serve to dissipate any discomfort. This may involve asking whether the participant has anything to add or how the participant experienced the interview. The researcher should also offer main points of the interview followed by requesting participant feedback about how thoroughly those main points were understood.

Thus far in this chapter we have discussed individual one-on-one interviews. However, interviews can be conducted with participants individually or in groups. Next we discuss the challenges in conducting group interviews.

Multiplying the Challenges: Interviewing Groups

Considered back in favor among social science researchers (Acocella, 2012), one popular form of group interview is the focus group. The purpose of a focus group is to expose differing points of view (Kvale & Brinkman, 2009), but these are unfortunately used inappropriately to generalize to an entire population. Focus groups are not appropriate for discussions of sensitive topics and, as will be discussed, may be appropriate for exploratory and scale development (Creswell, 2013; Kvale & Brinkman, 2009) "since the lively collective interaction may bring forth more spontaneous expressive and emotional views than in individual, often more cognitive interviews" (Kvale & Brinkman, 2009, p. 150). The focus group is an opportunity to engage the public self (Acocella, 2012). Too often, group interviews are used only as a supposed easy and inexpensive means of collecting data (Acocella, 2012). Rather, the focus group method must be integral to the purpose of the study and its methodology.

The role of the focus group facilitator is complex. One challenge for the interviewer is to refrain from group members feeling they need to come to consensus (Kvale & Brinkman, 2009) or group members becoming polarized (Acocella, 2012). Acocella (2012) further noted that the role of the facilitator is a relational one, ensuring that group members participate, engage in, understand, and are able to clarify the discussion. In focus group interviews, the interviewer must prevent a person or persons from dominating the group and encourage reserved participants to engage, ensuring balanced contribution (Fontana & Frey, 2008). Pacing, too, can be a challenge when the conversation moves so rapidly that clarification is missed and depth is replaced by topic jumping.

Acocella (2012) differentiated between a focus group and a group interview. In focus groups, participants are not asked questions individually but rather the facilitator offers a topic about which the group exchanges ideas, experiences, and perspectives. Because of the group exchanging ideas, only four to five good questions are needed. Acocella (2012) recommended utilizing a somewhat homogenous group to avoid inhibitions, yet one that will elicit various perspectives. However, this conflicts with researchers who advocate for embracing diversity in every phase of the research process (Teddlie & Tashakkori, 2011). It is recommended that researchers invite participants who are very familiar with the topic unless the purpose is to gain understanding of stereotypes or common sense understanding (Acocella, 2012).

The previous discussions have primarily considered face-to-face interviews. Current technology allows for group and individual interviews to be conducted via formats other than face to face. We discuss below some of the complexities associated with conducting interviews that are not face to face.

Using Alternatives to Face-to-Face Interviewing

Obviously, personal interaction is lost when interviews are conducted through electronic means. One major challenge is missing or misunderstanding meaning when there is no body language to assist in communicating meaning. However, this lack of face-to-face interaction has been known to work well with participants who have body image concerns because "the physical presence of a problematic body can represent an unwanted disturbance" (Kvale & Brinkman, 2009, p. 149). According to Kvale and Brinkman there is opportunity for fictional characters or characteristics to impede on data collection. Deceit unfortunately can be a two-way street, however, as researchers also could deceive participants (Fontana & Frey, 2008). Markham (2008) suggested,

> The construction of identity must be initiated more deliberately or consciously. Offline, the body can simply walk around and be responded to by others, providing the looking glass with which one comes to know the self. Online, the first step toward existence is the production of discourse, whether in the form of words, graphic images, or sounds. (p. 249)

The construction of identity on-line requires more explicit and diligent interaction.

Interviews can occur over the telephone. Though not used frequently, interviewing via the telephone is another means of data collection. Similar to digital interviews, interviewing via the phone has the disadvantage of not seeing nonverbal cues (Lechuga, 2011). However, advantages include that it is less costly, there are no geographic constraints, participants can be more autonomous and are typically more willing to discuss sensitive topics, and the researcher is able to take notes as eye contact is not assumed (Lechuga, 2011). In her study with faculty at for-profit institutions, Lechuga found that phone interviews "overcame behaviors that impede researcher access" (p. 255). Interviewing over Skype has the advantage of seeing participants as well as the advantages that phone interviews offer. Yet, when using technology, it is important to consider alternatives if the technology fails. Also, might using Skype deter access to participation? Contrarily, using Skype is attractive when considering samples in rural or international locations, but researchers should consider the width of broadband available and the quality of the connection. Poor audio quality and dropped connections are particularly disruptive in a research context.

To summarize our discussion in this chapter thus far, we have described complexities involved with collecting data that include guidance by theoretical perspective, methodological influences, selecting the appropriate type of interview, and creating interview questions. In Table 6.5, we examine a published example by Baxter Magolda, King, Taylor, and Wakefield (2012) of how all of these aspects of research intersect. Congruence among the elements of the research design is evident in their relationships to one another and in the ways in which each addresses the research purpose. The interview questions demonstrate the type of interview (open and then semi-structured), which is congruent with the constructivist-developmental methodology, which is informed by a constructivist theoretical perspective—all of which are purposeful in informing a developmental research interest.

We now turn to other types of data collecting methods beyond the interview and the challenges they present researchers.

Table 6.5 Congruence of Data Collection Methods

Compelling Interest	Decreasing authority dependence during the first year of college
Theoretical Perspective	Constructivist
Methodological Influences	Constructivist-developmental
Type of Interview	Informal conversational
Questions	*In-situ* Opening—personal history, relationships, ways of constructing knowledge Second phase—describe their educational experiences, how they made sense of these experiences, how these experiences influenced what to believe, how to view themselves and their relationships Third phase—how their collective experiences shaped their view of the world and themselves

Challenges in Observations: More Than Simply Watching

Even if researchers obtain data primarily through interviews, they are making observations of participants' body language and the interview setting (Glesne, 2011). However, there are occasions when researchers may choose to collect data through observation to triangulate other data (as explored in Chapter Two) or because interviewing people might taint their natural behaviors. Observations can and should be conducted when they allow the researcher to address the research question (Glesne, 2011) and are informed through theoretical framework (Marshall & Rossman, 2011). Glesne (2011) stressed that the goal of participant observation is to make the "strange familiar and the familiar strange" (p. 67). This could include recording events (differentiating daily from special), detailing surrounding conversations (gestures, postures, and space), exposing formal and informal routines, and elucidating sensory perceptions, while noting patterns (Glesne, 2011; Marshall & Rossman, 2010). The researcher constantly must ask "Am I making judgments rather than observations?" and "What am I seeing that I have never noticed before" (Glesne, 2011, p. 91).

Glesne (2011) suggested a continuum of participant observation from solely observer to full participant. An example of researcher as solely observer is found in a study to explore explicitly how basketball pick-up game players form teams at outside courts on campus where the researcher has no interaction with the basketball players. Angrosino and Rosenberg (2011) referred to this as naturalist observation, which began from a postmodern view of promoting objectivity. One of the challenges of naturalistic observation is the question of whether the basketball players wanted to be observed. Should they have been offered the chance to give their permission? Also, what of possible cultural differences? Can researchers of a different culture authoritatively interpret observed behaviors sufficiently without discussing their meaning with those who enacted them?

Addressing those ethical questions has led ethnographers, in particular, to seek interaction simultaneously while observing (Angrosino & Rosenberg, 2011). Observer as participant and participant as observer (Glesne, 2011) described data collection where researchers increasingly interact with participants. Referring to a study introduced in Chapter Five, Merchant (a White researcher) and Zurita's (a Mexican American research assistant) experiences in a Texas high school provides an example of participant as observer. *My Freshman Year* (2005), in which Nathan lived in a residence hall and took first-year courses is an example of being a full participant. Nathan's work was criticized because college students were not aware that they were being observed. The challenge is determining the degree of observation and participation appropriate to address the research question while maintaining ethical obligations to the participants. The context and focus of the study determines the degree of interaction and observation. Glesne (2011) advised that the less the researcher holds in common with the participants, the less the interaction so as not to intrude on or deceive participants.

Reviewing documents is another means of collecting data. Used in conjunction with participant observation, researchers can ask participants about the meaningfulness of documents.

Challenge of Analyzing Documents and Artifacts as Data: More Than Reading

Documents as data can include meeting minutes, memos, wills, memoirs, photographs, old letters, scrapbooks, films, paintings, archives, employments records, drawings, websites, dairies, graffiti, tombstones, membership lists, newsletters, newspapers, bulletin boards, crime reports, trash, pottery, clothing, court cases, strategic plans, financial records, policy statements, budgets, personal letters, textbooks, and speeches. As in observations, using documents as a method of data collection should be adopted when they address the focus of the study (Glesne, 2011) and are consistent with the theoretical framework (Marshall & Rossman, 2011). Documents can confirm other data and expose additional perspectives. Documents also assist researchers in telling a story (Glesne, 2011) and uncovering values and beliefs, such as how budgets reveal values of policy makers (Marshall & Rossman, 2011). According to Glesne,

> Visual data, documents, artifacts, and other unobtrusive measures provide both historical and contextual dimensions to your observations and interviews. They enrich what you see and hear by supporting, expanding, and challenging your portrayals and perceptions. (p. 89)

Document analysis can challenge researchers by presenting contradictions. Therefore, researchers should ensure that documents are not being used out of context. Documents can be analyzed through objective means, such as counting the use of specific use of a word or term. However, a constructivist, constructionist, interpretive, and post-structural frame to analysis is currently more favorable. These approaches focus on patterns, discourse, and relationships (Marshall & Rossman, 2011). As in analyzing interviews, researchers must describe the rationale for their interpretations. Analysis can also include "the stories that surround" the documents, how "they are made, how they are used, and what . . . they mean to people" (Glesne, 2011, p. 88).

In analyzing documents and artifacts, an ethical issue erupts in considering how those who created the documents might be harmed by their use in a study. Of course, the digital age has ushered a whole host of new documents and the means by which to produce and allow access to them. Hence social media and technology offer exciting additions to means of collecting data.

Challenges Involved With Using Social Media and Other Digital Documents

In the fourth edition of *The Sage Handbook of Qualitative Research* (Denzin & Lincoln, 2011), a chapter by Davidson and di Gregorio is titled, "Qualitative Research and Technology: In the Midst of a Revolution." Although focused primarily on the evolution of Qualitative Data Analysis Software (QDAS), they also address the intersection of data analysis management programs with other issues emanating from the presence of access to the Internet. For example, they noted:

> The rise of Web 2.0 applications, such as YouTube, Flickr, Twitter, and Facebook, allows anyone with access to the Internet to upload their own data—be it photos, video, or chat—to share with others, to comment, and to organize . . . . How does one deal with unstructured data of many formats? How does one best organize, search, sort, pattern, and manipulate this kind of data? (Davidson & de Gregorio, 2011, p. 636)

The use of social media sites and digital documents has raised salient challenges for researchers. Digital documents include blogs, digital stories, social media (e.g., Facebook, Twitter, MySpace), time-use dairies, video sharing sites such as You Tube™, and photovoice (Bouwma-Gearhart & Bess, 2012; Flores & Garcia, 2009; Hart-Davidson, 2007; Marshall & Rossman, 2011; Rolón-Dow, 2011), and even images from microscopes, x-rays, and MRIs (Prosser, 2011). Prosser (2011) noted, "The combination of improved software and training capacity enabled researchers with metadata to store, analyze, map, measure, and represent complex human communication with other interconnected entities" (p. 482).

In their edited book on digital writing research (examining how digital technologies influence research), McKee and DeVoss (2007) posed the following questions: How do methodologies need to be adopted to accommodate digital data collection methods? What changes in the approval process to research human subjects are necessary due to digital technologies? How is the view of collaboration and single authored work changing? In what ways are on-line journals changing the distribution of research findings? What might the future hold in digital writing research? With the rapid changes in technology, answers to these questions are dynamic, and, in fact, there may be several appropriate answers. Nonetheless, we attempt to address these questions below.

Prosser (2011) noted that using images in research promotes theory building and the critical analysis of everyday contemporary culture. Digital storying and testimonies have been used as means for individuals and groups to portray their oppression through "deliberately chosen images" (Angrosino & Rosenberg, 2011, p. 473). However, the means by which to analyze digital documents are in essence similar to that of traditional transcripts. Selecting a sampling strategy and defining a unit of data to then sort and code remains similar; however, boundaries or where one document begins and another ends becomes more difficult in wikis, blogs, and websites (Blythe, 2007). Are different pages from the same URL always different documents? In essence, these documents, too, allow for the illumination of patterns, description of relationships such as the cause and effect relationships, and offer new and imaginative collaborative insights (Bouwma-Gearhart & Bess, 2012; Marshall & Rossman, 2011). Misinterpretation of digital documents is as potentially problematic as in paper documents. Hence, Marshall and Rossman (2011) recommended sharing images with participants and inviting them to offer their interpretations if researchers can follow up with participants.

As mentioned earlier, digital documents allow forums where social identities can be "disembodied" (Marshall & Rossman, 2011, p. 182). A particular challenge in utilizing digital documents is protecting anonymity and privacy, especially considering the common place of hacking and back-ups that are automatically saved and may remain accessible even when researchers want to destroy them (Angrosino & Rosenberg, 2011; Marshall & Rossman, 2011).

Institutional Review Board (IRB) policies require researchers to gain approval to study human subjects when their research will "contribute to 'generalizable knowledge'" and when research involves a "living individual" about which a researcher collects data through interaction with the individual or when a researcher obtains "identifiable individual information" (Banks & Eble, 2007, p. 32). But when studying digital documents such as blogs, chats of on-line communities, and websites, at what point does the writer or creator become a research participant? Banks and Eble (2007) wrote,

> Ultimately, any research that includes human subjects—even as authors—should be reviewed by the IRB so as to ensure the research and researcher(s) are protected from possible unwitting violations of the federal regulations and from possible lawsuits. (p. 33)

Moreover, according to Phillips (2012), it is unclear if postings on social media are public or private. Is authors' consent necessary for what many users consider private but is publicly available? Due to the confusion, the American Psychological Association (APA) recommended obtaining permission to collect data from writers of social media in publicly available accounts and not to use personal accounts associated with the researcher as avenues for data collection (Phillips, 2012).

Certainty of authorship and ownership of blogs can be limiting. So too can be determining the level of contribution of those involved in blogs. Blogs and other digital opportunities for publishing defy traditional notions of individual achievement. Bouwma-Gerhart and Bess (2012) promoted the collaborative advantages of digital documents, particularly blogs. Because digital documents allow for the "rapid exchange of ideas, manuscript drafts, and associated research materials . . . instead of involving only a few collaborators inside one's approximate and accustomed academic research circle, ongoing research can be informed by the contemporaneous researchers whose traditional role has been post-publication reviewers" (pp. 240–250). This is called anticipatory participation.

According to Blythe (2007), analyzing multimedia sources could include codes for light and color, two or three dimensional space, time motion, sound, and links. The frequent updating of websites and the policy changes and practices of social media and websites present difficulties for researchers. For example, those studying institution or student organization websites could have their research impeded by such changes (Blythe, 2007; Glesne, 2011; Phillips, 2012).

Another concern of using digital documents is that instances of group think have been identified (Bouwma-Gearhart & Bess, 2012).

Nonetheless, these digital sources allow for an opportunity to provide a voice for the underrepresented and for community problem solving. Blogs allow researchers working on similar problems within a similar discipline to collaborate. This is evidenced by the increase in multi-authored research papers that provide substantial opportunity for collaboration in research, particularly in higher education (Bouwma-Gerhart & Bess, 2012). Blogs provide a "voluntary division of labor" (p. 252) and potentially "more egalitarian communities of academic collaborators (Bouwma-Gerhart & Bess, 2012, p. 258). Moreover, social media offers opportunities to study student behaviors in real time (Phillips, 2012).

An excellent example of research on social networking was done by Martínez Alemán and Wartman (2009). In their study, they sought to investigate the "nature of online campus culture" and thus required consideration of electronic communications among students. These researchers used an ethnographic approach to present the meaning students gave to text, images, and the function of social networking. There are several important lessons that are worthy of considering in their study. First, they noted that this research "requires a more deliberate exchange of information because the researcher and participant are not in the same physical space" (p. 51). Second, in order to use Facebook as a data point, the researchers had participants open their profiles and explain the content and respond to questions regarding what the researchers observed. This form of data collection was described as merging "the concept of traditional research (where the researcher and participants are both present) with the direct observation of the online environment, in this case, participants' Facebook accounts" (pp. 51–52).

Challenge of Open-Ended Survey Items: More Than a Question

The ability to collect data from a large sample makes using open-ended survey items very attractive. Open-ended survey items can provide text from participants, and specific items can elicit data in the forms of stories or explanations that can be analyzed using qualitative analysis techniques. Yet, there are many challenges that come with this form of data collection. When considering the use of a survey as a method for data collection, three critical aspects must be addressed. First, the instructions need to be as crystal clear as possible. Participants will either have concerns clarified or become discouraged by the instructions. Second, how the information will be used must be made clear to participants. To solicit rich responses, participants must have a level of trust as to how responses will be used. And finally, researchers should pilot items with a few participants prior to sending out the survey. Soliciting feedback on how the item was interpreted and what approach the participant used in responding is important. To better inform researchers, this next section will delve into the writing of open-ended items, issues with interpreting responses, and the challenges involved with using social media.

Creating an Open-Ended Survey Item

Much like the effort that goes into creating good interview questions, creating open-ended survey questions also requires great attention. For many researchers, the goal of having an open-ended question is to solicit a long, more detailed response about the phenomenon being discovered (Patton, 2002). Although Chapter One touched on the role that existing literature has on the theoretical framework of a study, knowledge of the literature is critical to creating open-ended questions. Researchers must have a sense of what type of answers they wish to solicit from participants in order to create a good survey item. Previous research informs the type of behaviors, feelings, actions, or reactions that apply to the phenomenon under investigation.

Some of the criteria used to create good survey items apply to creating a good open-ended item (Dillman, 2007). One of the main criterion in creating surveys is whether the question requires an answer. Answers to open-ended items cannot be yes or no, or promote a categorical response; rather, the item should solicit a reflection, an explanation of a behavior, or a reaction to a situation. This can be done by asking for examples or explanations about previous responses. This type of question allows the researcher to garner longer and richer responses.

A second criterion to consider is whether the respondent can answer the questions (Dillman, 2007). This is very important when seeking information about processes. It is essential to consider whether the phenomenon being investigated is something participants will recall or be willing to report. This consideration should also include whether there is motivation to respond to the survey and open-ended item. As discussed in Chapters Five and Nine, the motivation, readiness, and willingness to respond to an open-ended question is critical. These criteria were used by Vasti and a team of Latina researchers when they wanted to conduct a study on adult Latino/as. Access to a broad-based sample was difficult, and therefore the team chose to use a survey with open-ended items (Torres, Martinez, Wallace, Medrano, Robledo, & Hernandez, 2012). Consistent with the criteria mentioned, the items asked for examples and explanations of certain topics. In writing the results, the team focused on the responses from the item "As an adult, have you experienced a life change that caused you to re-evaluate the meaning of your identity?" (Torres et al., 2012, p. 8). The other questions in the survey allowed the research team to enhance the interpretation of the responses, but the main data came from this one question.

Interpreting Responses to Open-Ended Items

Even when a good open-ended item is created, the interpretation of the responses can be challenging. The main reason is that researchers are not likely to go back and ask for clarification from the respondent. The researcher is left to make judgments about how genuine the responses are or if there was an element of social desirability (Dillman, 2007) in the responses. Social desirability refers to responses that reflect what the participant thinks the researcher wants to hear. This is particularly true when using open-ended items in evaluation of a service—if the respondent wants to please the service provider, then socially desirable responses are likely (Dillman, 2007). For example, if a researcher is conducting a survey about alcohol use in college and there is an open-ended item such as "Please use this space to provide additional comments," and a respondent writes "I'm drowning in alcohol here," should this be considered a cry for help? Should this be considered a joke by a college student wanting to make fun of the topic of the survey? Both of these interpretations are viable, yet without going back to the respondent, it would be difficult to say what was meant by the student.

Analysis of open-ended items can be done using many of the techniques explained in Chapter Seven. A common technique used is open and axial coding (Strauss & Corbin, 1998), which is associated with grounded theory. The challenge comes with interpreting what the codes mean across participants. Oftentimes, open-ended items result in broad codes, and therefore there is an inherent limitation of the study.

Challenges in Negotiating Power During Data Collection

Issues discussed previously in this chapter mostly dealt with the processes of data collection, but here we consider complex issues of how we are to be with participants while collecting data. One of the most important challenges in collecting data regards negotiating issues of researcher power over participants, regardless of the data collection methods. Certainly, maintaining confidentiality of the interview and deciding what of the interview will be repeated, how, and when (Kvale & Brinkman, 2009) are issues of researcher power. As discussed in Chapter Two, the ways participants are involved in a study, how information is gained, and what is reported are controlled by the researcher. According to Kvale and Brinkman (2009) "It is time to stop treating the interviewee as a 'clockwork orange,' that is, looking for a better juicier (techniques) to squeeze juice (answers) out of the orange (living person/interviewee)" (p. 117). Furthermore, how might qualitative research "seduce" participants "to disclose information they might later regret" (Kvale & Brinkman, 2009, p. 73) because the interviewer is "historically and contextually located, carrying unavoidable conscious and unconscious motives, desires, feelings, and biases—hardly a neutral tool" (Kvale & Brinkman, p. 117). Consequently, neutrality is not possible and not owning a stance is improbable. For that reason, Fontana and Frey (2008) advocated for *empathetic interviewing* where researcher and participants co-create findings and share a similar perspective. For example, Moustakas (1994) referred to his participants as co-researchers. Contrarily, *polyphonic interviewing* describes an interviewing style where the researcher offers little engagement during the interview and reports participants' comments holistically rather than collapsed with others' voices (Kvale & Brinkman, 2009). This makes participants less hidden or made over by the researcher. Expecting or promoting the goal of creating friendship through the interview is also problematic. Such friendship is "illusionary and fleeting" (Fontana & Frey, 2008, p. 119) and appears as only using the participant for the researcher's gain. This must be differentiated from establishing rapport with participants as well as gate keepers (those who grant access to research sites, as defined in the previous chapter) which is crucial (Creswell, 2013; Fontana & Frey, 2008). Establishing rapport requires thoughtfulness about how a researcher presents oneself. Imagine conducting a life history or single narrative study, and the single participant loses faith and trust in the researcher. The study then must be abandoned. Sincerity is crucial as the researcher's initial presentation cannot be solely about "a ruse to gain trust," but rather trust must be reciprocated (Fontana & Frey, 2008, p. 136) and is created through shared language and meaning (Fontana & Frey, 2008).

We described above many means of collecting data. However, some researchers decide to mix methods. Next we explore the challenges mixing methods imposes.

Challenge of Mixed Methods: More Than Using an Interview and Survey

The pressure from funding sources for quantitative studies in research (Creswell, 2011; Denzin, 2011) has resulted in considerable increase of interest in mixed methods research. Recently, a growing number of handbooks (Tashakkori & Teddlie, 2003) and other types of how-to books (Howard, 2007) that focus on doing mixed methods are available. For this reason, in this section we highlight the challenges and review the ongoing controversies surrounding mixed methods research.

The use of mixed-method research design is generally accepted as appropriate in applied disciplines such as education, evaluation, and nursing (Covell, Sidani, & Ritchie, 2012; Teddlie & Tashakkori, 2011). When the term mixed methods is used in this chapter, we refer to the use of qualitative and quantitative methods within a single study. Generally, two or more forms of data are merged or one set added to the other within more than one philosophical stance and theoretical perspective (Creswell, 2003).

The issue that arises from this mixing of methods is that few researchers take the time to understand the philosophical issues and challenges that occur when methods from different traditions are combined. A major criticism of mixed methods research is that the expertise is more focused on quantitative methods rather than on the broad spectrum of methods available (Denzin, 2011; Denzin & Lincoln, 2008). The use of qualitative methods is encouraged within the assessment literature, but the discussion has mainly focused on method (e.g., interviews and focus groups) (Schuh & Upcraft, 2000; Schuh, 2008), rather than the conflicting philosophical foundations that come with the type of methodology associated with the methods. Whether conducting institutional assessment or large-scale research studies, when qualitative and quantitative methods are used together in a study, the researcher must consider the unique philosophical, theoretical, and methodological issues that arise in the research process.

Disciplines, including the field of higher education, advance misconceptions about what constitutes mixed methods research, and these misconceptions are fueled by the varied definitions of what "mixing" is actually happening in the research process. This results in mixed-method research within the field to be published with no connection between method, methodology, and epistemology. And finally, because the concept of paradigmatic orientation is more closely considered in the literature for qualitative research (Denzin, 2011), it is likely that those trained solely in quantitative methods will pay little attention to the tenets of methodology that are needed to conduct good mixed-method research. As a result, when researchers say they conduct mixed-method research, it is the qualitative portion of the research that often suffers because the focus is placed only on the method (e.g., focus groups or interviews) while paradigmatic issues are neglected.

According to Teddlie and Tashakkori (2011) current characteristics of mixed-method research include methodological eclecticism, which is when researchers select the most appropriate tools from a myriad of options and then integrate them to address the research questions under consideration. The research question determines the method and methodology utilized. However, the researcher must be knowledgeable about the options. The second characteristic is paradigmatic pluralism, in that "a variety of paradigms may serve as underlying philosophy for the use of mixed methods" (Teddlie & Tashakkori, 2011, p. 287). The third characteristic is advocating for diversity throughout the research process. Still another characteristic is considering research on a continuum rather than opposite polarities. An example of the middle ground approach is Preissle (2011), who wrote,

> I have been accused by some of philosophical schizophrenia. Research approaches are mental models that we formulate for our study of the world. Although I value coherence, consistency, and other such elements under some circumstances, I also believe that innovation and creative problem solving often mean finding ways of putting things together that convention has separated. (p. 695)

The caution offered when combining paradigms deals with the shared elements between the paradigms. For example, it is virtually impossible for a researcher to see reality as both attainable through statistical controls and contextually constructed. However, within mixed methods, this may be appropriate. An example of this would be to test theoretical concepts that emerged from a constructivist-grounded theory study by creating a model and analyzing it for model-fit with structural equation modeling. Vasti used this approach to create a new model that considers the intent to persist in college without using traditional academic achievement measures (Torres, 2006). Because Vasti's longitudinal study has many first-generation college students in the sample, she found that few of the Latino/a students felt academically prepared to do college level work. The issue that emerged during data analysis, using grounded theory techniques, was that students built up their own capacities through other support mechanisms. Seldom did students mention their low academic preparation. This emergent issue became the impetus to consider support issues as strong influences on the intent to persist. Using this insight, Vasti set out to gain a better understanding of this phenomenon. While reading supporting materials on this phenomenon, she began to explore the role of social cognitive theory (Bandura, 1986) in interpreting how students enhanced their capacities within the college environment. The combination of emerging themes in the qualitative data and aspects of social cognitive theory helped conceptualize a new model that considers the impact of environmental and support factors on the intent to persist. Using structural equation modeling, Vasti tested the model to see if it had good model fit. This example respected both traditions by allowing the model to emerge from the data and then using a quantitative technique that tested model-fit rather than manipulated or controlled aspects of the data.

Negotiating Mixed Methods Research as Paradigm

Paying attention to paradigmatic concerns is the first strategy in negotiating the methodological issues in mixed methods. Two primary questions guide the discussion about negotiating the paradigmatic issues in mixed-method research.

Question One: Is there one paradigm that is best suited for mixed-method design?

The response to the first question comes from two perspectives. First, there are significant references in the literature on mixed-method research advocating for the sole use of pragmatism as a paradigm that accommodates both qualitative and quantitative methods while rejecting the incompatibility thesis (Creswell, 2011; Teddlie & Tashakkori, 2011). The second approach to this question requires a closer look at the notion that a paradigm reflects a researcher's worldview; therefore, the researcher must make an individual choice. Both of these perspectives provide insight into the management of mixed-method research.

Addressing the first approach of using pragmatism, it is clear that recently the mixed-method literature tends to advocate for the use of pragmatism as a single paradigm to guide mixed-method studies (Creswell, 2011; Johnson & Onwuegbuzie, 2004; Tashakkori & Teddlie, 1998, 2003). The attractive aspects of pragmatism in mixed-method studies include: (a) rejection of the need to force a choice between contradicting epistemologies, (b) more importance placed on the research question instead of the method or paradigm, and (c) the acceptance of "a problem-solving, action oriented inquiry process based on a commitment to a democratic values and progress" (Teddlie & Tashakkori, 2011, p. 290).

The second approach to the first question views paradigms as a choice that relates to the researcher's worldview and therefore can vary depending on the individual investigator (Creswell 2011; Teddlie & Tashakkori, 2011). If a researcher values the perspective that paradigm choice is relevant to a researcher's worldview, then each investigator must search for his or her own voice within various epistemologies. Again, this search becomes part of the evolution of the researcher and is critical to framing the research that uses both quantitative and qualitative methods (Torres & Baxter Magolda, 2002). Nonetheless, Teddlie and Tashakkori (2011) more recently advocated for the consideration of methodological eclecticism and paradigmatic pluralism in that they may provide sources of "divergence and dissimilarity" which in turn offers opportunity for new understanding (p. 287).

Question Two: **What mixing actually occurs in mixed-method research and how should this be identified?**

The second question deals with the type of mixing that is occurring during the research process and focuses on the confusion that exists in mixed-method research (Creswell, 2011). Many researchers do not use consistent language, making it difficult to understand what mixing is actually occurring. Three terms are most often associated with the different ways mixed-method research can be conducted: *multimethod, mixed method,* and *mixed model.* Each of these terms has slightly different connotations about the research process.

Multimethod.   This research term uses two or more methods or procedures (e.g., observations and oral histories) from the same qualitative or quantitative paradigm (Creswell, 2011). Because the methods are from the same tradition, there is little mixing at the paradigm level and often, when the methods are quantitative, there is little, if any, mention of a paradigm orientation. In multimethod research, mixing methods does not necessarily require mixing of research paradigms.

Mixed method.   This term includes those studies that use both qualitative and quantitative data collection and analysis (methods) in either a parallel or sequential manner. "The mixing occurs in the methods section of the study" (Tashakkori & Teddlie, 2003, p. 11) and because the analysis of the data is usually done separately, this type of study does not always require the consideration of distinctions between the constructivist or positivist paradigms associated with qualitative and quantitative research (Tashakkori & Teddlie, 2003).

Mixed-method research considers four strategies to guide how the research is conducted (Creswell, 2003):

1. This first strategy involves implementation of the data collection. Qualitative and quantitative data can be collected concurrently or sequentially.
2. The second strategy involves deciding whether more importance is placed on the data collection and analysis of the qualitative or quantitative data or if equal importance is given to both. This priority is determined by "the interest of the researcher, the audience for the study, and what the investigator seeks to emphasize" (Creswell, 2003, p. 212). This strategy implies an important

distinction because it allows the researcher to express her or his preference towards one tradition of research, yet it does not require the use of a paradigm to guide this decision.

3. The third strategy focuses on the point where data would be integrated or at what point the qualitative and quantitative information is merged. The integration can occur during data collection, data analysis, data interpretation, or some combination of these. Choosing a preference between the quantitative or qualitative tradition would also influence the integration strategy. This strategy could also allow for separate analysis of data.

4. The final, strategy is that the theoretical perspective can be either explicit or implicit. This strategy considers whether there is a theoretical perspective that guides the research design. Creswell (2003) acknowledged that all research designs have an implicit theoretical perspective, yet it seems unclear if this perspective has to be made explicit at some point in the research process. This strategy is applicable because in a *mixed-method* approach, the level of concern is in the method. Although Creswell's stance constitutes one guideline, we advocate that, in order to maintain quality in all aspects of the research process, the theoretical perspective should always be clear. Because the term *mixed method* focuses on the mixing of methods only, it does not deal with the potential paradigmatic tensions between the research traditions as data integration can be done sequentially.

Mixed model. This is the term used for studies that have a higher level of mixing of the paradigms (Tashakkori & Teddlie, 1998). The mix is done at all stages of the research process and therefore mixed-model studies have to meet a "much more stringent set of assumptions than does multimethod or even mixed method" studies (Tashakkori & Teddlie, 2003, p. 11). Creswell (2011) called this an integrated design. Mixed-model research can use multiple paradigms in a single study or it can use a single paradigm to frame the researcher's worldview. There are no exemplary examples of mixed-model research in the higher education literature.

Doing Mixed-Method Research

Although there are several process models within mixed-method research literature, this section focuses on three primary decisions that inform the design of a research study. These decisions deal with the implementation (data collection), the priority (which method is given precedence), and integration (process of analysis and incorporation of findings) (Creswell, 2003). The implementation aspect of the study indicates whether the data were collected at the same time (concurrent) or one at a time (sequential). This first aspect of the research process, then, determines the potential strategies that can be used. Although these strategies do not represent all the possible strategies, they do provide insight into the type of design issues that must be considered in this type of research (Creswell).

Strategies for mixed-method designs.   The following strategies illustrate the decisions about data collection, priority, and analysis:

- Sequential explanatory—This design strategy is straightforward in the sense that quantitative data are collected and analyzed, which is then followed by the collection and analysis of qualitative data. As Creswell (2003) noted, "The priority typically is given to the quantitative data, and the two methods are integrated during the interpretation phase" (p. 215). This type of strategy is considered when the qualitative data assume the role of explaining the quantitative data.
- Sequential exploratory—This design strategy also has data collection in two separate phases, with priority given to whichever type of data is collected first. Generally this strategy tends to have qualitative data collected first and the integration of the two types of data (qualitative and quantitative) is done at the interpretation phase. This strategy is used when the goal is to test elements of an emerging theory from the qualitative data (Creswell, 2003).
- Sequential transformative—This design strategy collects data in two separate phases and priority is given to either qualitative or quantitative methods depending on the theoretical perspective that guides the study. The theoretical perspective would provide the framework as to the manner in which interpretation would be handled. This "strategy may be more appealing and acceptable to those researchers already using a transformative [e.g., critical race theory] framework" (Creswell, 2003, p. 217). This strategy is seldom seen in published research.
- Concurrent triangulation—This strategy collects data at the same time, and the goal is to confirm or substantiate findings within a single study. The goal in this type of strategy tends to offset the weakness of one method with another method. Priority can be given to either, and integration occurs at the interpretation phase by providing convergence in the findings or explaining the lack of convergence (Creswell, 2003).
- Concurrent nested—In this strategy, the data are collected simultaneously, but priority is given to one method that guides the research decisions in the study. This type of strategy can be used to broaden the understanding of a phenomenon by using more than one method (Creswell, 2003). This strategy has much more potential for researchers but should be used with care since many research decisions must be justified in the process.
- Concurrent transformative—Although the data are collected at the same time with this strategy, the priority and integration is guided by the researcher's theoretical perspective. Like the sequential transformative strategy, this process is heavily guided by the transformative nature of the research question and theoretical perspective (Creswell, 2003).

The example given earlier in this chapter of Vasti's study on the intent to persist for Latino/a students represents a concurrent nested strategy because qualitative and quantitative data were gathered concurrently, and the qualitative data took priority in making research decisions about how to view and analyze the quantitative data. In a different example, Creamer, Baxter Magolda, and Yue's (2010) study that created a quantitatively reliable instrument measuring self-authorship (as defined in Baxter Magolda's longitudinal qualitative study) is an example of a sequential transformative mixed methods. This study focused on creating items within a survey on Career Decision Making (CDMS) that would specifically consider self-authorship in the Diverse Viewpoints and Decision Making scale. The items were created based on previous research and expert review by Baxter Magolda (Creamer, Baxter Magolda, & Yue, 2010). The transformative nature of the study was found in the ability to assess "the impact of interventions designed to promote self-authorship, particularly during the process of making personal and educational decisions such as choosing a major or a career" (p. 552).

Summary

This chapter provided guidance on aspects of data collection and insight into what researchers should consider. While not every issue could be addressed, thinking through some of the messiness that comes with data collection will help the researcher design and implement a stronger study.

Exercises

Chapter-related

1. Pay attention to the "interviews" that take place in everyday life, like on television or YouTube. How are these interviews different from those conducted in research contexts? What skills and competencies do researchers need to develop in order to conduct effective interviews?
2. How do you see technology facilitating data collection? What are the potential drawbacks?
3. Identify the strengths and limitations of different data collection strategies.

Research Process

1. Identify the data collection methods that make most sense given your research design.
2. Articulate how your data collection methods flow and connect with your compelling interest, worldview, epistemology, and methodology. Refer to previous chapters if necessary.

3.   Design an interview protocol and interview questions. Conduct a pilot interview (verbal or through an on-line chat) with several willing peers. Be thoughtful about the type of interview and questions asked. Be sure they are directly connected to your research question. Ask the peers for feedback. Were any of the questions leading? Closed? In what ways did you establish trust and rapport? Did you allow for periods of silence for the peer to consider thoughts before answering? What were strengths and weaknesses? What did you learn?

4.   Design a protocol for an observation of some phenomenon in your immediate surroundings. What will you observe? How will you keep track of what you see, notice, hear, feel, and think? Given your world-view, assumptions about your topic, and prior experiences, what might you miss in your observations? What might you overemphasize?

5.   Create a transcript from your interview and/or your observation. Transcribing is a tedious yet central research procedure, and gets easier (and faster) with practice. After you finish transcribing, consider what you learned about your data collection methods from your transcription, about yourself as a researcher, and about your participant's responses or the nature of the observations.

7   Issues in Analysis and Interpretation

To report data is not enough, researchers must also provide interpretation. The action of interpretation conveys the understanding the researcher makes of phenomena reported by participants (Corbin & Strauss, 2008). Interpretation allows for "elucidating meanings" from data (Patton, 2002, p. 477). According to Schwandt (2007a), analysis involves the "activity of making sense of, interpreting, and theorizing data" (p. 6). This requires "a radical spirit of openness" to new potential (Crotty, 1998, p. 50). However, how data are interpreted is not a stand-alone decision, the process must be considered in light of previous research design choices. Common errors occur when data analysis techniques are considered separately from epistemology, methodology, or theoretical perspectives. The selected analysis technique must be congruent with these elements in order to have a high quality research study. The interpretation of data should be tailored to honor the philosophical assumptions inherent in the chosen research strategies (Creswell, 2003). While several common interpretation techniques that can be used in various types of studies will be covered in this chapter, the researcher must provide a rationale as to why the chosen techniques are consistent and congruent with previous choices in the research design.

Serving as discussants at research conferences, we have, on more than one occasion, received a paper that provided only a statement such as "participant observations were done and constant comparative techniques were used for analysis of data." This kind of statement causes more confusion than clarification regarding what research decisions were made. Participant observation as a method for gathering data is common among many qualitative research studies (Wolcott, 2002), as is constant comparison as a technique of analysis. Thus, there is no clarity about epistemological and methodological decisions that influenced the study by simply making a passing reference. The lack of information leaves the reader wondering what contributions the participant observation made in interpreting the findings. The findings have less meaning when the research was not situated within methodological or epistemological underpinnings. In essence, the findings were presented in the abstract without knowing how the researcher approached the research process. This creates concerns about the trustworthiness of the study.

This chapter addresses the analysis and interpretation of data and how other elements of the research process influence interpretation of various forms of data. In beginning this discussion, we stress that to maintain congruence in the research process, a researcher must be concerned with issues of continuity among all the elements in the research study. Continuity is the ability of the researcher to be consistent throughout the research process (Lincoln & Guba, 2000). Although the idea of continuity may seem like an easy and logical task, accomplishing this is what makes research decisions particularly difficult in the qualitative research process.

To represent how interpretations emerge from data analysis, this chapter begins with an explanation of the role of methodology and the role of previous literature in analysis. Then, common analysis techniques will be presented drawing parallels with terms used across methodologies. The techniques presented are open and initial coding, axial and focused coding, constant comparison, bracketing, hermeneutic circle, narrative analysis, and memo writing. The chapter will end with discussions of possible analytic tensions, issues of ethics, and challenges of the researcher–participant relationship in the interpretation process.

The Role of Methodology

It is through analysis of various forms of data that the researcher gains insights into the phenomenon under investigation. Analysis breaks down data into parts that can be used to make interpretations about what is being observed among participants. Methodology needs to direct how data are broken down and what is done to the data after the initial coding to generate interpretation. Generally, the various qualitative traditions range from the deeply interpretive, which offer meaning beyond what is said, to purely descriptive findings that report only what was observed. Different methodologies call for varying levels of analysis and structure depending on the goal of interpretation. For example, in phenomenology the goal is to understand the lived experience— this in turn requires offering meaning beyond what participants stated. On the other hand, the goal of grounded theory is typically for theory to emerge from the data and, as a result, requires a certain level of structure in the analysis process. Hence, methodology provides direction about the level of abstraction needed to analyze data or how much "face value" (credence) to give data. Few grounded theory studies would provide examples of data for all open codes— there would be too many, and therefore the face value is diminished with so much data and little reduction, or interpretation, of data. Instead, examples from the data would more likely come once the open codes were grouped and re-considered to define their properties and dimensions. In phenomenology, rather than reporting everything, the researcher seeks to create broad ideas that provide rich interpretations about how these ideas are linked. This is accomplished through drafting, writing, and rewriting thick descriptions so that particular and complex phenomenon can be understood. Interpretation tells the reader when, why, and under what conditions the units of analysis occur (Ryan & Bernard, 2000).

Analysis and interpretation should be fluid and reflect themes or ideas emerging rather than focusing only on fixed categories. This fluidity in the breaking down of data into manageable parts can feel ambiguous but is a necessary part of the process for the voices of the participants to be heard and for new understandings around the phenomenon to emerge.

In some methodologies, models are created to illustrate the interpretation of the units of analysis, such as the Model of Multiple Dimensions of Identity (Jones & McEwen, 2000). Other methodologies may refer to constant comparison, and key quotes are used to illustrate and exemplify the analysis. These quotes allow the reader "to understand quickly what it may have taken the researcher months or years to figure out" (Ryan & Bernard, 2000, p. 784), such as in the work of Baxter Magolda (2001). An important distinction that should be understood is the difference between describing what is observed and interpreting what is said about the phenomenon.

Description and Interpretation

As has been discussed above, methodology influences how data are presented in a study. Decisions made are explained within the context of their congruence with the methodology selected and allow the researcher to explain why data are presented in one manner or another. Two common ways to present data are through description and interpretation.

In essence, a descriptive analysis would provide the factual pieces that are contained in the data (Schwandt, 2007a). Within a research study, one typically uses descriptions to account events or actions. This can be helpful when considering a particular event in history or a particular policy. But, a descriptive scheme is also concerned "with how (not what) people do what they do. This second type of description takes the reader to the setting and reveals who the actors are, what they are doing, and so forth" (Schwandt, 2007a, pp. 65–66). Descriptive analysis can often leave the reader asking, "So what does this mean?" Most methodologies expect researchers to provide some context (description), but more importantly, they expect an interpretation of how data explain the phenomenon.

Interpretation of data "is the act of clarifying, explicating, or explaining the meaning of some phenomenon" (Schwandt, 2007a, p. 158). Interpretation answers questions about what the phenomenon means to participants, how and why it is salient, and what readers are to make of it. Interpretation moves beyond describing what is said and provides deeper clarifications. In order to accomplish this, the researcher engaged in interpretation of data also provides examples of quotes that the researcher finds to be strong illustrations of the theme, which demonstrates both the evolution of analysis and interpretations as well as provides a greater understanding of what is happening in the data. Too often, novice researchers provide only descriptions and not interpretations.

An example that clearly demonstrates both methodological and analysis decisions is Kezar's (2000) article on pluralistic leadership. In this study on leadership perspectives in higher education and understanding the differences that exist in meeting leadership challenges, Kezar (2000) used an in-depth case study methodology examining multiple levels of campus organizational leadership. The theoretical framework used in this study was positionality theory, which "assumes that power relations can change and that social categories are fluid and dynamic, affected by historical and social changes" (p. 726). She described her data collection technique as follows:

> Studies of leadership have identified multiple sources of evidence and triangulation of data as helpful in understanding complex phenomena such as leadership (Yukl, 1989). Thus, I utilized multiple methods to understand leadership including interviews, document analysis (records extending back twenty-five years at the school-wide, division, and department level; e.g., strategic plans, accreditation reports, minutes from meetings, consultant reports), observations and an analysis of the physical environment. (p. 729)

Following this extensive list of data gathering techniques, she described the choice she made for analyzing the data. Within the text she stated, "I used categorical and componential analysis to understand shared trends among people of different positionality" (Spradley, 1979, as cited in Kezar, 2000, p. 729). In the footnote we find the more complete description of how this analysis technique was consistent with her previous research choices. Her explanation of the analysis technique was: "Categorical analysis emphasizes the identification of categories and patterns. Componential analysis is the 'systematic search for the attributes (components of meaning) associated with cultural symbols' and in language (Spradley, 1979, p. 174)" (as cited in Kezar, 2000, p. 741).

This example illustrates the study of a broad phenomenon (leadership) within the theoretical framework of positionality theory and the use of categorical and componential analysis to break down the data and put it back together in a manner that explained attributes associated with cultural symbols. Throughout the article, the reader can understand why a specific decision was made and why it was consistent with previous research decisions. While the analysis techniques may be considered non-traditional, the approach taken by the researcher is accepted as a result of her effort to explain how these decisions emerged and how they were consistent with her research question and theoretical framework (previous literature). This work highlights how method, too, influences interpretation.

As demonstrated above and discussed in Chapter Six, data are gathered through a number of means, including structured and unstructured interviews, conversations, document reviews, observations, visual realities (i.e., film and photos), first person life histories, narratives, biographies, and focus groups. Whether to prioritize one data source over another can become an issue in interpretation. A study that uses only one method for data collection, say interviews, will allow the researcher to concentrate solely on the data derived from the interviews. On the contrary, when a researcher uses multiple forms of data, it is important to avoid treating one form of data as a sole source for all interpretation (Atkinson & Delamont, 2005). The question of interest and methodology can provide insight into how to treat multiple methods.

Another confusing element of analysis for researchers is the role of previous literature. The next section will discuss the tensions and considerations that should be well thought-out as the researcher engages in analysis and interpretation.

Role of Previous Literature

In order to clarify and maintain consistency with the previous chapters in this text, we will clarify the use of terms. The theoretical framework, or conceptual framework, consists of previous research studies, or existing research, on the topic of interest (as introduced in Chapter One). It is this type of research that is considered in a review of the literature, which is a common element of research articles and illustrates the understanding the author has about the phenomenon of interest by providing an overview of the existing research. Most, if not all, journal and dissertation guidelines require the inclusion of a literature review. This overview of previous research also comes with a responsibility to explain how previous research influences the research design and methodology as well as to be explicit about how a study compares with previous studies. In many cases, the review of literature is expected to illustrate the researcher's knowledge about the subject and critique the existing literature to justify the rationale for the present study (Hittleman & Simon, 2002). The issue that is seldom considered as part of the literature review is how previous research or theories should or should not influence one's own perspective or the research design. For example, researchers who see themselves as constructivists believe that meaning is constructed as a result of the interaction between humans and their world (Crotty, 1998). This epistemological belief can create an inherent tension between what is known from previous research that was conducted from a different epistemological belief and what is constructed as a result of the interaction of humans and their world. The use of previous research is the process of linking "our research—and ourselves—with others" (Wolcott, 2002, p. 94). Too strong an emphasis on what is previously known can be viewed as having an a priori(presumptive) foundation, which has specific implications for the research design and analysis techniques used in the study.

Because the theoretical framework in higher education research is used to designate the previous research that may influence the study at hand, it is critical to understand the central issue involved in linking one's research study with the work of other researchers. This central issue revolves around understanding how a researcher can use previous research to enhance, and not constrain, emerging findings. In grounded theory, this is referred to as balancing one's theoretical sensitivity (Corbin & Strauss, 2008; Glaser & Strauss, 1967/ 1999). Theoretical sensitivity is the insight (knowledge of existing research) a researcher has about the area of research that allows the researcher to make sense of emerging categories. Although a researcher would need to have sufficient theoretical sensitivity to conceptualize and formulate the study, there is also a need to not constrain possible new interpretations as a result of having this previous knowledge. Often, the tension about what has emerged that is new and what is assumed from previous research may not seem evident until the study is underway. As a result, decisions about how to use previous research can be complex.

The approach that seems natural to many researchers is to treat the process of learning from previous research as independent from the linking of the elements within the research design (epistemology, theoretical framework, methodology, and method). This tendency does not address the potential influence that previous research can have on understanding the phenomenon under consideration.

Wolcott (2002) suggested that researchers choose when links should be made and intentionally explain these choices to the reader. Examples of selecting when to link previous research with the present study would be to state the influence previous research may have on the present study or to use previous research in making sampling decisions as necessary in grounded theory (Strauss & Corbin, 1998). In some studies, the linking of previous research may not occur until the discussion of the findings. Whatever choices researchers make, the key is to make them explicit with sufficient explanation for the reader to understand the approach selected.

The placement of theory in a qualitative study (e.g., in the beginning as a literature review or later after the findings) indicates the role theory is playing in the study (Creswell, 2003). Researchers who expect to create theory use an inductive approach to theory building and are likely to consider existing theories towards the end. The interplay between theory and the data must be considered as an influence rather than a barrier to emerging conditions. Whether using theories *a priori* (presumptive) or *tabula rasa* (not at all, such as in a blank slate), the researcher should clearly delineate and explain them in terms of the influence this choice has on the phenomenon under consideration.

The Torres and Hernandez (2007) study on the influence of ethnic identity on the self-authorship of Latino/a college students provides examples of explicit statements connecting how previous research influenced the theory building process during the analysis of data. Because the researchers used a constructivist grounded theory, epistemology and methodology, they needed to explain the use of previous theories on the findings on this study. They begin this explanation with a succinct statement within the first paragraph of the methodology section: "The use of self-authorship as a framework was not *a priori;* rather it emerged as a plausible lens during the coding process" (Torres & Hernandez, 2007, p. 560). They went on to point the reader to the analysis section for further explanation.

In the analysis section, Torres and Hernandez (2007) described the process that led to use of an existing theory within this study. They stated "much discussion occurred about whether it was appropriate to use holistic development with this population of students [Latino/a] and within the methodology being used in this study" (p. 561). They described the decision to return to the cases and to consider whether existing theory could be used as a framework for analysis. They also stated that "this decision was made with the understanding that, if the emerging data did not seem to fall into the framework appropriately, then the analysis [using the theory] would be thrown out and the team would start over" (p. 561). They also cited Strauss and Corbin (1998), a primary text on grounded theory that explicitly addressed what they were considering, and wrote that "it is not that we use the experience or literature as data but rather we use the properties and dimensions derived from the comparative incidents to examine the data in front of us" (p. 80 as cited in Torres & Hernandez, 2007, p. 561). The explanation was completed with the statement "the properties of holistic development were not applied to the data, rather they were used as a means to examine it" (p. 561).

In this example, Torres and Hernandez (2007) went on to explain that the experiences of Latino/a students were not previously included in studies on self-authorship. For this reason, the findings of this study extended what was known about the theory and allowed new concepts to emerge for others to understand how the experiences of the Latino/a students differed from those of previous studies.

As mentioned earlier, the use of previous research can also influence the interpretation of the findings. An example of explicitly stating the influence of existing research in the analysis and interpretation phase can be found in a study of Black college students' faith development (Stewart, 2002). This study was grounded in Afrocentric philosophy and influenced by hermeneutic theoretical perspectives. In this published article, Stewart (2002) explicitly stated in her analysis and findings section that

> Although Fowler's (1981) and Parks' (2000) faith-identity typology theory is presented as a means of interpreting and understanding the students individually and collectively, the faith-identity typology was not used as an a priori framework; rather, in the midst of the interviews, I searched for more literature related to the area of faith and spiritual development. The faith-identity typology stood out as being the most responsive to the stories that the students were telling me. (p. 584)

This statement clarifies the process the researcher considered in regards to looking at existing research as well as its use and placement within the study.

In the first example, Torres and Hernandez (2007) used an inductive approach to existing theories and provided information about previous research because it was expected by the reviewers of the academic journal (Creswell, 2003). In this case, the audience was considered as part of the writing process and therefore a short review of the literature was provided. In the second example,

Stewart (2002) illustrated the interplay between data and existing theory that allows propositions to be considered while also keeping a particular framework in mind. The key is to not let existing research become the mold for the data, but instead to maintain the fluidity of the interplay (Lather, 1986). This constant interplay is difficult to maintain yet critical for congruency of the study.

This interplay emerges while using analysis techniques. As a way to introduce the various techniques that can be used, this next section will focus on common analysis techniques used in qualitative studies within higher education and student affairs.

Techniques in Data Analysis

Of the various elements of the research process, analysis is perhaps the most pivotal. It is here where the researcher struggles to make meaning of the varying forms of data collected. Some qualitative methodologies provide guidance about how analysis and interpretation should be conducted, while others are not as clear about how the process should occur. There are numerous techniques for analyzing qualitative data and several books that mainly cover the analysis of data. It is strongly recommended that in-depth study about analysis techniques be done prior to starting a research study. Books that provide summary comments will cover only the surface of what is involved with any particular technique. Because this book is focused on process and not an in-depth treatment of particular analysis techniques, this chapter offers general information regarding the techniques and provides citations for additional reading that can assist with understanding the techniques.

Analysis techniques allow the researcher to notice and identify descriptive, common, or unusual ideas, phrases, or words, and then attach those to a broader meaning of the phenomenon. Ryan and Bernard (2000) discussed a number of general strategies through which to analyze data, including systematic elicitation, in which lists are generated of "items that belong in a culture domain" (Ryan & Bernard, 2000, p. 770) and then relationships between the items are assessed. In addition, they discussed componential analysis where models are created based on relationships between features. These models do not include what the differences in meaning may contribute, rather they focus on a type of classification of a theme or term. What is captured in this type of analysis is the hierarchical structure in sets of terms, and key-words-in-context that lists the places where a particular word or phrase appears and notes the words that come before or after it. For example for the term "dogs" the classifications may include big, medium, little, or breed names.

Next, we briefly describe some specific techniques. Some of these techniques are discussed in other chapters in this book; however, we revisit them here because of their importance to an understanding of the analytic and interpretive processes. The order in which they are presented is not meant to represent any particular importance. Rather, they are grouped because they may commonly be used together, but not always.

Open and Initial Coding

According to Charmaz (2006), "coding means categorizing segments of data with a short name that simultaneously summarizes and accounts for each piece of data" (p. 43). A common technique that emerged from grounded theory methodology is referred to as open coding, which "requires a brain-storming approach to analysis because, in the beginning, analysts want to open up the data to all potentials and possibilities contained within" (Corbin & Strauss, 2008, p. 160). This process breaks data into manageable pieces and allows the researcher to explore the ideas contained within the in-depth aspects of the data. The common ideas are then put together to create poten-tial concepts that represent what was found in the data (Corbin & Strauss, 2008). Charmaz (2006), in her more recent work, referred to open coding as initial coding, the first of two main phases of coding. Initial coding is accomplished by doing coding line by line or word by word, thereby sticking very close to the data (Charmaz, 2006). The essential process at this level of coding is to remain open, putting aside preconceived notions about what is expected to be found (Corbin & Strauss, 2008). Researchers call the concepts that emerge "themes" or "initial codes," which represent the labels given to segments of data that describe aspects of the phenomenon. This process has some commonalities with the unloosing of data expected in phenomenologi-cal studies (Charmaz, 2006).

Few studies end analysis with open coding. This is because it is not unusual to have hundreds of open or initial codes, and reporting out so many codes would be both difficult and render description rather than an interpretation that addresses the question(s) of interest. From open coding, or unloosing of data, the researcher will likely use some type of further data reduction tech-nique to group the codes together in order illustrate how the codes relate to each other. This data reduction technique can be called axial coding, constant comparison, or hermeneutic circle.

Axial and Focused Coding

Another technique from grounded theory focuses on the process of relating concepts to each other. This is referred to as axial coding (Corbin & Strauss, 2008) or focused coding (Charmaz, 2006) and is the part of putting back together the open codes into categories (larger concepts) that relate to one another. While considered a completely separate process from open coding in earlier editions of Corbin and Strauss's grounded theory text, the third edition describes this process as going "hand in hand" and the distinctions between these techniques as "artificial" (Corbin & Strauss, 2008, p. 198). By linking the earlier codes according to the relationship between them, axial coding provides categories that have properties or concepts within them. This analysis strategy can be accomplished using a constant comparison technique that is explained later. Axial coding techniques are similar to focused coding (Charmaz, 2006) or hermeneutic circle (Schwandt, 2007a).

As an example, in an advanced student development theory class taught by Vasti, the students (researchers) grouped the open codes into categories that described certain conditions in the process of developing interpersonal relationships. This process reduced over 75 open codes into three conditions. Once the conditions were determined, the open codes were used to describe what happens within the three conditions. For example, among first-year students, the proximity of friends "condition" was found to include 1) friendships that were within living communities, 2) friends from student groups and classrooms, and 3) friends from home. Further information on this process is included in the constant comparison example.

Recommended Reading:

Bryant, A., & Charmaz, K. (2007). *The Sage handbook of grounded theory.* Thousand Oaks, CA: Sage.

Charmaz, K. (2006). *Constructing grounded theory: A practical guide through qualitative analysis.* London: Sage.

Corbin, J., & Strauss, A. (2008). *Basics of qualitative research* (3rd ed.). Los Angeles, CA: Sage.

Constant Comparison

This analysis technique involves comparing incidents in order to find similarities and group together codes under broader descriptive concepts (Corbin & Strauss, 2008). By comparing incidents, the researcher can differentiate between categories or themes and then identify the properties specific to a certain category. When there is a unique incident, then it may be appropriate to use theoretical comparisons where further information is used to explain the incident through metaphors or similes. Comparisons between incidents, respondents, or locations are a natural part of human nature; however, here researchers use a systematic approach in constant comparison. This requires that the researcher explain how the comparisons were made and why the comparison is appropriate within the study.

In the example brought up of axial coding, students in Vasti's advanced student development course used constant comparison to determine if the "conditions" identified for developing interpersonal relationships in axial coding applied to all class levels (sophomore, junior, etc.). By doing this, the researchers were able to see how conditions changed between the class levels and that some conditions applied only to participants in one class level.

Recommended Reading:

Corbin, J., & Strauss, A. (2008). *Basics of qualitative research* (3rd ed.). Los Angeles, CA: Sage.

Bracketing

Within phenomenological studies, bracketing is sometimes called epoché (but as differentiated in Chapter Four, these are not identical concepts). This technique requires that the researcher "suspend judgment about the existence of the world and 'bracket' or set aside existential assumptions made in every-day life and in the sciences" (Schwandt, 2007a, p. 24). This technique allows the researcher to focus on the phenomenon being investigated. van Manen (1990) saw bracketing as a part of the larger reduction process where research-ers become compelled to study what they find mysterious, then suspend their assumptions about the topics, then strip away all theories of the topic, and finally see past the individual lived experience toward a structure of the universal experience. The challenge here is of course to put away or suspend one's assumptions. Is this really humanly possible? Bracketing requires that research-ers interrupt their beliefs in order to explore structures. For example, research-ers suspend their memories of their own struggles with deciding upon a major so that they can detect the structures of struggling with such decisions.

Recommended Reading:

Moustakas, C. (1994). *Phenomenological research methods.* Thousand Oaks, CA: SAGE.
van Manen, M. (1990). *Researching lived experience.* Albany, NY: State University of New
   York Press.

Hermeneutic Circle

Moustakas (1994) wrote that it is through the hermeneutic circle that the preju-dices of researchers are dismantled. By hearing what participants say, research-ers are led to "new prejudgments" (p. 10). But these are constantly viewed with skepticism, looking for additional evidence to confirm or disconfirm these new prejudgments. The hermeneutic circle allows researchers to bring new understanding from behind the researcher's awareness. Within the circle, the researcher reflects "the experience as it appears in consciousness but also [offers] an analysis and astute interpretation of the underlying conditions" (p. 10). The bringing back together of separate aspects of data into their con-textual whole is the completion of the hermeneutic circle. The interpretation of trajectory relationships, such as similarity, difference, analogy, and metaphor, is mutually dependent upon the larger context. Interpretation allows the reduced data to be brought back into the larger context (Schwandt, 2007a).

For example, in a study currently underway on the experiences of student veterans, Jan as co-researcher with Tomoko Grabosky, expected to hear partici-pants describe their transition issues to the higher education culture from the military culture. That was the case. But, in listening deeper and disregarding their assumptions (submerging into the hermeneutic circle), Jan and Tomoko discovered ways that student veterans created military culture on campus. This initially became apparent as participants described how important the veterans club was to them as well as what happened at meetings. As the researchers submerged deeper in the circle, they also heard of veterans using recreational facilities as they would have in the military and "attacking" their academics. The researchers had to pay attention to what was happening behind them to come forward in the circle of new insight. Such attention demands a focus that some researchers may find difficult. The hermeneutic circle occurs simultaneously with conducting conversations, studying transcripts, and writing drafts of the analysis. In drafts researchers ask questions that then in subsequent drafts they attempt to address.

Recommended Reading:

Moustakas, C. (1994). *Phenomenological research methods.* Thousand Oaks, CA: SAGE.

Schwandt, T.A. (2000). Three epistemological stances for qualitative inquiry: Interpretivism, hermeneutics, and social constructionism. In N. K. Denzin and Y. S. Lincoln (Eds). *Handbook of qualitative research* (2nd ed., pp. 189-213). Thousand Oaks, CA: SAGE.

Wertz, F. J., Charmaz, K., McMullen, L. M., Josselson, R., Anderson, R., & McSpadden, E. (2011). *Five ways of doing qualitative analysis: Phenomenological psychology, grounded theory, discourse analysis, narrative research, and intuitive inquiry.* New York, NY: The Guilford Press.

Narrative Analysis

Because narrative analysis as a data collection method is associated with interviews, autobiographical, conversational, life story research, and storytelling,the interaction between the participants' experiences and those of the researcher are central. For this reason, much of the analysis discussion around narrative inquiry is focused on epistemological beliefs of the researcher. Chapter Four referred to this as "Researcher as Narrator" and requires that analysis decisions be made about how to represent the voices (stories) of the participants.

In studies that use narratives as the method for data collection, the procedures for analysis vary. Interpreting narratives tends to include two major possibilities. One aspect can be analyzing how the story is organized, how it developed, and what is happening or "doing" (Schwandt, 2007a). This approach is useful for setting up the context within an event or phenomenon and how that event was interpreted by the participants. The second approach is to focus on "what is being told in the story" (Schwandt, 2007a, p. 202). This approach is much more interpretative in nature and is focused on infusing the social context within the narrative of the participant. Examples of the use of narrative analysis are provided in Chapter Four.

Recommended Reading:

Clandinin, D. J. (2007). *Handbook of narrative inquiry: Mapping a methodology.* Thousand Oaks, CA: SAGE.

Memo Writing

This is the technique of elaborating on the coded categories that are developed during data analysis. Memos are expected to "capture the thoughts of the" researcher during the analysis process (Schwandt, 2007a, p. 189). The intent is for the memo to be conceptual in nature and is written by the researcher for the use of the researcher. As Charmaz (2006) discussed, "memo writing constitutes a crucial method . . . because it prompts you to analyze your data and codes early in the research process" (p. 72). This can be accomplished through a researcher journal, actual memos, or memos within analytic software.

Memos can be used in a variety of ways during the analysis phase. For example, memos can be sorted to assist in the comparison between incidents or conditions. This can provide additional insight into a condition and how these insights arose during the study. In longitudinal studies, memos are critical to remembering research decisions and why a certain direction or approach was used at a given point in the study. Memos are often portrayed in the analysis as part of the researcher's interpretations of a particular event or circumstance.

Recommended Reading:

Charmaz, K. (2006). *Constructing grounded theory: A practical guide through qualitative analysis.* London: Sage.

Lempert, L. B. (2007). Asking questions of the data: Memo writing in the grounded theory tradition. In A. Bryant & K. Charmaz (Eds.), *The Sage handbook of grounded theory* (pp. 245–264). Thousand Oaks, CA: Sage.

This introduction to commonly used techniques illustrates the overlap among methodologies but also the importance of explicitly explaining why the technique is being used and the connection to the specific methodology. As a way to continue to illustrate processes, the next section will expand on ethical considerations of analysis.

Ethics of Adequate Evidence

One of the ways to consider the quality of the study is to highlight the behavior of the researcher during the analysis process to make sure an ethical approach was taken. Several strategies exist to check the researcher's analyses and interpretations. Building on the theme of continuity and congruence introduced in the first four chapters of this book, the readers of qualitative studies must see a clear connection between what is presented as data and what is offered as interpretations of the data. Most typically, rich description and many quotations from transcripts are offered so that the reader may join the researcher inside of the data. It is not acceptable to simply offer one quote for each theme because this does not provide the kind of evidence that a reader needs to trace the claims the researcher makes back to the data itself. According to Erickson (1986) "evidentiary inadequacy" is in fact an ethical issue as it relates to the integrity of data analysis and interpretation. Erickson detailed five types of evidentiary inadequacy that come from both data collection decisions and analytic strategies:

1. *Inadequate amounts of evidence.* The researcher has too little evidence to warrant certain key assertions.
2. *Inadequate variety in kinds of evidence.* The researcher fails to have evidence across a range of different kinds of sources (e.g., direct observation, interviewing, and site documents) to warrant key assertions through triangulation.
3. *Faulty interpretive status of evidence.* The researcher fails to have understood the key aspects of the complexity of action or of meaning perspectives held by actors in the setting due to inadequate time in the field or interviewing that was insufficient.
4. *Inadequate disconfirming evidence.* The researcher lacks data that might disconfirm a key assertion or lacks evidence that a deliberate search was made for potentially disconfirming data (leading to the critique that the researcher looked only for evidence to support his/her own interpretations).
5. *Inadequate or discrepant case analysis.* The researcher did not scrutinize the set of disconfirming instances, examining each instance (i.e., discrepant case) and comparing it with the confirming instances to determine which features of the disconfirming case were the same or different from the analogous features of the confirming cases. Such comparative feature analysis often reveals flaws in the original assertion. (Erickson, 1986, p. 140)

Implicit in a discussion of providing sufficient evidence for the claims the researcher makes is the evidence that an analytic process is thoroughly discussed. Data analysis typically involves a process of moving from concrete words and categories to more abstract ones. This process results in the naming of themes intended to interpret or capture what is going on in the data. Therefore, these themes should offer a glimpse into the richness of the data rather than simply conveying a non-descriptive generic name.

Another aspect that contributes to assessing the trustworthiness of the findings is the explicit explanation of the role of previous literature on the results of the study. While theoretical sensitivity is needed to be able to see relationships between data concepts and understand the potential of new meaning (Corbin & Strauss, 2008), being open to new findings requires a balanced approach.

Role of Researcher

Most researchers enter the data analysis phase with excitement about the interesting information they will learn from their participants. What is seldom addressed in the research methodology literature is the evolving relationship between researcher and participant and issues that can arise regarding congruence, consistency, and interpretation. The role of the researcher in the data analysis process is an implicit aspect of the epistemology and methodology chosen. The specifics of this relationship evolve as the data are collected, and the relationship with the participants is explored in analysis rather than just conceptualized.

During the data analysis process, this implicit aspect inherent in the researcher–participant relationship moves to the foreground and presents potential concerns that were not previously considered. The qualitative research literature refers to these issues using terms like subjectivity (Peshkin, 1988), "feeling right" (Corbin & Strauss, 2008, p. 45) or trustworthiness (Lincoln & Guba, 1985). Most of the literature in qualitative research encourages some level of involvement with participants as a way to increase trust and rapport, yet the literature cautions the researcher to "also step back and see their own stories in the inquiry" (Clandinin & Connelly, 2000, p. 81). The tension between building rapport and maintaining appropriate distance to see your own story requires constant attention. This type of tension was experienced by Vasti in her longitudinal study of Latino/a students in college. As a response to managing this tension, she chose to talk to a qualitative mentor and eventually wrote about her experiences in a journal article (Torres & Baxter Magolda, 2002). In this article, Torres explored how her own ethnicity and similarity of experiences to those shared in the students' stories made her reflect on herself as the instrument of the research. Having a false sense of control over the process gave way to an understanding of how these issues can be managed in the research process. How a researcher manages subjectivity is greatly influenced by the view of knowledge (epistemology) and the process used to create knowledge (methodology).

Congruence and consistency in the research design must include consideration of how the role of the researcher will be managed and how the researcher understands the relationship between participants and researcher. Two researchers reflected on their own development as researchers engaged in longitudinal studies about how the relationship between participants and the researcher changed (Torres & Baxter Magolda, 2002). Baxter Magolda admitted that, at the onset of her study, she was concerned with "treating participants fairly and ethically," and after 15 years of sustained interaction, her relationship evolved greatly and moved towards the mutual construction of knowledge between researcher and participants (Torres & Baxter Magolda, 2002, p. 481). Torres admitted to feeling an ethical obligation to help students who had negative images about being Latino/a and helping them process the influence of these messages. This evolving role of the researcher should be expected in qualitative research and described as part of the congruence and consistency of the research process.

Feminist researchers embrace the development of a relationship with participants as a way for greater engagement and understanding into the phenomenon of interest (Reinharz, 1992). Generally accepted within the feminist methodology literature is the idea that "personal experiences [are] a valuable asset for feminist research" (p. 258). This type of research values the connection between the research project and the researcher's experiences because one usually is "starting with one's own experience" (p. 259). As a result, many feminist researchers look for research topics that stem from their own personal experiences. If a researcher is using a feminist theoretical perspective, then the issues involved with the researcher–participant relationship would always be at the forefront of the research process.

Lather (2007) reflected on her own feminist ethnography among women with HIV/AIDS and stated that perhaps her co-author and she were,

> agents of displacement, making representations only to foreground their insufficiencies. We do this in order to resist the women in our study being consumed without remainder by some sense-making machine. Our task is not so much to unpack some real as to enact the ruins of any effort to monumentalize lived experience. Such reflection on ungraspable meaning is not about ineffability but about how the ambiguities of knowing are the structure of our grasp. (pp. 39–40)

Another example of this tension between self as a researcher and the participants can be found in Frank Harris's study of men's identity (2010). In the trustworthiness section of this article, Harris reports this tension:

> I routinely reflected on my own salient identities as a college-educated heterosexual African American man while conducting this study. Doing so allowed me to recognize how these identity dimensions informed my beliefs and assumptions about college men and masculinities and shaped my interactions with the participants. Being reflexive also helped to ensure that my gender identity and experiences did not lead to hasty or shallow interpretations of the data. (p. 304)

In this text, Harris explicitly stated his own role in the research and the influence this can have on data analysis. In this section of the article, he shared with the reader the techniques he used to manage this tension. The techniques he selected were consistent with his epistemology and methodology, thus maintaining congruence and consistency in the research process.

Summary

This chapter provided insights into issues that emerge during the analysis phase. Many more concerns may emerge as researchers embark on their study. The simultaneous interplay between data collection and analysis is highlighted among various methodologies (Corbin & Strauss, 2008). In this chapter we attempted to provide some strategies for data analysis and interpretation as well as guidance and thoughts on issues that may emerge from the analysis and interpretation of data.

Exercises

Chapter-related

1. Select an analysis technique, such as open coding, and attempt to distinguish how it may be implemented within different methodologies (e.g., grounded theory, case study, etc.).

2. Consider various data collection methods and how they would each influence the analysis process.

3. As a memo-writing exercise, explain why you would select a particular analysis technique that is consistent with your epistemology and methodology. In other words, what rationale would you provide for specific analytic techniques?

Research Process

1. Using the transcript you generated through the exercise in Chapter Six (or using a portion of a transcript from a research project), complete a first read through of the entire transcript, reading thematically. As you read, jot down notes about the major themes you see.

2. Then, go back to the transcript and do a line-by-line coding of the text, trying to, as Charmaz suggests, stay close to the data and code using gerunds (words that reflect action).

3. After you complete your initial coding, identify the new insights you gained about what kind of data to collect next. What leads would you pursue next? How would you go about this?

4. Finally, come together in a small group and examine how you each approached coding this data chunk. What differences and/or similarities are there? Compare what you saw when you read thematically as an entire narrative with what you gained when you did line-by-line coding. What preconceptions might you have brought to the coding process?

5. Consider how different analytic techniques may vary your analysis and interpretation processes.

8 Anticipating and Navigating Ethical Issues

> Clearly, researchers need both cases and principles from which to learn about ethical behaviors. More than this, they need two attributes: the sensitivity to identify an ethical issue and the responsibility to feel committed to acting appropriately in regard to such issues. (Eisner & Peshkin, 1990, p. 244)

Qualitative inquiry, like most endeavors involving human relationships, is replete with ethical issues at every step of the process. Developing the kind of ethical sensitivity that long-time qualitative methodologists Eisner and Peshkin refer to in the quotation above involves both knowledge of ethical principles guiding research decisions and then ample practice in applying principles to the real dilemmas that emerge in a qualitative research context. Knowledge and practice do not, of course, guarantee that a researcher will then behave ethically when issues emerge, but paying attention to ethical issues and making good judgments increase the likelihood of behaving ethically.

An important first step in developing ethical sensitivity is anticipating where and when ethical issues may emerge in the research process. And indeed, the potential is great for ethical issues to emerge in all areas of the research design, including the statement of purpose and research questions, data collection, data analysis and interpretation, presentation of results, and the role of the researcher. For example, being clear with the reader about your epistemological, theoretical, and methodological grounding, as discussed in Chapter One, are ethical issues, as are developing criteria and integrating strategies for assuring trustworthiness of the entire research design, as detailed in Chapter Two. Issues of trust and rapport, as discussed in Chapter Five on sampling, are ethical issues, as are being clear with the ways of demonstrating participants' historical and cultural situatedness, as stated in Chapter Seven. There are ethical dimensions to making explicit the researcher's personal investments in the research, the various biases a researcher brings to the work, a researcher's surprises in the process of the research endeavor, and/or the ways in which one has avoided or suppressed certain points of view, as explicated in Chapter Seven. Nearly every research decision and action carries with it an ethical dimension for which the researcher must be prepared.

The purpose of this chapter is to provide an overview of ethical issues that intersect with qualitative research designs, principles that guide decision making when resolving ethical dilemmas, and examples from research that illuminate the issues and nature of the dilemmas. As Eisner and Peshkin (1990) appropriately suggested, ultimately, ethical sensitivity and behavior depend upon the good judgment of the researcher, which emerges "from the convergence of principle, experience, and reflection" (p. 245). To that end, every research project requires that the researcher think through the nature of the study and what ethical behavior should look like given a particular set of research circumstances.

Ethical Principles at Stake

Ethical conduct is not just the simple matter of avoiding placing at risk those whom in our research projects we variously call the researched "others," "subjects," and "respondents." It is the infinitely more complex challenge of *doing good* [emphasis added], a consideration that places researchers at odds with one another as they raise entirely different questions about the location of good in the conduct of research. And it is as well, the identification of what constitutes proper behavior in the range of roles, settings, and circumstances where qualitative researchers are apt to find themselves. (Eisner & Peshkin, 1990, p. 243)

The ethical imperative to *do good,* rather than simply doing *no harm* in the context of qualitative inquiry significantly increases the obligations of the researcher to understand the ethical principles at stake in conducting research. Although many of these principles hold true for quantitative research as well, the nature of the relationships developed in most qualitative studies between the researcher and participants or between the researcher and the research context creates unique dilemmas and issues that must be considered and integrated into research practices. Simply stated, L. M. Smith (1990) captured the essence of ethics in qualitative research by suggesting that "At a commonsense level, caring, fairness, openness, and truth seem to be the important values undergirding the relationships and the activity of inquiry" (p. 260). These ethical imperatives are often safeguarded through principles and promises, such as confidentiality, anonymity, informed consent, avoidance of deception, respect, privacy, and do no harm. Often, researchers remain complacent about ethical issues, thinking that if they simply comply with expectations and procedures dictated by the Institutional Review Board (IRB), then their obligations are met (Magolda & Weems, 2002). But as Schwandt (2007b) articulated in a chapter on growing controversy surrounding IRB in a time of highly regulatory practices, "behaving ethically in research is not a simple exercise in rule following" (p. 96). The following discussion of ethical principles and practices demonstrates the considerable elusiveness behind these principles when tested in the complicated contexts of qualitative research.

Confidentiality refers to the treatment of information that an individual has knowingly disclosed in a research relationship or context with an expectation that this information will not be disclosed to unauthorized parties without consent. In principle, confidentiality guarantees respondents that the information they provide in the research context will not be shared. *Anonymity* suggests that if and when information is shared, no identifiable data will be disclosed. When personal data are provided, it is only "behind a shield of anonymity" (Christians, 2000, p. 139). Stated differently, Patton (2002) made this distinction: "Confidentiality means you know but won't tell. Anonymity means you don't know, as in a survey returned anonymously" (p. 408). Both confidentiality and anonymity are part of the larger issue of protecting a participant's *right to privacy* and making promises that disclosure of any kind of information will not occur without a participant's consent. It is important to note that there is a paradigmatic influence on these principles as some argue that the principles of anonymity and confidentiality reflect a belief in value-neutral science (Christians, 2011) rather than reflecting "a set of ethical principles that are feminist, caring, communitarian, holistic, respectful, mutual (rather than power imbalanced), sacred, and ecologically sound" (Denzin, Lincoln, & Smith, 2008, p. 569). However, we advocate understanding these basic principles, which are at the heart of most statements of ethical principles and IRB procedures, because this is the research context in which most researchers in higher education need to function and because understanding of what one is critiquing is integral to a responsible critique.

The principles of confidentiality, anonymity, and privacy are typically operationalized in research through the statement of *informed consent,* which participants must sign before engaging in the research process. For example, in the institutional guidelines provided for human subjects review, a statement of informed consent is prepared and reviewed with each participant prior to the collection of any data. Guidelines may differ by institution, so it is important to understand the policies, procedures, and expectations of the institution sponsoring the research. Further, multi-institution studies may require that the researcher also go through a human subjects review at those institutions where data are collected. What follows in Table 8.1 is a general example of an informed consent form, modeled after the one used at The Ohio State University, with excerpted portions that address directly the ethical principles of confidentiality, anonymity, and consent (see http://orrp.osu.edu/irb/).

By signing this form, the participant signals and verifies that the researcher has met the obligation to inform participants of the nature of the study and their involvement in it, and that the participants understand and agree with what has been communicated to them. Typically, this conversation ends with the signature. More problematically, however, as Weis and Fine (2000) pointed out:

> The consent form sits at the contradictory base of the institutionalization of research. Although the aim of informed consent is presumably to

Table 8.1 Sample Statement of Informed Consent

Statement of Informed Consent

This is a consent form for research participation: It contains important information about this study and what to expect if you decide to participate.

Your participation is voluntary: Please consider the information carefully. Feel free to ask questions before making your decision whether or not to participate. If you decide to participate, you will be asked to sign this form and will receive a copy of the form.

Purpose: The purpose of this study is to investigate students' understanding of _____ [insert clear statement of purpose of study].

Procedures: By agreeing to participate in this study, you will take part in an individual interview, lasting no more than 90 minutes. You may be asked to participate in follow-up interviews of approximately 30 minutes each.

Duration: You may leave the study at any time. If you decide to stop participating in the study, there will be no penalty to you, and you will not lose any benefits to which you are otherwise entitled.

Confidentiality: All information obtained in this study is strictly confidential. However, there may be circumstances where this information must be released. For example, personal information regarding your participation may be disclosed if required by state law. The results of this study may be used in reports, presentations, and publications, but the researchers will not identify you. Only [researcher's name] will have access to individual data. All data will be encrypted and stored in a secure location and then destroyed one year after completion of the study.

Risks: Any discomfort you might experience should be no more than typically experienced during a small group discussion [include clear statement of any risks associated with participation]. If you are not comfortable with the discussion and wish to discontinue participation in the study, you will be free to leave without penalty.

Benefits: The potential benefits of your participation include the opportunity to [insert benefits, such as self-knowledge, reflection, generation of new understanding].

Incentives: [insert any incentives, such as a gift card, entry to a lottery for prize, books that participants will receive upon completion of participation].

Questions and Contacts: For questions or concerns about the study, you may contact [researcher's name and contact information], or you may also contact [insert name and contact information] in the Office of Responsible Research Practices.

Signing the Consent Form: I have read (or someone has read to me) this form and I am aware that I am being asked to participate in a research study. I have had the opportunity to ask questions and have had them answered to my satisfaction. I voluntarily agree to participate in this study.

Participant Name (please print)

Signature   Date

Investigator Signature   Date

protect respondents, inform them of the possibility of harm in advance, and invite them to withdraw if they so desire, it also effectively releases the institution or funding agency from any liability and gives control of the research process to the researcher. (pp. 41–42)

The issues of control and power in qualitative research are important ones for researchers to consider. On the one hand, most qualitative methodologies emphasize relationship building and reciprocity between researcher and participant as well as the co-construction of meaning in the analysis phases. On the other hand, and important to the integrity of research, more bureaucratic processes, such as informed consent, seem to serve as subtle—and not so subtle— reminders that, ultimately, power resides with the researcher. However, even with power held by the researcher, some scholars maintain the impossibility of realizing the promises suggested by informed consent. For example, Eisner (1991) wrote, "We might like to secure consent that is informed, but we know we can't always inform because we don't always know. We would like to protect personal privacy and guarantee confidentiality, but we know we cannot always fulfill such guarantees" (p. 225).

As noted earlier, these principles and the procedures to realize them are anchored in objectivist approaches to scientifically based research. Researchers approaching their work from critical lenses promote a different conceptualization or "a reflexive, critical ethics [which] could include a concern for: transformative egalitarianism, attention to the problems of representation, and continued examination of power orientations" (Lincoln & Cannella, 2007, p. 76). Navigating the tensions of informed consent is an important consideration— one that Weis and Fine (2000) reconciled by focusing on informed consent as "a conscience—to remind us of our accountability and position" (p. 42). This idea of informed consent as conscience reminds researchers that there is much at stake for researchers as well as participants in the research process.

Challenges in Applying Principles to Practice

Although nearly all codes of ethics and institutional review board requirements will call for the demonstration of strategies in place to preserve confidentiality, anonymity, privacy, and informed consent, many qualitative researchers stress these principles are nearly impossible to guarantee (Christians, 2011; Lincoln & Cannella, 2007; Patton, 2002; Shaw, 2008) and thus difficult to apply to practice. Several areas of concern are particularly challenging, including assuring confidentiality and anonymity, the use of pseudonyms, and the promise to do no harm.

Confidentiality and Anonymity

Several key questions emerge from the realities of actually providing assurances of confidentiality and anonymity. First, as Patton (2002) identified, "What are reasonable promises of confidentiality that can be fully honored?" (p. 408). In some cases, participants may want to be identified or fully described in the setting. In other cases, researchers may inquire about changing certain details of a particular story line (e.g., names, locations, and demographic identifiers) to which a participant may or may not agree. The most important principle in thinking about this question is to promise only those assurances and guarantees that the researcher is confident can be delivered and to always honor and respect the wishes of participants. This requires a process of negotiation between the researcher and participants and may continually evolve as the research progresses. However, this maxim is not always straightforward, and, like all ethical dilemmas, may be fraught with complexities. For example, in a study that uncovered racism in higher education, anonymity and confidentiality needed to be considered in relation to continued harm done to those involved. As described by the researcher:

> To what extent should I reveal the ugly parts of racism to acknowledge the experiences of the victims and to portray the effects of racism in an authentic way? Who should I "out," or could I tell a truthful, historical account without having to reveal the true identity of the players involved? Is it fair to talk about the actions of people who may now regret their actions or have a different perspective twenty or more years later? (E. Hernandez, personal communication, August 16, 2012)

This issue relates to a second question: Are there ever any circumstances in which the researcher would not honor a participant's request for confidentiality or not promise confidentiality? (Patton, 2002). Examples of such circumstances might include a researcher learning from a participant about significant substance abuse, domestic violence, or theft. In some situations, for example, the reporting of child abuse or sexual assault, a researcher may be legally obligated (and ethically required) to disclose information. Research, like all else in higher education, is influenced by the larger sociocultural context of the time, so we suspect that in this era of the Penn State sexual abuse case, legal and ethical obligations regarding reporting will only increase. It behooves the researcher to consider his or her research in the context of these situations and to evaluate the likelihood of any of these issues emerging. If there is any likelihood that these serious issues might emerge, the researcher should consider discussing these issues in advance rather than waiting until a situation occurs and risking the perception of violating what was promised at the outset of the study. If any legal obligations may become a factor, these too should be included in the consent form.

In an investigation of lesbian identity development, the researcher listened as one of her young college student participants described suicidal thoughts and ideation. In consultation with her dissertation advisor, the decision was made to call the director of the counseling center at the university where the research was conducted. The director had agreed prior to the beginning of the study to serve as a consulting psychologist to the researcher if the need arose. The researcher was then able to talk through with a highly skilled professional, in a confidential environment, the nature of the suicidal talk from her participant and make a decision about how to best handle the situation. These kinds of situations call for a researcher to think about ethical obligations to participants as well as to the research and to exercise ethical sensitivity and professional responsibility. If, in the example just provided, the researcher had simply "turned the student in," then any relationship of trust would most likely have been violated and the participation of this student in the study would have ended. On the other hand, if the researcher had chosen to ignore the participant's suicidal talk and considered it as data for her study, the risks she assumed were great and the potential consequences disastrous.

Another example that illustrates the tension in providing assurances of confidentiality and privacy (a related issue to confidentiality as it relates to a researcher holding personal information private) focused on the location of research. Despite the promise of confidentiality and privacy, much research is conducted in public spaces or in office settings with public waiting areas, sometimes at the request of a participant. Although the "coffee shop interview" was suggested by a participant, the researcher should take care to think through all the possible consequences of interviewing in a highly trafficked area. Despite a researcher's inquiry about a participant's comfort and perception of safety in a certain research space, confidentiality and privacy cannot always be guaranteed.

The Use of Pseudonyms

Because of the nature of qualitative research, it is very difficult to always disguise the research context or the identity of the respondents participating in the study. Typically, pseudonyms are used, but this does not always guarantee anonymity. When pseudonyms are used, the researcher usually asks participants to choose their own, which may make them more likely to be identifiable to those who know them and are reading results of the research. Furthermore, in some cases, participants may choose *not* to disguise information, suggesting that such a practice is inconsistent with the goals of the research project or with participants' needs to fully express who they are. For example, in a study on the importance of the coming-out process to gay, lesbian, bisexual, and transgender (GLBT) identity, a participant may believe that to disguise one's identity further marginalizes and silences the experiences of GLBT individuals and runs counter to the purpose of the study. This is particularly true in projects with emancipatory goals or when using collaborative approaches such as participatory action research.

Patton (2002) aptly summarized some of the tensions inherent in a promise of confidentiality in relation to participant informed consent and use of pseudonyms:

> ... the norms about confidentiality are changing and being challenged as the tension has emerged between the important ethic of protecting people's privacy and, in some cases, in their desire to own their own story.

Informed consent, in this regard, does not automatically mean confidentiality. Informed consent can mean that participants understand the risks and benefits of having their real names reported and choose to do so. Protection of human subjects properly insists on informed consent. That does not automatically mean confidentiality. (p. 412)

The Promise to Do No Harm

Even the ethical imperatives of "do no harm" (Kitchner, 1985) and respect in the research relationship carry with them challenges and tensions. As Magolda and Weems (2002) aptly suggested, a sole reliance on meeting the requirements of IRB procedures can provide the researcher with a misguided sense of security with regard to harm. Furthermore, they wrote, "Because the IRB narrowly defines harm as physical and mental abuse, blatant violation of privacy, and ill-informed consent, the review process implicitly communicates that qualitative inquiry is relatively innocuous on the harm continuum" (p. 492). However, given the nature of the relationships between researchers and participants, which is at the core of most qualitative inquiry, even the best of intentions can lead to the unintended consequence of harm or disrespect. For example, interview questions that are culturally inappropriate and insensitive may constitute a microassault on a participant's self-esteem, or interpreting results in an unfavorable light may bring further harm to a group already experiencing marginalization in their setting. Further, the role of the researcher uncovering harm in the research context may pose difficult ethical dilemmas. In a study on the process of facilitating difficult dialogues about race, a researcher wondered about the boundaries defining his role as a researcher when he perceived the potential for harm in the class setting he was observing:

> During the second dialogue, a White student made a comment that was perceived as offensive by a student of color in the room. There were some back-and-forth comments between the students, and then the student of color became silent. The facilitator then moved on and asked another question of the group. Throughout the remainder of the dialogues, the student of color did not say anything at all, even when directly asked questions. What makes this an ethical issue is that this student was obviously shaken and harmed by the exchange during the dialogue. A question I often reflected on following the "incident" was, "What is my role as a researcher to intervene and talk with the facilitators about how to support this student?" I chose not to say anything throughout the course of the dialogue given my role as a researcher and observer. However, I have continually felt unsettled by my decision and wondered if I should have said something. Yet, by saying something, I was also concerned that I would push the facilitators to do something they might not have done otherwise (thereby "influencing" the dialogue), and the purpose of my observation was to watch facilitators in the moment (not to promote change). Thus, to what

extent is a researcher supposed to intervene when she/he believes a participant is silenced or harmed? How does a researcher balance the role as researcher with a person who wants to support participants? (S. J. Quaye, personal communication, August 27, 2012)

In their provocative article entitled "Doing Harm: An Unintended Consequence of Qualitative Inquiry?" Magolda and Weems (2002) argued through the use of confessional tales from their own research that the potential for harm is present for those serving as gatekeepers in qualitative studies, for participants in a study, for the cultural communities of interest in a particular study, and for researchers themselves. In summary, their tales suggest that, although it is incumbent on the researcher to fully disclose and discuss the potential for harm in a study, it is not possible to ever fully anticipate the complexities, and therefore harm, that may emerge as the research progresses. Likewise, although participants often quickly provide consent to participate in a study, which signifies that they understand the risks involved and the potential for harm, "safeguard measures . . . cannot ensure that respondents will fully understand (or care about) potential harm to themselves" (Magolda & Weems, 2002, p. 498).

As results of research are prepared, interpreted, and disseminated, issues of harm are also associated with how results will be received and perceived. And finally, the researcher runs the risk of harm through exposing oneself to others, bumping up against strongly held notions that are counter to research findings, and entertaining compromises to negotiate the complicated terrains of qualitative research contexts. Because the influence of social identities is omnipresent in qualitative studies, researcher self-disclosure can also be a difficult ethical issue. In their ethnographic study, Magolda and Ebben Gross (2009) wrote about the ethical challenges represented by the "major differences in researchers' and participants' ontologies and epistemologies" (p. 36) and the frustrations and quandaries such differences presented them. In particular, their differences revolved around competing assumptions about the nature of the world and how knowledge is constructed (e.g., socially constructed or from God's Word). Magolda and Ebben Gross reflected:

> Often, we wondered whether it was futile to study the SSC [Students Serving Christ] group, given that our constructed reality (i.e., our interpretations) of the group may not be valid in the eyes of SSC members, for whom God's Word was the only authentic source of wisdom. We worried that we might not be able to fulfill a major goal of the study, which was to share our interpretations with the SSC in the hopes that social change might occur. (p. 37)

What this example also demonstrates is the influence of theoretical perspective on ethics. Magolda and Ebben Gross's (2009) ethnographic study drew upon critical theories and hence their interest in social change. As Kelemen and Rumens (2008) argued, "the researcher's epistemological positioning has a heavy bearing on the actual course of action for engaging in and eventually resolving ethical dilemmas" (p. 2). Thus, the personal ethics and epistemological beliefs involved in negotiating such tensions in the research process are both central to and complicated by the ethical dimensions inherent in qualitative research projects. In summary, a number of complex issues, often taken for granted by researchers, such as those involving promises of confidentiality, anonymity, and to do no harm, make applying ethical principles to the realities of conducting qualitative research challenging as well as worthy of researchers' ethical sensitivity and skill in responding appropriately.

Phases of the Research Process and Ethical Issues

The ethical principles of confidentiality, anonymity, informed consent, privacy, respect, and do no harm are central to the process of conducting qualitative research and emerge as dilemmas throughout the research process. An understanding of these principles is important in the development of ethical sensitivity, but is not enough to effectively anticipate and resolve ethical dilemmas. As Eisner and Peshkin (1990) suggested principles must be interwoven with practice and reflection for the development of good judgment. In this section of the chapter, phases of the research process are examined in concert with ethical principles at stake. Examples from research projects are offered as a pathway for reflection upon the ethical issues involved and how a researcher might think about and deal with such issues. It is important to note that these examples are illustrative in nature and that every research project is unique and contextual; thus, there are no simple templates or recipes to follow when working through ethical dilemmas. Ethical principles provide helpful guidelines for thinking about issues—-they do not offer answers. Individual researchers, then, must learn to recognize ethical issues, discern what is most important in the situation, and act accordingly. To drive home the ubiquitous nature of ethics in qualitative research, L. M. Smith (1990) emphasized:

> At the most microlevel, every decision and every act in a qualitative research project can be placed against one's ethical standards. From the very conception of the problem to the entry procedures to the kind and place of sampling and data collecting on through to publication—the entire research process can be viewed in terms of its implications for the people involved. (p. 273)

Statement of Purpose and Research Questions

The statement of purpose and guiding research questions provide the organizing framework for a study. They provide participants and researcher alike with guideposts for what it is the researcher would like to learn more about. Although nearly every text on qualitative research design emphasizes participants' rights to be informed about the purpose of the study and what the researcher is asking from participants, these are not always easily accomplished because what is clear to the researcher may not be so clear to participants. Further, this ethical obligation is not simply providing the statement of purpose via the informed consent form, but is about the purpose statement itself. The importance of clarity in the writing of these statements of purpose and direct communication with participants about the goals of the researcher cannot be underestimated because participants do need to know something about the nature of their contributions and participation and what it is the researcher will ask of them in order to evaluate an invitation to participate. However, this kind of communication must be ongoing because some aspects of the research design may shift as the study unfolds.

Embedded in the need for clarity in the statement of purpose and research questions are two related ethical issues: the ethical imperative to "do good" and the need to create a purpose statement that is consistent with the chosen methodology. "Doing good" suggests that care must be taken to assure that the focus of a study does not in any way contribute to the marginalization or disempowerment (Creswell, 2013) of participants and that, in fact, there exists the potential for benefit to participants. Doing good is more than simply "doing no harm" in that striving for goodness suggests that the research works toward participant authority, fulfillment, and social change. This is particularly important when conducting research with or about traditionally underrepresented or disenfranchised individuals and/or communities or when a study is situated within a critical framework. Weis and Fine (2000) articulated this ethical responsibility well: "Because we write between the poor communities and social policy and because we seek to be taken seriously by both audiences, we know it is essential to think through the power, obligations, and responsibilities of social research" (p. 33). These commitments are first articulated in the statement of purpose and research questions for a study. In studying an underrepresented student population, a researcher would not want to use language in a statement of purpose that suggests presumed challenges, barriers, or deficits (even though real challenges may be experienced by such a population).

For example, in a study on an understudied population, college students who were homeless as adolescents, Jarrett Gupton (2009) explained that his purpose was "to understand the macro and micro influences that define the identity and life experiences of homeless youth and how those influences have constrained and enabled their educational pathways to postsecondary education" (p. 3). We see his continued careful attention to honoring his participants' life experiences by not further contributing to their marginalization in his research questions:

1. What is the relationship between the cultural narratives of homeless youth and the cultural repertoires homeless youth develop to gain access to higher education?
2. Do structure and agency interact to define a homeless identity and if so how?
3. Does a homeless identity mediate a student's perception of their educational experiences and pathways to higher education? (pp. 3–4)

By emphasizing a structural and cultural perspective rather than one that focuses on "the psychological detriment and physical harm that follows from the instability of homelessness" (Gupton, 2009, p. 4), we see an intentional effort to avoid harm to participants through the use of appropriate language that does not marginalize or devalue them or their experiences. This also conveys the respect the researcher has for understanding the experiences of those serving as participants in a study.

A second ethical issue connected to the statement of purpose and research questions resides in the relationship between the focus of the study and the chosen methodology. This issue has an ethical dimension to it because, if a researcher presents in the statement of purpose, for example, that a study is a critical ethnography, then this suggests a certain relationship between the researcher and participants as well as an emancipatory goal for the project. In essence, the methodological approach, which is reflected in the statement of purpose, communicates important information to participants about how they will be interacting with the researcher and about promised outcomes from participation. An example of this issue is found in the ethnographic study conducted by Magolda and Ebben Gross (2009) in which their interpretivist approach was at odds with the evangelical lens through which many of their participants viewed their participation in the study. Magolda and Ebben Gross (2012) described Matthew, the director of the Students Serving Christ (SSC) ministry, and his view on what the purpose of their study was to be: "Matthew assumed we would focus on the SSC's doctrine and mission, more so than its members' perceptions" (p. 240). Magolda and Ebben Gross found themselves navigating these epistemological differences between themselves and their participants in every stage of the research design, yet these negotiations began with differing viewpoints on what exactly the focus of the study was to be.

Further, an ethnographic inquiry suggests to participants the inclusion of participant observation and prolonged engagement. No shortcuts for meeting these methodological criteria are acceptable, although there may be instances when an ethnographer goes "undercover" as an unknown observer in some settings. However, a stated purpose of research should alert participants to the nature of their involvement with the researcher and their roles in data collection and analysis. Regardless of methodological approach, the researcher must be able to deliver on the promises communicated implicitly or explicitly in the statement of purpose and research questions.

One last issue relates in a more indirect way to the statement of purpose and research questions and that is the scope and timing of a study. As noted in earlier chapters, the focus of a study must be defined enough to be not only clear, but realistic. Once a study is initiated, the purpose has been communicated to participants, and consent has been granted, the researcher then has an ethical responsibility and obligation to follow through on the project in a timely way. Although many projects often take longer than initially planned due to a variety of factors that may not be anticipated at the early stages of design or always under the control of a researcher, failure to complete a project once initiated is a breach of trust, respect, and commitment made to participants, as well as an abuse of the power in the researcher–participant relationship. Researchers must be cognizant of the fact that following through on research projects is not just a function of—or reaction to—one's own commitments and time considerations, but also an obligation owed to participants who shared their time and expertise at the request of the researcher.

Data Collection

Ethical issues may emerge in the data collection phases of research because of how data are collected, where data are collected, and why data are collected. Once again, these factors are guided by methodological choice so that, for example, ethical issues related to participant observation will emerge more potently in ethnographic studies than in narrative inquiry. More importantly, these decisions must be anchored in a fundamental respect for research participants and research sites. Although researchers are deeply invested in and very familiar with the phenomenon they are investigating, participants may be less so and therefore vulnerable to what might be perceived as intrusions on their space, both physical and psychological. Whether collecting data via interviews or observations, researchers must be sensitive and attuned to how participants might receive and perceive interview questions and the scrutiny of observations. Any signs of discomfort, resistance, or other indications of emotional distress must be recognized and appropriately negotiated.

Some studies may elicit the revelation of painful memories or experiences that require the researcher to both respond empathically and know when consultation or referral to counseling is warranted. In a study involving college students working with people living with AIDS during an alternative spring break trip, several of the participants were moved to tears when talking about their interactions with the residents on the HIV/AIDS floor of a health center (Jones, Robbins, & LePeau, 2011). For one participant in particular, because of the perceived terminal nature of this disease, her interactions evoked great sadness and memories of loss in her life. A participant in another study discussed painful memories of a time when she suffered from sexual assault (Robbins, 2012). In instances such as these, the researcher must draw upon counseling skills and professional judgment to determine whether consultation with a professional or referral is warranted. Conducting research and conducting counseling sessions are not one and the same, although the personal nature of many topics and the relationships formed between a researcher and participant may give the perception that these boundaries are blurred. The researcher has an ethical obligation to respond humanely to these instances, but not to act as professional counselor.

Another potential ethical issue related to data collection revolves around the collection of data that the researcher *hopes* to gather. The researcher necessarily frames the focus of the study through the statement of purpose and research questions and then goes out to ask questions and/or observe the phenomenon under investigation in order to elicit some answers and responses to these questions. Interview questions, for example, then have the potential to lead participants in a certain direction in their responses. Although some of this is unavoidable by the sheer construction of questions, care must be taken not to direct participants so much that they are telling the researcher's story rather than their own. Weis and Fine (2000) referred to this as the "voyeuristic search for 'good' stories" (p. 48). They went on to explain how these stories got constructed among their research team:

> While engaging in interviewing, the research assistants would gather informally and share stories. We talked about respondents not showing up for interviews, the lives of interviewees, "funny things that happened along the way," our pain, and our early understanding of the material. The words and phrases thrown around included: "interesting," "boring," "nothing out of the ordinary," "you should have heard this," and "this one has great stories." (p. 48)

These somewhat natural and human reactions to what has been heard also assign judgment to the stories told that reflect the researcher's perspective and point of view and must be checked because they could lead to missing important, though perhaps unexpected, themes in the data. For example, in a narrative study on the perceived outcomes of a high school service-learning graduation requirement, Jones, Segar, and Gasiorski (2008) were initially struck by the absence of a "story" in relation to the way in which the benefits of such requirements were discussed in the literature on service-learning. What was "storyworthy" (Chase, 2005, p. 661) in their data was not what was expected. That is, the participants focused their stories on meeting the requirement for graduation (similar to their other graduation requirements) rather than on any benefits associated with service-learning.

One of the reasons researchers are drawn to the "good story" is because data collection is erroneously constructed as a one-way conversation, leaving no room for reciprocal conversations with participants. Opportunities for reciprocal dialogue and conversations, even in those methodological approaches that call for a more structured approach to interviewing, create the space for researchers and participants to reflect on the meaning-making process together. In reflecting on an ethical principle that guides her research practices, Elisa Abes wrote,

> I don't think I should expect participants to discuss anything with me that I would not discuss with them. Although in the context of teaching, this quote from bell hooks (1994) about engaged pedagogy remains very prominent in my thinking on this matter. "Empowerment cannot happen if [professors] refuse to be vulnerable while encouraging students to take risks" (p. 21). Although my earlier research was not critical in nature, I did

want it to be empowering for participants. But even more so, it felt like I was exploiting them if I asked them to talk about things I wouldn't talk about (and it reinforced the power difference). Although this was usually very comfortable for me, there were times when they asked me questions about topics I typically wouldn't discuss with people I don't know well. And I shied away from their questions of me. My experience with this conundrum guides me as I now advise newer researchers about the ethics of reciprocity and empowerment. (E. S. Abes, personal communication, October 1, 2012)

The issue of researcher disclosure in the data collection process is an important one to consider. Some research contexts or cultures may make this decision even tougher.

Conducting international research or research across cultural and linguistic differences can pose another set of ethical dilemmas. In addition to grounding of informed consent in Western values, and therefore not always understood in the way U.S. IRB intends, gatekeepers involved in access to participants and data collection may influence participation and the quality of the data collected. In conducting case studies of higher education institutions in international contexts, Kristen Renn captured the ethical intersections of consent, access, and data collection:

I worried about obtaining genuinely informed consent when, although the concepts about which I was inquiring translated linguistically and conceptually into local languages, the concept of "informed consent" is not one that translates into all cultures. As I was gaining access to participants through institutional gatekeepers (as is common in qualitative research), I was worried about ethical questions related to presumably "voluntary" participation when I did not understand the local language. For example, at one campus I was invited to do a focus group with students from a particular section of a course. The institutional gatekeeper asked the instructor to make the students available to me. The instructor was present during the focus group and translated a few questions into the local language when it seemed clear that the students did not fully understand what I was asking. My ethical concerns thus centered on the voluntary nature of participation in a culture where teachers are not to be questioned or disobeyed and the quality of the data obtained when an authority figure was present during the focus group. (K. A. Renn, personal communication, August 15, 2012)

Given the many strategies for data collection as well as the near endless array of settings in which data may be collected, attention to the ethical issues and dilemmas that may arise are important researcher considerations, in part because the quality of data collected is inextricably linked to data analysis and interpretation.

Data Analysis and Interpretation

Analyzing and interpreting data carry with them a significant ethical responsibility to tell the story of the research and the participants who are part of a study in a way that participants themselves recognize as their story (Jones, 2002). This is particularly important when the researcher claims a constructivist approach. Critical studies complicate this ethical tenet because of the emphasis on structures of inequality that pattern individual lives. Moreover, some scholars would further question the criteria for what constitutes a "true" story. Despite the prevailing wisdom that researchers should negotiate their interpretations of data with participants, Talburt (2004) suggested that this presumed negotiation "promises a true story through participant verification . . . by privileging as a goal of research the representation of the emic, or insider, views that participants offer" (p. 88). She and others acknowledge that, by telling a story that mirrors the way in which participants would tell it, other stories are left out.

An example of the influence of theoretical perspective on data analysis and interpretation is found in a narrative study focused on students' experiences as participants in an alternative spring break trip working with people living with HIV/AIDS. Data was analyzed once, once using a constructivist approach and the second using a critical lens. This analytic shift changed the research questions and the stories told as evidenced by descriptions of each:

Constructivist approach: The purpose of this study was to investigate students' narratives about the meaning they made as they crossed physical and developmental borders on an ASB program focused on HIV/AIDS. In particular, specific research questions included: (a) what is to be learned about the nature of the experience through stories told over time?; (b) what are the narratives associated with the participants' sense of self, relationships with others, and future plans?; and (c) what difference did a trip focused on HIV/AIDS make to the narratives told? (Jones, Robbins, & LePeau, 2011, p. 29).

Critical approach: The purpose of this study was to explore the possibilities and limitations of service-learning by deconstructing the narratives about HIV/AIDS that emerged among college students who participated in an alternative spring break (AB) program. To unmask the conditions that cultivated these narratives, we investigated the following questions: (a) what structures of power and privilege surrounded and shaped students' experiences around HIV/AIDS and the meaning they made of those experiences?; (b) what narratives, including silent or implicit narratives, emerged about HIV/AIDS?; and (c) what do these narratives suggest about the possibilities and limitations of service-learning? (Jones, LePeau, & Robbins, 2013).

It is clear that results from a constructivist approach will more likely be recognizable to participants and reflect back to them, even in an analytic way, their experiences and the meaning made of them. A critical approach is more likely to yield narratives and interpretations that illuminate unstated sentiments or even stories that are not recognized by participants and thus surfaces ethical decisions a researcher must make related to presenting participants in a light they might not intend or understand.

Another example that illustrates the complexities of connecting theoretical perspectives to data analysis is found in the study about required service-learning mentioned earlier (Jones, Segar, & Gasiorski, 2008). As noted, we were initially struck by what we perceived to be the absence of a "story." In a constructivist study, this phenomenon could imply that there really wasn't anything to co-construct because there weren't any "good stories." However, using a critical lens to interrogate silences and implicit stories, much can be analyzed in terms of the problematic nature of mandating service-learning in high schools. If the critical lens is not applied, the constructivist researcher may unwittingly end up with a "victim-blaming" narrative (e.g., "these students sure are superficial") compared with one that emphasizes more structural and policy domains (e.g., "this requirement is not accomplishing its objectives and is doing social harm"). These decisions regarding data analysis and how to interpret what don't appear to be "good stories" are ethical ones.

One important point implied in these examples is that data analysis and interpretation are much more than simply reading transcripts and describing what is there. Novice qualitative researchers often identify this as "looking for themes." Data analysis is a time-consuming and labor intensive process that requires immersion in the data and continual reading and rereading of transcripts as codes, themes, patterns, and categories are generated. The more time (both in terms of quantity of time and quality of time) the researcher is immersed in the data, the stronger the analyses and interpretations will be. This time is required to meet the ethical obligations the researcher has to participants and to the research project. Respecting participants and assuring the integrity of the research process are ethical imperatives that guide analysis and interpretation.

Several strategies exist to check the researcher's analyses and interpretations. Building on the issues addressed in Chapter Seven regarding evidentiary inadequacy, the readers of qualitative studies must see a clear connection between what are presented as data and what are offered as interpretations of the data. Most typically, rich description and many quotations from transcripts are provided so that the reader may join the researcher on the inside of the data. It is not acceptable to simply tell the reader what is important or offer one quote for each theme because this does not provide the kind of evidence and analysis that a reader needs to trace the claims a researcher is making back to the data itself. As fully presented in Chapter Seven, "evidentiary inadequacy" (Erickson, 1986) is in fact an ethical issue because it relates to the integrity of data analysis and interpretation.

Implicit in a discussion of the importance of providing sufficient evidence for the claims the researcher makes is that evidence of an analytic process is also provided. Data analysis typically involves a process of moving from concrete words and descriptions to more abstract conceptualizations. This process results in the naming of themes intended to capture what is going on in the data. Therefore, these themes should offer a glimpse into the richness of the data rather than simply convey a non-descriptive generic name. For example, in a master's thesis exploring the experiences of allies to GLBT students, an early draft of the presentation of results included theme names such as *awareness of self* and *advocacy as allies*. Neither of these theme names gives the reader any idea of the texture or nuances of awareness or advocacy. Was it increased awareness? Shifting awareness? Highly visible advocacy? Limited advocacy? Subsequent versions, after going back to the data and taking a more critical and analytical look included a much more complex picture of what was really going on for these self-perceived allies. The resulting analysis included theme names such as *perceived consequences to self, rationalizing non-ally behavior*, and *influence of religious and political contexts*. This is the truth-telling dimension in the ethics of qualitative inquiry—the researcher must spend significant time with the data and the analytic process to get the interpretation of the data close to shedding analytical light on the phenomenon of interest.

Accurate interpretations (although we recognize that even this word accurate is contested and influenced by epistemological and theoretical considerations) are advanced through the use of trustworthiness strategies (as discussed in Chapter Two). One central strategy is to involve the participants in data analysis and interpretation. This is often referred to as *co-construction*, yet the mechanics of truly accomplishing co-construction are both time consuming and complicated. Abes captured these dynamics:

> In thinking about how I use interview transcripts, it's important to me that I consider them to be life stories, rather than only "data." As I write, I am investing in co-constructing these stories. But as well-intentioned as I might be, I fear I've taken ownership of the participants' stories for my own research agenda. As I have interpreted, reinterpreted, and re-written the stories, they become less co-constructed . . . . Co-constructing stories requires, at a minimum, at the very minimum, asking the participants to review and discuss my interpretations. Needing them to be part of this process has raised several ethical concerns.
>
> First, some analysis that has shaped how I tell their stories focused on my understandings of the students' cognitive complexity. Some of my interpretations have been grounded in inconsistencies within and omissions from their stories. Students cannot provide any check on interpretations that exceed their cognitive capacity. These interpretations are thus ultimately based on my own biased understanding of how they make meaning of their identity. More recently, I have applied queer theory and intersectional analyses to some of the participants' stories. Doing so raises concerns because the participants might not be conscious of, or necessarily interested in, the ways in which I perceive power structures to shape their stories. To what extent then ought I involve participants in co-constructing

these stories when I am overlaying onto their interviews a theoretical perspective that tells "their" story in a way they might not think or know to tell it. Despite this quandary, I will still tell a critical theory story out of an ethical obligation to reveal how power shapes reality, but know I need to be respectful of the participants in doing so.

I have also questioned how much time I ethically can expect participants to invest in a study. Asking for time beyond data collection sometimes feels selfish, and even exploitative, knowing that whatever personal benefits they initially reaped from this research are diminishing. Yet not working with them to co-construct the story also feels disrespectful. At a minimum, I invited them to review and discuss the analysis and manuscript and trust they will not do so only out of a sense of obligation. One particular issue I ran into during this process was that I could not locate one of my participants when writing a manuscript that incorporated her stories. Despite some discomfort around the ethics of using her stories, I have continued to do so for several years because I believe she has an important story to tell that can benefit others, which was her motivation for participating in the study. I hope I am telling a version of her story with which she would be comfortable. (E. S. Abes, personal communication, October 1, 2012)

The ethics of data analysis are at the heart of good qualitative research. Reflection on the ethical obligations to fully engage in the analytic process is crucial before, during, and after the research process. As summarized well by Soltis (1990)," Description is not neutral. It is the interpretive result of an interpersonal engagement with others and as such has the potential to be ethically sensitive, especially with regard to the principle of respect for persons" (p. 252).

Writing and Publication

Lamott (1994) connected ethics and the writing process with this cogent passage:

> Becoming a writer is about becoming conscious. When you're conscious and writing from a place of insight and simplicity and real caring about truth, you have the ability to throw lights on for your reader. He or she will recognize his or her life and truth in what you say, in the pictures you have painted . . . . Tell the truth as you understand it. If you're a writer, you have a moral obligation to do this. (pp. 225–226)

Although writing is central to the communication of results and discussion in both qualitative and quantitative studies, writing and rewriting are the primary means of communication in qualitative research. It is in and through the writing process that meaning takes shape and insights are sharpened. Therefore, excellent writing skills are crucial to qualitative research in order to "throw the lights on" for readers. Good writing requires significant practice and benefits from multiple perspectives. We never submit anything for publication that several others have not read and proofed for us and on which they have not offered feedback and commentary. This not only improves our writing but also assures that we are communicating clearly and succinctly. What becomes known about your research comes through what is written, and, therefore, the writing process carries with it a great responsibility. Telling and not telling are equally powerful, and this power most often resides with the researcher. What one writes—or withholds—has significant consequences for the research and to the participants. This can get complicated if, for example, what the researcher writes is not received well by participants. They might quibble with what is written but might be more concerned that it does not reflect well on them. Related, if the research is funded by an external source and/or by individuals with specific expectations about the findings, the researcher may experience pressure to soften or suppress certain findings (Creswell, 2013). This dilemma may be a test of the researcher's integrity if continued funding is in jeopardy and should be negotiated in the initial stages of the research process.

Ethical issues also exist as researchers consider the dissemination of results. For example, is there an ethical obligation to share results and publish findings in a reasonable amount of time? We would suggest that the answer is yes because herein lies the public good in research. However, researchers cannot always control what consumers of research actually do with the results. It is important for researchers to consider the possible uses for their results and the potential consequences for their participants or the setting in which the research was conducted.

Strategies for Working Through Ethical Issues

No simple recipes or templates exist for definitively anticipating and responding to ethical issues in qualitative inquiry. However, the combination of knowledge, reflexivity, and experience (action) increases the likelihood that researchers will be sensitive to the ethical dimensions of research and respond appropriately. Lincoln (1990) offered this overarching principle, which has stood the test of time, referred to as a "categorical imperative" to guide action:

> Behave as if the principle underlying your action were to become—by your will alone—a universal law of nature. That is, act in such a way that you would not be distressed to discover that the principle undergirding your own action were now a law that could be enacted by others upon you. (p. 291)

Using this underlying principle, we offer the following strategies as a beginning place:

- Anticipate ethical issues that may come up and integrate these into the research design process.

- Develop rapport with participants and work on sustaining relationships through ongoing and honest communication and dialogue about the research process.
- Identify an ethics "mentor" or those with whom you can consult as issues emerge.
- Join a writing group or research team so that you can learn from others' ethical dilemmas and gain experience in resolving them.
- Familiarize yourself with and adhere to ethical codes (ACPA-College Student Educators International) and ethical guidelines provided in style manuals (e.g., American Psychological Association [APA]) and by professional associations such as the Association for the Study of Higher Education (ASHE) and the American Educational Research Association (AERA).
- Take seriously the reflective process on ethical issues, which helps connect ethical sensitivity to action.
- Your greatest ethical commitment must be to the participants in your study. All research decisions must be evaluated against the likelihood of avoiding harm and doing good. This is the ethical injunction to *care*, which is not simply, as Noddings (1984) wrote, putting yourself in others' shoes, but instead receiving the other into oneself such that their reality "becomes a real possibility" for you (p. 14).

Summary

No researcher can escape the ethical dilemmas posed by qualitative inquiry. The purpose of this chapter was to highlight some of the overarching ethical principles at work in qualitative research as well as particular issues that emerge at each stage of the research process. As was mentioned in this chapter, the ethical terrain is not a static one, but rather shifts with changing policy, procedures, and contemporary situations that increase attention to ethical issues at stake. For example, as discussed in Chapter Six and again in Chapter Nine, the use of the Internet and technology in research is raising ethical issues not considered previously. How does a researcher treat data that are easily accessible via domains such as Facebook? What does consent look like in these publicly available mediums? Does authenticity matter in a social media environment in which an individual can create and re-create (several times a day) the persona they present on-line? These kinds of questions contain ethical dimensions and require careful consideration. Our hope is that the knowledge advanced in this chapter will increase the ethical sensitivity of researchers and improve the skills needed to connect sensitivity to action, even in the face of previously unconsidered issues. Ultimately, both sensitivity and skill depend upon respect—for the research process, the research setting, and the people in it. When respect is diligently and deliberately practiced, all involved in the research process benefit because, as Lawrence-Lightfoot (1999) noted, "Respectful relationships also have a way of sustaining and replicating themselves" (p. 10).

Exercises

Chapter-related

1. What makes an issue an ethical one? How does a researcher develop ethical sensitivity?
2. Identify 3–4 ethical principles central to the conducting of qualitative research.
3. Identify specific challenges that may emerge as a researcher applies ethical principles to the realities of conducting qualitative research. What strategies might a researcher use to help navigate and resolve these issues?

Research Process

1. As you have conceived your research project thus far (e.g., statement of purpose, research questions, sampling strategies, data collection, and data analysis and interpretation), consider each step in your research design for the ethical issues that may emerge. Identify 2–3 specific ethical issues that you anticipate at each stage.
2. For each ethical issue that you identify, jot down notes about what principles will guide your thinking about each issue as well as specific steps you will take to address each issue.
3. How does your worldview and theoretical perspective intersect with the defining of and working through ethical issues? For example, how does a study designed as feminist inquiry raise a different set of ethical issues from one designed as constructivist?

9 Lessons Learned and Future Directions

As we acknowledged in the Preface, we came to this project through different life and research experiences. However, throughout our writing and rewriting process, we maintained our commitment to providing a good and helpful resource on qualitative inquiry for higher education and student affairs researchers and practitioners. As we prepared for writing this second edition, we reflected upon what we have learned about qualitative inquiry in the years between the first and second editions from our own research, from using the first edition with graduate students and practitioners interested in learning about qualitative research, and from reading the work of others published in scholarly outlets. As we conclude this second edition of the book, we use this final chapter to identify several new lessons learned, which come out of our evolving understanding of qualitative inquiry and ability to engage with research in more sophisticated ways. We also discuss what we see as future directions in qualitative research and speculate on the impact of these directions on research practice in higher education and student affairs.

Before we turn to the *new* lessons learned, we revisit those lessons learned discussed in the first edition of this book. We do so because examining the new lessons learned in relation to the *old* lessons provides a glimpse into both our evolution as researchers and methodologists as well as into the evolving questions evident in the area of qualitative inquiry.

Lessons Learned

What follows is the list of lessons learned we created in the first edition of *Negotiating the Complexities of Qualitative Research in Higher Education* (Jones, Torres, & Arminio, 2006). We developed these lessons from our experiences conducting research as well as in dialogue with one another to determine overlapping themes and points of complementarity. Each lesson contains suggestions to the reader that we hoped would provide guidance and be helpful to researchers. Although we will next offer *new* lessons learned, we think that the suggestions embedded in the initial lessons learned are still useful ones.

1. Consider your experience as something that provides inspiration—or consternation—and situate your research in that dynamic. Tap into an abiding concern you carry with you. If you can't figure this out, talk with trusted friends and colleagues about their perceptions of your patterns of interest and curiosities. Reflect on and analyze your past experiences—where do your commitments lie? What stirs you or gets you fired up? What aspects of your professional practice need improvement or just don't make sense to you? Research is too often experienced as a burden rather than as the possibility of illuminating practice and providing direction for improved practice.

2. Identifying your abiding concern also requires that you acknowledge the presence of self in the research process. The tendency to avoid our own experiences in research is a remnant of a more quantitative objectivist stance and is contrary to the tenets of interpretivist qualitative inquiry. We believe that all research, quantitative and qualitative alike, comes out of the subjectivity and worldview of the researcher. Placing this in the foreground of research is a strength of qualitative inquiry. However, truly understanding how one's positionality influences the research process requires constant attention and thoughtfulness.

3. Another strength of qualitative research is the opportunity to delve into the complexities of life. This includes the possibility of illuminating multiple perspectives or an intensive look at one perspective. Qualitative research, when conducted congruently with philosophical and methodological elements, and when it meets the criteria of goodness and responds to ethical considerations, offers insight beyond what is obvious, assumed, or floating on the surface of phenomena. Researching a complex phenomenon is not easy. Rarely do we engage in qualitative research to prove a point or affirm what is known. Rather, questions suitable to qualitative inquiry provoke, illuminate, complicate, surprise, and emancipate that which we are coming to know and understand. This more dynamic process calls for both flexibility and clarity of focus. The lesson we offer here is not to be content with obvious or expected interpretations, but rather to push yourself to stretch and work toward what is interrelated, webbed, complicated, and difficult to put into words. Unfortunately, there are plenty of examples from published qualitative research that are merely descriptive and barely skim the surface of what is going on in the data. The challenge is to go deeper than what a casual read would provide—to delve into greater meaning making and interpretation.

4. We know our work benefits from the perspectives of others who read and provide feedback to our interpretations and writing. As you conceptualize and design studies, and then as you write the results of your work, always consult with others. These should be individuals both familiar and unfamiliar with your area of focus because all perspectives contribute to the overall strength of research. We would never submit anything for publication without first having it reviewed by trusted colleagues and then

responding to their feedback. Identify individuals who have strengths in different areas to read and evaluate your work: someone who writes better than you do and can edit and proof your work, someone who you know will challenge your ideas and interpretations, someone with greater knowledge of the context of your research than you have, and someone who has no background in your focus to ascertain how clear your work is to those reading about this area for the first time. Qualitative research benefits from multiple perspectives in all phases. (Jones, Torres, & Arminio, 2006, pp. 189–190)

New Lessons Learned

We now turn to new lessons learned; that is, what the past six years of work as researchers, methodologists, teachers, and educators has taught us about conducting qualitative inquiry. As noted previously, in some ways, the lessons that follow represent how we have evolved as researchers in our thinking and knowledge base, the kinds of questions about which we are wondering, the issues with which we struggle, and the experiences we have had in conducting qualitative inquiry.

1. Even though the quantity of published qualitative research has increased and the quality somewhat improved, quantitative approaches still rule. This can be seen in the publication of very poorly designed and executed qualitative studies as well as in the quantitative and positivist principles used to critique some very good qualitative studies. For example, a qualitative manuscript may get flat out rejected because an editorial board member views a "very small sample size" as a fatal flaw (in that it can't be corrected in a revised version of a manuscript unless the researcher goes back out to the field to add participants). In a grant application, Susan and a colleague proposed a grounded theory study on the process of developing civic identity. The proposal was rejected because a reviewer critiqued the design as "sampling on the dependent variable."

Demerath (2006) recalled a keynote address at the Congress of Qualitative Inquiry by Linda Tuhiwai-Smith who made the point that "Qualitative researchers know more about [quantitative researchers] and their work, than they know about us and ours" (p. 100). Indeed, we have learned that, despite the growing attention to qualitative research approaches in many fields, the prevailing sentiment is that real scientists conduct quantitative research and that anyone can do qualitative work. Ask anyone engaged in qualitative research if it is "easy" and we suspect you will get a resounding no. Yet, in interviews for faculty positions, for example, qualitative researchers are often asked if they are qualified to advise quantitative dissertations, but the corresponding question asked of quantitative researchers is rarely uttered. At the end of a research talk as part of an interview for a faculty position, Susan was queried by a faculty member in attendance about her data analysis. The question was something like, "How did you come up with these results?" The implication, of course, was that Susan had simply made them up, rather than the more precise and scientific approach of statistical analysis. Susan proceeded, by way of response to this question, to painstakingly detail every step of the analytic process so that the questioner could see the systematic approach to data analysis used.

Demerath (2006) proposed several strategies that qualitative researchers might adopt in order to function effectively in a climate characterized by limited conceptions of what constitutes scientifically based research (SBR). These include understanding the ideological and methodological underpinnings of the SBR movement; educating peers about what constitutes qualitative research and it's unique value; developing greater transparency in research design, presentation of findings, and development of trustworthiness criteria; utilizing mixed methods research designs; and engaging in research that advances public interests and public good (Demerath, 2006). The important lesson is that it is important to be multi-vocal when it comes to scientifically based research. That is, good qualitative researchers must be impeccably knowledgeable about qualitative approaches but also well versed in quantitative rationales and research strategies. The most effective defense against the presumption of quantitative superiority is to understand quantitative approaches while also producing high quality qualitative research. The importance of doing good work is paramount in part because there will be some individuals who will never be convinced of the contributions of qualitative approaches. Thus, qualitative researchers must stand by their own high quality research rather than put all their effort into swaying skeptics to a different point of view.

2.   We have learned more about the contribution of blending methodological approaches and incorporating theoretical perspectives into research designs, which add to the complexity and sophistication of analysis and interpretation. However, as the quote that follows suggests, you first need to know "the rules" before you can begin amending them. We think this holds true to conducting qualitative research as well.

> Some set great value on method, while others pride themselves on dispensing with method. To be without method is deplorable, but to depend on method entirely is worse. You must first learn to observe the rules faithfully; afterwards, modify them according to your intelligence and capacity. (Sze & Wang, *The Tao of Painting*, 1963/1701, p. 17)

This lesson results in two observations. The first is that many qualitative researchers do not draw from primary methodological sources when designing studies and writing methodology sections in manuscripts. As much as we think our book is a useful resource, it is not a primary source. Reading primary sources will enable researchers to both understand the historical and disciplinary foundations for particular approaches and design elements, but will also enable a more sophisticated treatment of both the topic under investigation and the methodological approach to it. What this means is that if a researcher proposes a grounded theory study, then we would expect to see citations from Strauss, Corbin, Charmaz, and Clarke, for example; or if a phenomenological study is described, then the philosophical foundations reflected in the works of Husserl, Heidegger, or Moustakas should be referenced.

However, the way in which primary sources are used is also important to consider. We find that when writing up methodology sections of research studies, some researchers simply pluck the classic explanatory lines from methodologists and stick them into their text, yet they appear disconnected from the actual study being described. That is, when a researcher describes a study as "constructivist" in nature, this quotation from Denzin and Lincoln (2000b) quickly follows: "The constructivist paradigm assumes a relativist ontology (there are multiple realities), a subjectivist epistemology (knower and respondent co-create understandings), and a naturalistic (in the natural world) set of methodological procedures" (p. 21). Augmenting one's claim of a constructivist study with a quotation from a primary source is important to do, but the researcher must go on to demonstrate an understanding of what exactly this means and how the quotation reference connects directly to the study described. In the example just provided, why is a constructivist approach appropriate for a specific study and how will co-construction be accomplished? It is not enough to indicate, for example, that the constant comparative method of data analysis described by Corbin and Strauss (2008) will be used. The researcher must explain and justify why this method is appropriate and how it will be implemented in the study at hand. Failing to draw from primary sources suggests both a surface understanding of the methodological approaches and designs proposed and executed as well as calls into question the credibility of the researcher. Yet, the researcher must both draw from primary sources as well as demonstrate an in-depth understanding of the material used in relation to his or her own research study. The reference list in this book points the reader to a number of primary sources to address this potential limitation.

The second observation related to the lesson about learning the rules first is that many novice researchers are attracted to critical and emancipatory approaches to qualitative inquiry. The draw of social justice research will be discussed in the next lesson learned, but we want to suggest again that beginning researchers need to learn the fundamentals of various approaches before blending multiple perspectives. For example, as just noted, a researcher conducting a narrative study must first be able to explain why a narrative methodological approach is suitable to the proposed study and demonstrate how the narrative approach is integrated into all elements of the research design (e.g., sampling, data collection, and data analysis should all take a narrative approach). Then, after settling into a thorough understanding of a particular approach, such as narrative inquiry, a researcher may decide to add the layer of a theoretical perspective, such as critical theory or critical race theory. Again, the use of a specific methodological approach and theoretical perspective should shift how each element of the research design is considered and implemented. The process just discussed is reflected in the narrative study discussed in earlier chapters exploring the influences of social identity on students' meaning making associated with a short-term immersion program focused on HIV/AIDS (Jones, Robbins, LePeau, 2011; Jones, LePeau, & Robbins, 2013). These researchers began by analyzing the data using constructivist approaches and then turned to a critical analysis to interrogate the taken-for-granted assumptions and implicit stories in students' narratives. However, the critical analysis followed the constructivist one because the researchers considered it important to begin by foregrounding the students' narratives as they understood them before taking them apart through a critical lens.

Similarly, mixed methods research is gaining in popularity, yet deciding to conduct a mixed methods study involves epistemological and philosophical considerations rather than simply adding a survey to an interview study or open-ended questions at the end of a survey. For example, Vasti and colleagues (Torres, Martinez, Wallace, Medrano, Robledo, & Hernandez, 2012) investigated the influence of adult experiences and life events on the development of Latino ethnic identity through the use of a grounded survey. However, the authors noted that the construction of the survey was based upon central characteristics of narrative inquiry and questions were designed to elicit participants' stories and meaning making. First learning, understanding, and practicing the "rules" enables a researcher to then move into more sophisticated designs and interpretations, such as the more pragmatic approach used by Vasti and her colleagues, which blended a constructivist emphasis on meaning making with the more positivist approach of survey design. Such blending is challenging to accomplish if done well because researchers must both pay attention to and understand how differing epistemological worldviews come together in such an approach and then also defend such blending with a rationale that incorporates both philosophical and methodological considerations.

3.   As noted above, many researchers in higher education and student affairs find the promise of social justice research appealing, and for good reasons. Denzin and Giardina (2009) described this time as an "historical present that cries out for emancipator visions, for visions that inspire transformative inquiries, and for inquiries that can provide moral authority to move people to struggle and resist oppression" (p. 11). However, what we have learned is that, even in the presence of good intentions, the realities of conducting social justice research with emancipatory results is far more complex than the rhetoric and discourse surrounding this aim suggests. How does a researcher *really* conduct emancipatory research? What does research that results in social justice outcomes actually look like? Who are the researchers best suited to conduct emancipatory research? These are some of the questions with which we have wrestled.

Celine-Marie Pascale (2011) also raised questions in relation to research that claims social justice as a goal. Her questions included the following:

> Is social research for social justice simply a matter of exposing inequalities? Is it a matter of supplying remedies for inequalities? Of producing knowledge that empowers people to act in their own best interests? Does social research that is sensitive to issues of social justice require an ethic of transparency? Of co-participation? To what extent does social research for social justice require us to expose the machinations of power? (p. 5)

Although writing primarily about observational research, Angrosino and Rosenberg (2011) tackled these questions and suggested three ways in which researchers may pursue the emancipatory outcomes of social justice research. The first strategy relates to the commitment the researcher has to a particular population and the presence of real empathy (which is much more than establishing rapport). Angrosino and Rosenberg described this relationship: "the researcher should be directly connected to those marginalized by mainstream society; that is, the researchers should feel some sort of kinship (be it political or emotional) with those being studied and not treat them solely as depersonalized objects of research" (p. 474). Researchers must think carefully about what this means; that is, how might one become "connected to those marginalized?" This does not necessarily mean that a researcher must be *of* this marginalized community, but that the relationship must be a real one, for both the researcher and participants, and that the questions investigated by a researcher must be significant to those marginalized, not only those of interest to the researcher.

The second way in which researchers can promote social justice, which is related to the first way, is in the kinds of data collected and considering where expertise and authority are located. That is, as Angrosino and Rosenberg (2011) pointed out, ". . . we are in the habit of asking questions based primarily of our scholarly (i.e., distanced) knowledge of the situation at hand. We move in a more productive direction if we begin to ask questions based on our experience of life as it is actually experienced in the community under study" (p. 474). This requires knowing enough about the community in which research is situated and grounding questions in this knowledge. Some researchers, when researching outside of their own communities, appear to be working out some of their own issues through conducting social justice research, which is rarely appropriate, especially in these contexts. The third point relates to the role of the researcher and points to the need for social justice researchers to become advocates, "which might mean becoming a spokesperson for causes and issues already defined by the community" (p. 474). This last point necessarily shifts the role of the researcher away from a recorder of events, patterns, behaviors, and meaning making to one who advances particular commitments and causes, which brings with it ethical questions (as discussed in Chapter Eight).

Even by paying attention to these three imperatives—becoming directly connected to the community under study, basing data collection on the knowledge within this community, and working *with* the community to advance a cause of importance to that community (Angrosino & Rosenberg, 2011)—results may not necessarily advance social justice and emancipatory outcomes because that is complicated work that involves more than a single researcher's investigation. For example, we see social justice researchers claiming to "give voice" to the experiences of those silenced in research. Yet, doesn't the language of *giving* voice foreground the power of the researcher? And how does one listen for what is silent? Or as Queer Crit researcher Mitsunori Misawa (2012) asked when writing about social justice narrative inquiry, "How can their unheard narratives be heard?" (p. 241). We raise these questions not to discourage social justice research, but instead to promote more discussion about just how complex this work can be. We do think that attention to the principles and strategies outlined in this lesson learned will enable researchers to get closer to these imperatives, but this also requires ongoing reflection about commitments and values, the kinds of relationships researchers have with those on the margins of mainstream society and how they are perceived by those communities, and how a research design would necessarily shift to incorporate emancipatory processes and potential outcomes. What we have learned is that it is far more difficult to turn one's commitments into reality, and some researchers accomplish this better than others because of their own identities, their knowledge of different communities, and their abilities to conduct reciprocal and respectful research.

Future Directions

We now turn to a discussion of what we see as potential future directions in the area of qualitative inquiry in higher education and student affairs. We do so not to offer predictions of what is to come but more so to advance discussion about the evolution of qualitative inquiry in higher education and student affairs contexts in a way that grapples with the complexities of this work. We also want to point readers in the direction of the multiple editions of *The Sage Handbook of Qualitative Research* (now in its fourth edition) because each edition ends with a section on the future of qualitative research. Reading each one provides a glimpse of evolving perceptions of future possibilities and issues, and the fourth edition offers the most recent iteration of "where we might go from where we've been," which is the title of the chapter written by Judith Preissle. We draw some of our ideas from this chapter but also situate the future directions we identify in the context of higher education and student affairs research. To that end, the future directions we discuss are using technology and social media, operating in a context that requires external funding and increasing viability for funding, and expanding thinking about the role of methodologies in qualitative inquiry.

Technology and Social Media

Although precisely predicting what changes technology and social media will bring to conducting qualitative inquiry is impossible given the speed with which change is occurring, we do know without a doubt that technology has the potential to transform some fundamental elements of research. Indeed, it was not that long ago that reference to the use of technology in qualitative inquiry referred to conducting interviews via email! Now, and into the future, qualitative researchers are faced with and engaged in uses of technology that change the shape and form of the boundaries of research sites; research question possibilities; sampling and data collection strategies; participant identities and representations; and ethical issues associated with privacy, informed consent, and interpretation, to name but a few. We have addressed technology in other chapters in this book (see Chapters Six and Eight); here, we raise several questions as we anticipate what the future holds in relation to technology, social media, and qualitative research in higher education and student affairs.

The first question relates to the phenomenon of distance learning in higher education. Currently there exist institutions of higher education that deliver their entire curriculum and educational program via distance learning. The overwhelming success (if success is measured by sheer numbers and the backing of elite universities) of Coursera and MOOCs (massive open online course) portends a future where the great majority of students will never step foot on the grounds of a campus, which for many years has served as the research site of many a higher education and student affairs researcher. As Dan Butin (2012) poignantly conveyed in relation to the teaching mission of colleges and universities,

> Indeed. If I can take the vast majority of my general education requirements from top-notch professors at famous universities in the comfort of my bedroom, why should I ever again have to pay $400 per credit to get dressed, drive 20 miles to my regional college, search for a parking space, and attend a lecture in a massive auditorium with 300 other students listening to an adjunct I don't know go through a PowerPoint lecture I could have scrolled through at 1.25X speed in the MITx course? In one fell swoop, every introductory college course in the country has been put on notice.

So what does this growing phenomenon have to do with qualitative research in higher education? Not only will access to students and their perceptions of their experiences change dramatically, but research questions that address student learning and development, student meaning making, perceptions of campus climate, and student engagement, to name a few, will all look very different in an on-line, distance learning environment. In fact, the core of what has long been considered "the student experience" will fundamentally change. This will require qualitative researchers to rethink all elements of a research design, including the ways in which data are collected given this changing context.

Technology also requires researchers to re-imagine themselves as researchers. Not only is the institution of higher education embracing technology in new and previously unimagined ways, and the majority of college students are adept at using multiple technology platforms and engaging in on-line environments and social networking, but also researchers must rethink their roles, skills, and research-based relationships. Angrosino and Rosenberg (2011) made this point in discussing the changing nature of "observation" given advances in technology. They suggested:

> Technological change is never merely additive; it is never simply an aid to doing what has always been done. It is, rather, *ecological* in the sense that a change in one aspect of behavior has ramifications throughout the entire system of which that behavior is a part. So the more sophisticated our technology, the more we change the way we do business. We need to begin to understand not only what happens when "we" encounter "them," but when "we" do so with a particular kind of powerful technology. (p. 472)

Although there is no one right way to "do business" when conducting qualitative inquiry, technological advances shift many of the taken-for-granted dimensions of research in localized and naturalistic settings. What is the nature of the researcher–participant relationship in a technological or virtual environment? How does technology alter power dynamics in such a relationship? How does the use of technology shift the presence of the researcher in the research process? How does technology shift the ways in which data may be accessed and collected? These questions, and many others, emerge as a researcher considers the possibilities of technology in the research process.

Finally, what does technology do to the sense of "place" or context that anchors much qualitative research? Some may argue that technology opens up the possibility of additional locations, places, or communities ripe for investigation; yet the explosion of on-line communities presents new challenges for qualitative researchers. As Angrosino and Rosenberg (2011) pointed out, on-line communities are "the 'location' for so many of the most interesting communities on the contemporary scene" (p. 473). They went on to point out some of the challenges of on-line and virtual worlds, such as their ephemeral nature, the ability (and sometimes desire) of those participating in virtual communities to create new identities or disguise existing ones, and the ethical issues that emerge (discussed in Chapter Eight) when conducting research in on-line contexts (Angrosino & Rosenberg, 2011). Higher education and student affairs qualitative researchers will need to consider research that has relied on "place" in this new and quickly growing technological context. Further, constructs that have been investigated by qualitative researchers in the past, such as sense of belonging, community, and involvement, will require rethinking as they have been tied to a physical space. What do these constructs look like in an on-line or virtual environment?

External Funding Viability

In looking to the future, it seems safe to say that the external funding environment in which higher education researchers exist will persist. That is, the press on all researchers is to succeed in securing outside funding for research projects. This emphasis is in part related to our economic times as many universities receive substantial financial gains when grants from outside funding agencies are awarded. External funding also increases the prestige of a university by presumably tying research efforts underway by researchers to larger national and international interests, represented by the research topics that funding agencies are interested in supporting. We do not see this trend disappearing in the near future.

What this future trend requires is that qualitative researchers learn to develop projects that are viable for external funding as the quantitative-post-positivist bias is clearly at work in funding agencies, and to do so without feeling as though they are selling their souls. Because many funding agencies are typically less interested in qualitative inquiry and because such studies are judged using quantitative criteria and thus perceived as limited in impact and generalizability, qualitative researchers must engage in collaborative and interdisciplinary research. This may mean participation on multi-institutional and/or interdisciplinary research teams on which a qualitative researcher carves out a qualitative piece of a large-scale project or development of a mixed methods approach to a topic for investigation. In the ever-popular area of research into STEM (science, technology, engineering, mathematics) topics, funding agencies such as NSF (National Science Foundation) support large-scale quantitative projects with qualitative components built in to contextualize statistical analyses and provide in-depth understanding. Such funding agencies do not yet appear willing to fund qualitative only projects, but the combination of statistical and interpretive analyses offer a compelling funding rationale that enhances funding viability.

One example of the kind of larger-scale research project that utilizes a mixed methods and collaborative design is that of the Wabash National Study of Liberal Arts Education, a national, multi-institutional, longitudinal study of student development and college impact (Seifert, Goodman, King, & Baxter Magolda, 2010). This study was designed by a research team comprised of both qualitative and quantitative researchers who thoughtfully considered the contributions of each approach. That is, the research team incorporated both the theoretical frameworks undergirding each approach and the kinds of questions to be pursued using quantitative and qualitative methods into their design. The study design also reflected a decision to integrate both quantitative and qualitative approaches and data collection equally so that one was not given priority over the other (Seifert et al., 2010). The point of mentioning the Wabash National Study here is not to detail the findings of this research on the impact of college on self-authorship and liberal arts learning outcomes, but to highlight the Wabash study as a model for collaborative, large-scale research that incorporates qualitative approaches in ways that are meaningful rather than "added-on." (For details on the collaborative process used to coordinate a large research team using qualitative inquiry, see Baxter Magolda, M. B., & King, P. M. (2012). *Assessing meaning making and self-authorship: Theory, research, and application. ASHE Higher Education Report, 38*(3). San Francisco: CA: Jossey-Bass.) This study is also well-funded—presumably because funders found that the mixed methods, national, and longitudinal design reflected an approach that offered a more complete and comprehensive investigation into their focus and the potential for more credible, transferable, and substantive results.

Of course, some of what we are suggesting by way of discussing future trends may not sit well with all qualitative researchers. Julianne Cheek (2011), in a chapter about the politics and practices of funding qualitative inquiry, wrote "For, no matter what type of qualitative inquiry we do, we are all selling, be it selling our time and/or our labor or/and our research projects" (p. 251). Although she goes on to suggest that all researchers need funding to conduct their research, the notion of selling our work seems counter to the perhaps now old-school notions about the more noble possibilities of creating knowledge and advancing new understanding through research. As we move forward into the future, some qualitative researchers will need to think about how to secure funding without compromising what is most important to them, the issues they care about and want to learn more about through qualitative inquiry, and the strategies they use to investigate such abiding concerns. This will require creative and innovative thinking. For example, what might it look like if qualitative researchers adopted the practice of quantitative researchers by establishing a large national database of qualitative data that researchers could use for secondary data analysis? The days of the lone researcher and single-authored publications are behind us as the need for meaningful and fruitful collaborations paves the way of the future. This may be required to assure not only the viability of the research but also of the researcher.

Role of Methodologies

What role does methodology play in qualitative inquiry? The term itself is a contested one. Methodology can be defined rather straightforwardly as "a theory of how inquiry should proceed" and to explicate and define the kinds of problems that are worth investigating (Schwandt, 2001, p. 161). Methodologies provide direction to framing areas of investigation and the related procedures (Schwandt). Those who confuse methodology with methods may declare methodology as unnecessary. There are others who engage methodology to convey both a process as well as a standpoint, such as feminist methodologists. Finally, some scholars endorse an approach of "post-methodology that bespeaks an end of grand narratives about research" (Lather, 2007, p. 69), which raises ontological and epistemological concerns. This connection is also conveyed by Pascale (2011):

> Whether or not researchers use the term epistemology, and regardless of whether or not researchers *understand* epistemology, we all draw from it each time we assert (or assume) that something counts as evidence. Every decision that we make about how to create valid knowledge about the world is an ontological and epistemological issue. (p. 5)

In some respects, this future direction returns us to a prevailing idea in this text. That is, all elements of a research decision are interrelated. A decision about one element (e.g., epistemology, methodology, or methods) influences decisions about other elements. Considering the role of methodologies in qualitative inquiry also reinforces the point made earlier in this chapter about the importance of knowing the rules (e.g., understanding the differences between different methodological approaches) before one breaks out of the structures such approaches provide.

In a discussion about definitional issues in qualitative research, Denzin and Lincoln (2011) provided useful language about the role of methodologies. Although interestingly, and to our point about future directions, they do not use that term but instead adopt the phrase "interpretive practices." They wrote:

> Qualitative research involves the studied use and collection of a variety of empirical materials—case study, personal experience, introspection, life story, interview, artifacts, and cultural texts and productions, along with observational, historical, interactional, and visual texts—that describe routine and problematic moments and meanings in individuals' lives. Accordingly, qualitative researchers deploy a wide-range of interconnected interpretive practices, hoping always to get a better understanding of the subject at hand. It is understood, however, that each practice makes the world visible in a different way. (pp. 3–4)

Our perspective in relation to the future is in the direction of the importance of maintaining methodological boundaries, even in the face of calls for more eclectic or hybrid practices. We see a trend among some researchers to name their own methodological approaches, yet not always with recognition of the traditions upon which they are drawing in this seemingly novel approach. We also underscore the point made by Denzin and Lincoln (2011) that methodological approaches convey and direct interpretive practices. All researchers engage in interpretive practices, whether or not they name them as such, and these practices shape all elements (or should) of a research design. Further, researchers who do adopt more eclectic methodological approaches must be sure to actually engage in such an approach, which is often challenging from a methodological perspective. That is, it may be far easier to write about a certain innovative approach, but actually conducting research using such an approach is much more difficult.

Methodological innovation may be appropriate but should flow from a solid foundation in what distinguishes certain methodological approaches or interpretive practices from one another. Related to and yet complicating the point made in the lessons learned section about following rules, Clandinin and Rosiek (2007) wrote:

> In the practice of research, however, such philosophical exactness is often a luxury. The actual business of interpreting human experience is messier. As

researchers we find ourselves drifting, often profitably, from one paradigm of inquiry into another. We do not cross borders as much as we traverse borderlands. (p. 58)

One of the strengths of qualitative inquiry is the opportunity for investigating messy and complicated issues at some depth. However, this point does not necessarily substantiate a claim that messy methodological approaches are appropriate. Instead, it calls for an ability to hold simultaneously competing ideas. On the one hand, methodological approaches provide structure around research questions, and these approaches can be distinguished from one another along certain categories, historical origins, philosophical foundations, and choices of methods. On the other hand, these distinctions should not be used to prematurely categorize or dichotomize methodological approaches; as Clandinin and Rosiek (2007) pointed out, "borders are abstractions" (p. 57) given the messiness of lived experiences. This requires researchers to inhabit "bumping spaces, conceptual spaces where different traditions of inquiry come together and where tensions become apparent" (p. 58). Navigating these methodological tensions represents a future direction in qualitative inquiry and the ability to inhabit this space an important research skill and disposition to acquire.

Summary

In this final chapter, we drew upon our ongoing experiences as qualitative researchers and added to our original list of lessons learned in the hopes of providing guidance, directions, and questions related to ongoing dilemmas and issues faced by qualitative researchers. We also discussed several areas of future direction (which are actually upon us) in qualitative inquiry, such as the changes brought by technology and social media, the press for external funding and viability, and the role of methodologies in conducting research. We offer these future directions more so to prompt discussion and to anticipate changes that are occurring rather than to declare definitively the direction in which qualitative inquiry is moving.

In concluding this second edition of *Negotiating the Complexities of Qualitative Research,* we hope that we maintained our original commitment to write a book that is both accessible and useful, while also raising questions and suggesting the complexities of qualitative approaches. We did not want to provide simplistic and overly structured steps involved in conducting qualitative inquiry, although we recognize the importance of understanding foundations before stepping out in a different direction. This second edition represents how our "futures" have evolved to enable us to tackle differently some of the issues raised in the first edition. We are confident that new futures will emerge that are the result of our changing world; sociopolitical occurrences; and the creativity, intelligence, and ingenuity of qualitative researchers to tackle the complexities of these times.

References

Abes, E. S. (2009). Theoretical borderlands: Using multiple theoretical perspectives to challenge inequitable power structures in student development theory. *Journal of College Student Development, 50,* 141–156.

———. (2012). Constructivist and intersectional interpretations of a lesbian college student's multiple social identities. *Journal of Higher Education, 83,* 186–216.

Abes, E. S., & Jones, S. R. (2004). Meaning-making capacity and the dynamics of lesbian college students' multiple dimensions of identity. *Journal of College Student Development, 45,* 612–632.

Abes, E. S., Jones, S. R., & McEwen, M. K. (2007). Reconceptualizing the model of multiple dimensions of identity: The role of meaning-making capacity in the construction of multiple identities. *Journal of College Student Development, 48,* 1–22.

Abes, E. S., & Kasch, D. (2007). Using queer theory to explore lesbian college students' multiple dimensions of identity. *Journal of College Student Development, 48,* 619–636.

Abma, T. A., & Widdershoven, G. A.M. (2011). Evaluation as a relationally responsible practice. In N. K. Denzin & Y. S. Lincoln (Eds.), *The Sage handbook of qualitative research* (4th ed.; pp. 669–680). Thousand Oaks, CA: Sage.

Acocella, I. (2012). The focus groups in social science research: Advantages and disadvantages. *Qual Quant, 46,* 1125–1136. doi: 10.1007/s1135–011–9600–4

Angrosino, M., & Rosenberg, J. (2011). Observations on observations: Continuities and challenges. In N. K. Denzin & Y. S. Lincoln (Eds.), *The Sage handbook of qualitative research* (4th ed.; pp. 467–478). Thousand Oaks, CA: Sage.

Arminio, J. L. (2001). Exploring the nature of race-related guilt. *Journal of Multicultural Counseling, 29,* 239–252.

Arminio, J. L., & Hultgren, F. H. (2002). Breaking out of the shadow: The question of criteria in qualitative research. *Journal of College Student Development, 43,* 446–460.

Arminio, J. W., & McEwen, M. K. (1996). White connections of family, place, race, and ethnicity: Implications for student affairs. *Journal of College Student Development, 3,* 315–323.

Atkinson, P. & Delamont, S. (2005). Analytic perspectives. In N.K. Denzin & Y.S. Lincoln, (Eds.), *The Sage handbook of qualitative research* (3rd ed.; pp. 821–840). Thousand Oaks, CA: Sage.

Ayala, J. (2000). Across dialects. In L. Weis & M. Fine (Eds.), *Speed bumps: A student-friendly guide to qualitative research* (pp. 102–105). New York, NY: Teachers College Press.

Ballard, K. (1996). Finding the ghost in the machine and giving it back to the body. In L. Heshusius & K. Ballard (Eds.), *From positivism and interpretivism and beyond* (pp. 100–107). New York, NY: Teachers College Press.

Bandura, A. (1986). *Social foundations of thought and action: A social cognitive theory.* Englewood Cliffs, NJ: Prentice Hall.

Banks, W., & Eble, M. (2007). Digital spaces, online environments, and human participant research: Interfacing with institutional review boards. In H. A. McKee & D. N. DeVoss (Eds.), *Digital writing research: Technologies, methodologies, and ethical issues* (pp. 27–48). Creskill, NJ: Hampton Press.

Baxter Magolda, M. B. (2001). *Making their own way: Narratives for transforming higher education to promote self-development.* Sterling, VA: Stylus.

———. (2003). Identity and learning: Student affairs' role in transforming higher education. *Journal of College Student Development, 44,* 231–247.

———. (2004). Evolution of a constructivist conceptualization of epistemological reflection. *Educational Psychologist, 39*(1), 31–42.

Baxter Magolda, M. B., & King, P.M. (2007). Interview strategies for assessing self-authorship: Constructing conversations to assess meaning making. *Journal of College Student Development, 48,* 491–508.

Baxter Magolda, M. B., King, P.M., Taylor, K. B., & Wakefield, K. M. (2012). Decreasing authority dependence during the first year of college. *Journal of College Student Development, 53,* 418–435.

Beck, C., & Kosnik, C. (2006). *Innovations in teacher education: A social constructivist approach.* Albany, NY: State University of New York Press.

Bergerson, A. A., & Huftalin, D. (2011). Becoming more open to social identity-based difference: Understanding the meaning college students make of this movement. *Journal of College Student Development, 53,* 377–395.

Berry, T. R. (2010). Engaged pedagogy and Critical Race Feminism. *Educational Foundations, 24*(3–4), 19–26.

Berube, M. S. (Ed). (1995). *Webster's II New Collegiate Dictionary.* Boston, MA: Houghton Mifflin.

Bhaskar, R, (1979). *The possibility of naturalism.* Atlantic Highlands, NJ: Humanities Press.

Blythe, S. (2007). Coding digital texts and multimedia. In H. A. McKee & D. N. DeVoss (Eds.), *Digital writing research: Technologies, methodologies, and ethical issues* (pp. 203–228). Creskill, NJ: Hampton Press.

Bouwma-Gearhart, J. L., & Bess, J. L. (2012). The transformative potential of blogs for research in higher education. *Journal of Higher Education, 83,* 249–275.

Bowleg, L. (2008). When Black + lesbian + woman ≠ Black lesbian woman: The methodological challenges of qualitative and quantitative intersectionality research. *Sex Roles, 59,* 312–325.

Brayboy, B. M. J. (2005). Toward a tribal critical race theory in education. *The Urban Review, 37*(5), 425–446.

Brightman, E. S. (1964). *An introduction to philosophy* (3rd ed.). New York, NY: Holt Rinehart Winston.

Broido, E. M., & Manning, K. (2002). Philosophical foundations and current theoretical perspectives in qualitative research. *Journal of College Student Development, 43,* 434–445.

Bronner, S. E. (1999). *Ideas in action: Political tradition in the twentieth century.* Lanham, MD: Rowman & Littlefield.

Bryant, A., & Charmaz, K. (2007*).* Grounded theory in historical perspective: An epistemological account. In A. Bryant & K. Charmaz (Eds.), *The Sage handbook of grounded theory* (pp. 31–57). Los Angeles, CA: Sage.

_____. Introduction ground theory research: Methods and practices. In A. Bryant & K. Charmaz (Eds.), *The Sage handbook of grounded theory* (pp. 1–28). Los Angeles, CA: Sage.

Buenavista, T. L., Jayakumar, U. M., & Misa-Escalante, K. (2009). Contextualizing Asian American education through critical race theory: An example of U.S. Pilipino college student experiences. In S. D. Museus & M. J. Chang (Eds.), *Conducting research on Asian Americans in higher education.* (New Directions for Institutional Research, No. 142, pp. 69–81). San Francisco, CA: Jossey-Bass.

Burr, V. (2003). *Social constructionism* (2nd ed.). New York, NY: Routledge.

Butin, D. W. (2012). What MIT should have done. *E-Learn Magazine.* doi: 10.1145/2241156.2263018

Cannella, G. S., & Lincoln, Y. S. (2011). Deploying qualitative methods for critical social purposes. In S. R. Steinberg & G. S. Cannella (Eds.), *Critical qualitative research reader* (pp. 104–114). New York, NY: Peter Lang.

Carpenter, S. (2003). Student affairs scholarship (re?) considered: Toward a scholarship of practice. *Journal of College Student Development, 42,* 301–318.

Carspecken, P. F. (2012). Basic concepts in critical methodological theory: Action, structure and system within a communicative pragmatics framework. In S. S. Steinberg & G. S. Cannella (Eds.), *Critical qualitative research reader* (pp. 43–66). New York, NY: Peter Lang.

Castagno, A.E., & Lee, S.J. (2007). Native mascots and ethnic fraud in higher education: Using tribal critical race theory and the interest convergence principles as an analytic tool. *Equity & Excellence in Education, 40,* 3–13.

Charmaz, K. (2000). Grounded theory objectivist and constructivist methods. In N. K. Denzin & Y. S. Lincoln (Eds.), *Handbook of qualitative research* (2nd ed.; pp. 509–535). Thousand Oaks, CA: Sage.

———. (2005). Grounded theory in the 21st century: Applications for advancing social justice studies. In N. K. Denzin & Y. S. Lincoln (Eds.), *Handbook of qualitative research* (3rd ed.; pp. 507–536). Thousand Oaks, CA: Sage.

———. (2006). *Constructing grounded theory: A practical guide through qualitative analysis.* Thousand Oaks, CA: Sage.

Chase, S. E. (2005). Narrative inquiry: Multiple lenses, approaches, voices. In N. K. Denzin & Y. S. Lincoln (Eds.), *Handbook of qualitative research* (3rd ed.; pp. 651–680). Thousand Oaks, CA: Sage.

———. (2008). Narrative inquiry: Multiple lenses, approaches, voices. In N. K. Denzin & Y. S. Lincoln (Eds.). *Collecting and interpreting qualitative data materials* (pp. 57–94). Los Angeles, CA: Sage.

———. (2011). Narrative inquiry: Still a field in the making. In N. K. Denzin & Y. S. Lincoln (Eds.), *The Sage handbook of qualitative research* (4th ed.; pp. 421–434). Los Angeles, CA: Sage.

Cheek, J. (2011). The politics and practices of funding qualitative inquiry: Messages about messages about messages. In N. K. Denzin & Y. S. Lincoln (Eds.), *The Sage handbook of qualitative research* (4th ed.; pp. 251–268). Los Angeles, CA: Sage.

Christians, C. G. (2000). Ethics and politics in qualitative research. In N. K. Denzin & Y. S. Lincoln (Eds.), *Handbook of qualitative research* (2nd ed.; pp. 133–155). Thousand Oaks, CA: Sage.

————. (2011). Ethics and politics in qualitative research. In N. K. Denzin & Y. S. Lincoln (Eds.), *The Sage handbook of qualitative research* (4th ed.; pp. 61–80). Los Angeles, CA: Sage.

Clandinin, D. J., & Connelly, F. M. (2000). *Narrative inquiry: Experience and story in qualitative research.* San Francisco, CA: Jossey-Bass.

Clandinin, D. J., & Rosiek, J. (2007). Mapping a landscape of narrative inquiry: Borderland spaces and tensions. In D. J. Clandinin (Ed.), *Handbook of narrative inquiry: Mapping a methodology* (pp. 35–75). Thousand Oaks, CA: Sage.

Clarke, A. E. (2005). *Situational analysis: Grounded theory after the postmodern turn.* Thousand Oaks, CA: Sage.

Coles, R. (1993). *The call of service: A witness to idealism.* Boston, MA: Houghton Mifflin.

Collins, P. H. (2000). *Black feminist thought: Knowledge, consciousness, and the politics of empowerment.* New York, NY: Routledge.

Coomer, D.L. (1989). Introduction to critical inquiry. In F. H. Hultgren & D. L. Coomer (Eds.), *Alternative modes of inquiry in home economics research* (pp. 167–184). Peoria, IL: Glencoe.

Coomer, D. L., & Hultgren, F. H. (1989). Introduction, considering alternatives: An invitation to dialogue and question. In F. H. Hultgren & D. L. Coomer (Eds.), *Alternative modes of inquiry in home economics research* (pp. xv–xxiii). Peoria, IL: Glencoe.

Corbin, J., & Strauss, A. (2008). *Basics of qualitative research* (3rd ed.). Thousand Oaks, CA: Sage.

Covell, C. L., Sidani, S., & Ritchie, J, A. (2012). Does sequential data collection influence participants' responses to closed and open ended questions? A methodological study. *International Journal of Nursing Studies, (49),* 664–671.

Creamer, E.G., Baxter Magolda, M., & Yue, J. (2010). Preliminary evidence of the reliability and validity of a quantitative measure of self-authorship. *Journal of College Student Development, 50,* 550–562.

Crenshaw, K. (1991). Mapping the margins: Intersectionality, identity politics, and violence against women of color. *Stanford Law Review, 43,* 1241–1299.

Creswell, J. W. (2003). *Research design qualitative, quantitative and mixed method approaches* (2nd ed.). Thousand Oaks, CA: Sage.

————. (2011). Controversies in mixed methods research. In Denzin, N. K. & Lincoln, Y. S. (Eds.), *The Sage handbook of qualitative research* (4th ed.; pp. 269–284). Los Angeles, CA: Sage.

————. (2013) *Qualitative inquiry & research design: Choosing among five approaches* (3rd ed.). Los Angeles, CA: Sage.

Crotty, M. (1998). *The foundations of social research: Meaning and perspective in the research process.* Thousand Oaks, CA: Sage.

Davidson, J., & di Gregorio, S. (2011). Qualitative research and technology: In the midst of a revolution. In N. K. Denzin & Y. S. Lincoln (Eds.), *The Sage handbook of qualitative research* (4th ed.; pp. 627–644). Los Angeles, CA: Sage.

Davis, T. L. (2002). Voices of gender role conflict: The social construction of college men's identity. *Journal of College Student Development, 43,* 508–521.

Delgado Bernal, D. (2002). Critical race theory, Latino critical theory, and critical raced-gendered epistemologies: Recognizing students of color as holders and creators of knowledge. *Qualitative Inquiry, 8(1),* 105–126.

Delgado Bernal, D., & Villalpando, O. (2002). An apartheid of knowledge in academia: The struggle over the "legitimate" knowledge of faculty of color. *Equity & Excellence in Education, 35(2),* 169–180.

Demerath, P. (2006). The science of context: Modes of response for qualitative research-ers in education. *International Journal of Qualitative Studies in Education, 19*(1), 97–113.

Denzin, N. K. (1989). *Interpretive interactionism.* Newbury Park, CA: Sage.

———. (2001). *Interpretive interactionism.* Thousand Oaks, CA: Sage.

———. (2011). The politics of evidence. In N. K. Denzin & Y. S. Lincoln (Eds.), *The Sage handbook of qualitative research* (4th ed.; pp. 645–657). Los Angeles, CA: Sage.

Denzin, N. K., & Giardina, M. D. (2009). Qualitative research and social justice: Toward a politics of hope. In N. K. Denzin & M. D. Giardina (Eds.), *Qualitative inquiry and social justice* (pp. 11–52). Walnut Creek, CA: Left Coast Press.

Denzin, N. K., & Lincoln, Y. S. (2000a). (Eds.), *Handbook of qualitative research* (2nd ed.). Thousand Oaks, CA: Sage.

———. (2000b). Introduction: The discipline and practice of qualitative research. In N. K. Denzin & Y. S. Lincoln (Eds.), *Handbook of qualitative research* (2nd ed.; pp. 1–28). Thousand Oaks, CA: Sage.

———. (2008). Introduction: The discipline and practice of qualitative research. In N. K. Denzin & Y. S. Lincoln (Eds.), *Collecting and interpreting qualitative materials* (pp. 1–43). Los Angeles, CA: Sage.

———. (2011). *The Sage handbook of qualitative research* (4th ed.). Los Angeles, CA: Sage.

Denzin, N. K., Lincoln, Y. S., & Smith, L. T. (2008). *Handbook of critical and indigenous methodologies.* Thousand Oaks, CA: Sage.

Dey, I. (2007). Grounding categories. In A. Bryant & K. Charmaz (Eds.), *The SAGE hand-book of grounded theory* (pp. 167–190). Thousand Oaks, CA: Sage.

Dill, B. T., & Zambrana, R. E. (2009). *Emerging intersections: Race, class, and gender in theory, policy, and practice.* New Brunswick, NJ: Rutgers University Press.

Dillard, C.B., & Okpalaoka, C. (2011). The sacred and spiritual nature of endarkened tran-sitional feminist praxis is qualitative research. In N.K. Denzin & Y.S. Lincoln (Eds.), *Handbook of qualitative research* (4th ed.; pp. 147–162). Thousand Oaks, CA: Sage.

Dillman, D.A. (2007). *Mail and internet surveys: The tailored design method* (2nd ed.). Hoboken, NJ: John Wiley & Sons.

Duneier, M. (2004). Finding a place to pee and other struggles of ethnography: Reflec-tions on race and method. In M. Fine, L. Weis, L. Powell Pruitt, & A. Burns (Eds.), *Off White: Readings on power, privilege, and resistance* (2nd ed.; pp. 206–214). New York, NY: Routledge.

Durant, W. (1961). *The story of philosophy.* New York, NY: Touchstone Books.

Duster, T. (2000). Foreword. In F. W. Twine & J. W. Warren (Eds.), *Racing researching, researching race: Methodological dilemmas in critical race studies* (pp. xi–xiv). New York, NY: New York University.

Edwards, K. E., & Jones, S. R. (2009). *"Putting my man face on:"* A grounded theory of college men's gender identity development. *Journal of College Student Development, 50,* 210–228.

Eisner, E. W. (1991). *The enlightened eye: Qualitative inquiry and the enhancement of educational practice.* New York, NY: Macmillan.

Eisner, E., & Peshkin, A. (1990). (Eds.), *Qualitative inquiry in education.* New York, NY: Teachers College Press.

Ellingson, L. L. (2011). Analysis and representation across the continuum. In N. K. Denzin & Y. S. Lincoln (Eds.), *The Sage handbook of qualitative research* (4th ed.; pp. 595–610). Los Angeles, CA: Sage.

Ellis, C. (2004). *The ethnographic I: A methodological novel about autoethnography.* Walnut Creek, CA: Alta Mira.

Ellsworth, E. (1997). *Teaching positions: Difference, pedagogy, and the power of address.* New York, NY: Teachers College Press.

Erickson, F. (1986). Qualitative methods in research on teaching. In M. C. Wittrock (Ed.), *Handbook of research on teaching* (3rd ed.; pp. 119–161). New York, NY: Macmillan.

———. (2005). Invited comments at plenary session, Scientifically based research and qualitative research methodologies, *Congress of Qualitative Inquiry,* Urbana-Champaign, IL.

Erikson, E. (1968). *Identity: Youth and crisis.* New York, NY: Norton.

Ewell, P. T. (2002). A brief history of assessment. In T. W. Banta (Ed.), *Building a scholarship of assessment* (pp. 3–23). San Francisco, CA: Jossey Bass.

Fine, M. (1994). Working the hyphens: Reinventing self and other in qualitative research. In N. K. Denzin & Y. S. Lincoln (Eds.), *Handbook of qualitative research* (pp. 70–82). Thousand Oaks, CA: Sage.

Finley, S. (2008). Arts-based inquiry: Performing revolutionary pedagogy. In N. K. Denzin & Y. S. Lincoln (Eds.), *Collecting and interpreting qualitative data materials* (pp. 95–114). Los Angeles, CA: Sage.

Flores, J., & Garcia, S. (2009). Latina testimonies: A reflexive, critical analysis of a 'Latina space' at a predominately White campus. *Race, Ethnicity and Education, 12,* 154–172.

Flyvbjerg, B. (2011). Case study. In N. K. Denzin & Y. S. Lincoln (Eds.), *The Sage handbook of qualitative research* (4th ed.; pp. 301–316). Los Angeles, CA: Sage.

Fontana, A., & Frey, J. H. (2008). The interview. In N. K. Denzin & Y. S. Lincoln (Eds.), *Collecting and interpreting qualitative materials* (pp. 115–159). Los Angeles, CA: Sage.

Freire, P. (1993). *Pedagogy of the oppressed* (30th anniversary ed.). New York, NY: Continuum Publishing. (Original work published 1970)

Gadamer, H. (1992). *Truth and method* (2nd ed.). (J. Weinsheimer & D. Marshall, Trans.). New York, NY: Crossroad. (Original work published 1960)

Gamson, J. (2000). Sexualities, queer theory, and qualitative research. In N. K. Denzin & Y. S. Lincoln (Eds.), *Handbook of qualitative research* (2nd ed.; pp. 347–365). Thousand Oaks, CA: Sage.

Geertz, C. (1973). *The interpretation of cultures: Selected essays.* New York, NY: Basic Books.

Giardina, M. D., & Newman, J. L. (2011). Cultural studies: Performative imperatives and bodily articulations. In N. K. Denzin & Y. S. Lincoln (Eds.), *The Sage handbook of qualitative research* (4th ed.; pp. 179–194). Los Angeles, CA: Sage.

Gibbs, G. (2007). *Analyzing qualitative data.* Los Angeles, CA: Sage.

Glaser, B. G., & Strauss, A.L. (1967; 1999). *Discovery of grounded theory: Strategies for qualitative research.* Chicago, IL: Aldine.

Glesne, C. (2011). *Becoming qualitative researchers: An introduction* (4th ed.). Boston, MA: Pearson.

González, K. P., Marin, P., Figueroa, M. A., Moreno, J. F., & Navia, C. N. (2002). Inside doctoral education in America: Voices of Latinas/os in pursuit of the PhD. *Journal of College Student Development, 43,* 540–557.

Gribbin, K. M. (2005). *Understanding the experiences of gay, lesbian, bisexual, and transgender (GLBT) allies: The influence of perceived consequences to self and others.* Unpublished thesis, The Ohio State University, Columbus, OH.

Guba, E. G. (1990). The alternative paradigm dialog. In E. G. Guba (Ed.), *The paradigm dialog* (pp. 17–30). Newbury Park, CA: Sage.

Gupton, J. (2009). *Pathways to college for homeless adolescents.* (Unpublished dissertation). The University of Southern California: Los Angeles, CA.

Habermas, (1984). *The theory of communicative action. Volume 1: Reason and the rationalization of society* (Thomas McCarthy, Trans.). Boston, MA: Beacon Press. (Original work published in 1981).

Hamera, J. (2011). Performance ethnography. In N. K. Denzin & Y. S. Lincoln (Eds.), *The Sage handbook of qualitative research* (4th ed.; pp. 317–330). Thousand Oaks, CA: Sage.

Hammersley, M. (1990). *Reading ethnographic research.: A critical guide.* New York, NY: Longman.

Hammersley. M., & Atkinson, P. (1983). *Ethnography principles and practice.* New York, NY: Routledge.

Harper, S. R., Patton, L. D., & Wooden, O. S. (2009). Access and equity for African American students in higher education: A critical race historical analysis of policy efforts. *Journal of Higher Education, 80,* 389–414.

Harris III, F. (2008). Deconstructing masculinity: A qualitative study of college men's masculine conceptualizations and gender performances. *NASPA Journal, 45,* 453–474.

———. (2010). College men's meanings of masculinities and contextual influences: Toward a conceptual model. *Journal of College Student Development, 51,* 297–318.

Hart-Davidson, W. (2007). Studying the mediated action of composing with time-use dairies. In H. A. McKee & D. N. DeVoss (Eds.), *Digital writing research: Technologies, methodologies, and ethical issues* (pp. 153–170). Creskill, NJ: Hampton Press.

Hays, D. G., & Mcleod, A. L. (2010). The culturally competent counselor. In D. G. Hays & B. T. Erford (Eds.), *Developing multicultural counseling competence: A systems approach* (pp. 1–31). Boston, MA: Pearson.

Hays, D., & Singh, A. A. (2012). *Qualitative inquiry in clinical and educational settings.* New York, NY: The Guilford Press.

Heidegger, M. (1962). *Being and time* (J. Macquarrie & E. Robinson, Trans.). New York, NY: Harper & Row. (Original work published in 1926).

Hernandez, E. (2012). The journey towards developing political consciousness through activism for Mexican American women. *Journal of College Student Development, 53,* 680–702.

Hittleman, D. R., & Simon, A.J. (2002). *Interpreting educational research: An introduction for consumers of research* (3rd ed.). Upper Saddle River, NJ: Pearson.

Hoad, T. F. (1986). *The concise Oxford dictionary of English etymology.* Oxford, UK: Oxford University Press.

Hogg, M. A. (2010). Social identity theory. In R. L. Jackson, II, & M. A. Hogg (Eds.): *Encyclopedia of identity* (pp. 749–753). Thousand Oaks, CA: Sage.

Honderich, T. (Ed.). (1995). *The Oxford companion to philosophy.* New York, NY: Oxford University Press.

hooks, b. (1990). *Yearning: Race, gender, and cultural politics.* Boston, MA: South End Press.

Howard, R.D. (2007). *Using mixed methods in institutional research.* Tallahassee, FL: Association for Institutional Research.

Howe, K., & Eisenhart, M. (1990). Standards for qualitative (and quantitative) research: A prolegomenon. *Educational Researcher, 19,* 2–9.

Ingram, D. (1990). *Critical theory and philosophy.* New York, NY: Paragon House.

Iverson, S.V. (2009). Crossing boundaries: Understanding women's advancement from clerical to professional positions. *Journal about Women in Higher Education, 2,* 140–166.

———. (2007). Camouflaging power and privilege: A critical race analysis of university diversity policies. *Educational Administration Quarterly, 43,* 586–611.

Jayakumar, U. M., Howard, T. C., Allen, W. R., & Han, J. C. (2009). Racial privilege in the professoriate: An exploration of campus climate, retention, and satisfaction. *Journal of Higher Education, 80,* 538–563.

Johnson, R.B., & Onweugbuzie, A.J. (2004). Mixed method research: A research paradigm whose time has come. *Educational Researcher, 33,* 14–26.

Jones, S. R. (2002). (Re)writing the word: Methodological strategies and issues in qualitative research, *Journal of College Student Development, 43,* 461–473.

———. (2009). Constructing identities at the intersections: An autoethnographic exploration of multiple dimensions of identity. *Journal of College Student Development, 50,* 287–304.

Jones, S. R., & Abes, E. S. (2003). Developing student understanding of HIV/AIDS through community service-learning: A case study analysis. *Journal of College Student Development, 44,* 470–488.

Jones, S. R., & Abes, E. S. (2013). *Identity development of college students: Advancing frameworks for multiple dimensions of identity.* San Francisco, CA: Jossey-Bass.

Jones, S. R., LePeau, L. A., Robbins, C. K. (2013). Exploring the possibilities and limitations of service-learning: A critical analysis of college student narratives about HIV/ AIDS. *Journal of Higher Education,84,* 213–238 .

Jones, S. R., & McEwen, M. K. (2000). A conceptual model for multiple dimensions of identity. *Journal of College Student Development, 41,* 405–413.

Jones, S. R., Robbins, C. K., & LePeau, L. A. (2011). Negotiating border crossing: Influences of social identity on service-learning outcomes. *Michigan Journal of Community Service Learning, 17*(2), 27–42.

Jones, S. R., Rowan-Kenyon, H. T., Ireland, M-Y., Niehaus, E., & Skendall, K. C. (2012). The meaning students make as participants in short-term immersion programs. *Journal of College Student Development, 53,* 201–220.

Jones, S. R., Segar, T.C., & Gasiorski, A. (2008). "It's like a double-edged sword": Understanding college student perceptions of their required high school "service- learning" experiences. *Michigan Journal of Community Service Learning, 15*(1), 5–17.

Jones, S. R., Torres, V., & Arminio, J. (2006). *Negotiating the complexities of qualitative research in higher education: Fundamental elements and issues.* New York, NY: Routledge.

Josselson, R. (2011). Narrative research: Constructing, deconstructing, and reconstructing story. In F. J. Wertz, K. Charmaz, L. M. McMullen, R. Josselson, R. Anderson, & E. McSpadden (Eds.), *Five ways of doing qualitative analysis: Phenomenological psychology, grounded theory, discourse analysis, narrative research, and intuitive inquiry* (pp. 224–242). New York, NY: Guilford Press.

Keeling, R. P., Wall, A. F., Underhile, R., & Dungy, G. (2008). *Assessment reconsidered: Institutional effectiveness for student success.* Washington, DC: National Association of Student Personnel Administrators.

Kelemen, M. L., & Rumens, N. (2008). *An introduction to critical management research.* London, UK: Sage.

Kellogg, A. H., & Liddell, D. L. (2102). "Not half but double": Exploring critical incidents in the racial identity of multiracial college students. *Journal of College Student Development, 53,* 524–541.

Kezar, A. (2000). Pluralistic leadership: Incorporating diverse voices. *The Journal of Higher Education, 71,* 722–743.

———. (2004). Wrestling with philosophy: Improving scholarship in higher education. *The Journal of Higher Education, 75,* 42–55.

———. (2010). Faculty and staff partnering with student activists: Unexplored terrains of interaction and development. *Journal of College Student Development, 51,* 451–477.

Kincheloe, J. L., & McLaren, P. (2000). Rethinking critical theory and qualitative research. In N.K. Denzin & Y.S. Lincoln (Eds.) *The Handbook of qualitative research* (2nd ed.; pp. 279–313). Thousand Oaks, CA: Sage.

Kincheloe, J. L., & Steinberg, S. R. (2012). Indigenous knowledges in education: Complexities, dangers, and profound benefits. In S. R. Steinberg & G. S. Cannella (Eds.), *Critical qualitative research reader* (pp. 341–361). New York, NY: Peter Lang.

Kitchner, K. S. (1985). Ethical principles and ethical decision in student affairs. In H. J. Canon & R. D. Brown (Eds.), *Applied ethics in student services* (New Directions for Student Services, No. 30, pp. 17–30). San Francisco, CA: Jossey-Bass.

Kromrey, J., Onwuegbuzie, A., & Hogarty, K. (2006). The continua of disciplined inquiry: Quantitative, qualitative, and mixed method. In S. Permuth & R.D. Mawdsley, (Eds.), *Research Methods for Studying Legal Issues in Education* (pp. 91–129). Dayton, OH: Education Law Association.

Kuhn, T. S. (1970). *The structure of scientific revolutions* (2nd ed.). Chicago, IL: University of Chicago Press.

Kvale, S. & Brinkmann, B. (2009). *Interviews: Learning the craft of qualitative research interviewing* (2nd ed.). Los Angeles, CA: Sage.

Ladson-Billings, G. (2009). Just what is critical race theory and what's it doing in a nice field like education? In E. Taylor, D. Gillborn, & G. Ladson-Billings (Eds.), *Foundations of critical race theory in education* (pp. 17–36). New York, NY: Routledge.

Lamott, A. (1994). *Bird by bird: Some instructions on writing and life.* New York, NY: Doubleday.

Lather, P. (1986). Research as praxis. *Harvard Educational Review, 56,* 257–277.

———. (1991). *Getting smart: Feminist research and pedagogy with/in the postmodern.* New York, NY: Routledge.

———. (2003). Issues of validity in openly ideological research: Between a rock and a soft place. In Y. S. Lincoln & N. K. Denzin (Eds.), *Turning points in qualitative research: Tying knots in a handkerchief* (pp. 185–215). Walnut Creek, CA: AltaMira.

———. (2006). Paradigm proliferation as a good thing to think with: Teaching research in education as wild profusion. *International Journal of Qualitative Studies in Education, 19*(1), 35–57.

———. (2007). *Getting lost: Feminist efforts toward a double(d) science.* Albany, NY: State University of New York Press.

Lather, P., & Smithies, C. (1997). *Troubling the angels: Women living with HIV/AIDS.* Boulder, CO: Westview.

Lawrence-Lightfoot, S. (1999). *Respect: An exploration.* Reading, MA: Perseus Press.

Lechuga, V. M (2011). Exploring culture from a distance: The utility of telephone interviews in qualitative research. *Journal of International Qualitative Inquiry, 25,* 251–268. doi: org/10.1080/095185.98.2010.529853

Lee, J., & Adler, L. (2006). Qualitative research redux: Researching contemporary legal issues concerning education. In S. Permuth & R.D. Mawdsley, (Eds). *Research Methods for Studying Legal Issues in Education* (pp. 25–56). Dayton, OH: Education Law Association.

Lempert (2007). Asking questions of the data: Memo writing in the grounded theory tradition. In A. Bryant & K. Charmaz (Eds.), *The Sage handbook of grounded theory* (pp. 245–264). Thousand Oaks, CA: Sage.

Lincoln, Y. S. (1990). Toward a categorical imperative for qualitative research. In E. Eisner & A. Peshkin (Eds.), *Qualitative inquiry in education* (pp. 277–295). New York, NY: Teachers College Press.

———. (1997). Self, subject, audience, text: Living at the edge, writing in the margins. In W. G. Tierney & Y. S. Lincoln (Eds.), *Representation and the text: Reframing the narrative voice* (pp. 37–55). Albany, NY: SUNY Press.

———. (1998). From understanding to action: New imperatives. *Theory and Research in Social Education, 26,* 12–29.

Lincoln, Y. S., & Cannella, G. S. (2007). Ethics and the broader rethinking/reconceptualization of research as construct. In N. K. Denzin & M. D. Giardina (Eds.), *Ethical futures in qualitative research: Decolonizing the politics of knowledge* (pp. 67–84). Walnut Creek, CA: Left Coast Press.

Lincoln, Y. S., & Guba, E. G. (1985). *Naturalistic inquiry.* Beverly Hills, CA: Sage.

———. (2000). Paradigmatic controversies, contradictions, and emerging confluences. In N. K. Denzin & Y. S. Lincoln (Eds.), *Handbook of qualitative research* (2nd ed.; pp. 163–188). Thousand Oaks, CA: Sage.

Lincoln, Y. S., Lynham, S. A., & Guba, E. G. (2011). Paradigmatic controversies, contradictions, and emerging confluences, revisited. In N. K. Denzin & Y. S. Lincoln (Eds.), *The Sage handbook of qualitative research* (4th ed.; pp. 97–128). Thousand Oaks, CA: Sage.

Linder, C., & Rodriguez, K. L. (2012). Learning from the experiences of self-identified women of color activists. *Journal of College Student Development, 53,* 383–398.

Magolda, P. M., & Ebben Gross, K. (2009). *It's all about Jesus! Faith as an oppositional collegiate subculture.* Sterling, VA: Stylus.

———. (2012). Misinterpreting the spirit and heart: Religious and paradigmatic tensions in ethnographic research. *Religion & Education, 39*(3), 235–256.

Magolda, P.M., & Weems, L. (2002). Doing harm: An unintended consequence of qualitative inquiry? *Journal of College Student Development, 43,* 490–507.

Markham, A. N. (2008). The methods, politics, and ethics of representation. In N. K Denzin & Y. S. Lincoln (Eds.), *Collecting and interpreting qualitative materials* (pp. 247–284). Los Angeles, CA: Sage.

Marshall, C. (1990). Goodness criteria: Are they objective or judgment calls? In E. G. Guba, (Ed.), *The paradigm dialogue* (pp. 188–197). Newbury Park, CA: Sage.

Marshall, C., & Rossman, G. B. (2011). *Designing qualitative research* (5th ed.). Los Angeles, CA: Sage.

Martínez Alemán, A.M., & Wartman, K. L. (2009). *Online social networking on campus: Understanding what matters in student culture.* New York, NY: Routledge.

Maykut, P., & Morehouse, R. (2001). *Beginning qualitative research: A philosophic and practical guide.* Philadelphia, PA: Routledge/Falmer.

Maynard, M. (2000). Methods, practice, and epistemology: The debate about feminism and research. In J. Glazer-Raymo, B. K. Townsend, & B. Ropers-Huilman (Eds.), *Women in higher education: A feminist perspective* (pp. 89–100). Boston, MA: Pearson Custom Publishing.

McCall, L. (2005). The complexity of intersectionality. *Signs: Journal of Women in Culture and Society, 30,* 1771–1800.

McKee, H. A., & DeVoss, D. N. (2007). Introduction. In H. A. McKee & D. N. DeVoss (Eds.), *Digital writing research: Technologies, methodologies, and ethical issues* (pp. 1–24). Creskill, NJ: Hampton Press Inc.

McNiff, J., Lomax, P., & Whitehead, J. (2003). *You and your action research project.* New York, NY: Routledge.

Merchant, B. M. (2001). Negotiating the boundaries and sometimes missing the mark: A White researcher and a Mexican American research assistant. In B. M. Merchant & A. I. Willis (Eds.), *Multiple and intersecting identities in qualitative research* (pp. 1–18). Mahwah, NJ: Lawrence Erlbaum Associates.

Merriam, S. B. (2009). *Qualitative research: A guide to design and implementation.* San Francisco, CA: Jossey-Bass.

Merriam, S. B., & Associates (2002). *Qualitative research in practice: Examples for discussion and analysis.* San Francisco, CA: Jossey-Bass.

Misawa, M. (2010). Musings on controversial intersections of positionality: A Queer Crit perspective on adult and continuing education. In V. Sheared, J. Johnson-Bailey, S. A. J. Colin, III, E. Peterson, & S. D. Brookfield (Eds.), *The handbook of race and adult education: A resource for dialogue on racism* (pp. 187–200). San Francisco, CA: Jossey-Bass.

———. (2012). Social justice narrative inquiry: A Queer Crit perspective. *Proceedings of the Adult Education Research Conference,* 239–246. Paper retrieved from www.adulterc.org/Proceedings/2012/papers/misawa.pdf.

Moos, R. H. (1979). *Evaluating educational environments.* San Francisco, CA: Jossey-Bass.

Morrow, R. A. (1991). Critical theory, Gramsci and cultural studies: From structuralism to poststructuralism. In P. Wexler (Ed.), *Critical Theory Now* (pp. 27–69). London, UK: The Falmer Press.

Morrow, S. L. (2005). Quality and trustworthiness in qualitative research in counseling psychology. *Journal of Counseling Psychology, 52,* 250–259.

Morse, J. M. (2007). Sampling in grounded theory. In A. Bryant & K. Charmaz (Eds.), *The Sage handbook of grounded theory* (pp. 229–244). Thousand Oaks, CA: Sage.

Morse, J. M., & Richards, L. (2002). *README FIRST for a user's guide to qualitative methods.* Thousand Oaks, CA: Sage.

Moustakas, C. (1994). *Phenomenological research methods.* Thousand Oaks, CA: Sage.

Museus, S. D., & Griffin, K. A. (2011). Mapping the margins in higher education: On the promise of intersectionality frameworks in research and discourse. In S. D. Museus & K. A. Griffin (Eds.), *Using Mixed Methods Approaches to Study Intersectionality in Higher Education.* (New Directions for Institutional Research, No. 151, pp. 5–13). San Francisco, CA: Jossey-Bass.

Nathan, R. (2005). *My freshman year: What a professor learned by becoming a student.* Ithaca, NY: Cornell University Press.

Noddings, N. (1984). *Caring: A feminine approach to ethics and moral education.* Berkeley, CA: University of California Press.

Olesen, V. (2011). Feminist qualitative research in the millennium's first decade. In N. K. Denzin & Y. S. Lincoln (Eds.), *The Sage handbook of qualitative research* (4th ed.; pp. 129–146). Los Angeles, CA: Sage.

Palmer, R. T., Davis, R. J., & Maramba, D.C. (2011). The impact of family support on the success of Black men at an historically Black university: Affirming the revision of Tinto's theory. *Journal of College Student Development, 52,* 577–597.

Pascale, C. (2011). *Cartographies of knowledge.* Los Angeles, CA: Sage.

Pascarella, E. T., Pierson, C. T., Wolniak, G. C., & Terenzini, P. T., (2004). First-generation college students: Additional evidence on college experiences and outcomes. *Journal of Higher Education, 75,* 249–284.

Patton, L. D., & Catching, C. (2009). "Teaching while Black": Narratives of African American student affairs faculty. *International Journal of Qualitative Studies in Education, 22,* 713–728.

Patton, M. Q. (1990). *Qualitative evaluation and research methods* (2nd ed.). Newbury Park, CA: Sage.

———. (2002). *Qualitative research and evaluation methods* (3rd ed.). Newbury Park, CA: Sage.

Peshkin, A. (1988). In search of subjectivity—One's own. *Educational Researcher, 17*(7), 17–21.

Peterson, R. D., & Hamrick, F. A. (2009). White, male, and "minority": Racial consciousness among White male undergraduates attending a historically Black university. *Journal of Higher Education, 80,* 34–58.

Phallas, A.M. (2001). Preparing education doctoral students for epistemological diversity. *Educational Researcher, 30,* 6–11.

Phillips, M. L. (2012). *Using social media in your research: Experts explore the practicalities of observing human behavior through Facebook and Twitter.* Retrieved from http://www.apa.org/gradpsych/2011/11/social-media.aspx.

Pinar, W. F., Reynolds, W. M., Slattery, P., & Taubman, P.M. (1995). *Understanding curriculum.* New York, NY: Peter Lang.

Pinnegar, S., & Daynes, J. (2007). My writing as inquiry. Locating narrative inquiry historically. In Clandinin, D. J. (Ed.) *Handbook of narrative inquiry: Mapping a methodology* (pp. 1–34). Thousands Oaks, CA: Sage.

Preissle, J. (2011). Qualitative futures: Where we might go from where we've been. In N. K. Denzin & Y. S. Lincoln (Eds.), *The Sage handbook of qualitative research* (4th ed., pp. 685–698). Thousand Oaks, CA: Sage.

Prosser, J. (2011). Visual methodology: Toward a more seeing research. In N. K. Denzin & Y. S. Lincoln (Eds.) *The Sage handbook of qualitative research* (4th ed.; pp. 479–498). Thousand Oaks, CA: Sage.

Quaye, S. J. (2012). Think before you teach: Preparing for dialogues about racial realities. *Journal of College Student Development, 53,* 542–562.

Radhakrishnan, R. (2003). *Theory in an uneven world.* Malden, MA: Blackwell.

Reason, R. D., Roosa Millar, E. A., & Scales, T. C. (2005). Toward a model of racial justice ally development. *Journal of College Student Development, 46,* 530–546.

Reinharz, S. (1992). *Feminist methods in social research.* New York, NY: Oxford University Press.

Renn, K.A. (2010). LGBT and queer research in higher education: The state and status of the field. *Educational Researcher, 39*(2), 132–141.

Robbins, C. (2012). *Racial consciousness, identity, and dissonance among White women in student affairs graduate programs.* (Unpublished dissertation). University of Maryland, College Park, MD.

Rockenbach, A. B., Walker, C. R., & Luzader, J. (2012). A phenomenological analysis of college students' spiritual struggle. *Journal of College Student Development, 53,* 55–74.

Rogers, J. L., & Love, P. (2007). Graduate student constructions of spirituality in preparation programs. *Journal of College Student Development, 48,* 689–705.

Rolón-Dow, R. (2011). Race(ing) stories: Digital storytelling as a tool for critical race scholarship. *Race, Ethnicity and Education, 14,* 159–172.

Rossman, G. B., & Rallis, S. F. (2010). Everyday ethics: Reflections on practice. *International Journal of Qualitative Studies in Education, 23,* 379–391.

Rumann, C. B., & Hamrick, F. A. (2010). Student veterans in transition: Re-enrolling after war zone deployments. *The Journal of Higher Education, 81,* 431–458.

Russo, C.J. (2006). Legal research: The "traditional" method. In S. Permuth & R. D. Mawdsley (Eds.), *Research Methods for Studying Legal Issues in Education* (pp. 5–24). Dayton, OH: Education Law Association.

Ryan, G. W., & Bernard, H. R. (2000). Data management and analysis methods. In N. K. Denzin & Y. S. Lincoln (Eds.), *Handbook of qualitative research* (2nd ed.; pp. 769–802). Thousand Oaks, CA: Sage.

Schlossberg, N. K. (1989). Marginality and mattering: Key issues in building community. In D.C. Roberts (Ed.), *Designing campus activities to foster a sense of community* (New Directions for Student Services, No. 48, pp. 5–15). San Francisco, CA: Jossey-Bass.

Schuh, J. H. (2008). *Assessment methods for student affairs.* San Francisco, CA: Jossey-Bass.

Schuh, J. H., & Upcraft, M. L. (2000). *Assessment practice in student affairs: An applications manual.* San Francisco, CA: Jossey-Bass.

Schwandt, T. A. (2000). Three epistemological stances for qualitative inquiry: Interpretivism, hermeneutics, and social constructionism. In N. K. Denzin & Y. S. Lincoln (Eds.), *Handbook of qualitative research* (2nd ed.; pp. 189–213). Thousand Oaks, CA: Sage.

———. (2001). *Dictionary of qualitative inquiry* (2nd ed.). Thousand Oaks, CA: Sage.

———. (2007a). *The Sage dictionary of qualitative inquiry* (3rd ed.). Los Angeles, CA: Sage.

———. (2007b). The pressing need for ethical education: A commentary on the growing IRB controversy. In N. K. Denzin & M. D. Giardina (Eds.), *Ethical futures in qualitative research* (pp. 67–84). Walnut Creek, CA: Left Coast Press.

Seidman, I. (1989). *Interviewing as qualitative research: A guide for researchers in education and social sciences* (2nd ed.). New York, NY: Teachers College Press.

Seifert, T. A., Goodman, K. M., King, P.M., & Baxter Magolda, M. B. (2010). Using mixed methods to study first-year college impact on liberal arts learning outcomes. *Journal of Mixed Methods Research, 4,* 248–267.

Shaw, I. (2008). Ethics and the practice of qualitative research. *Qualitative Social Work, 7*(4), 400–414.

Shields, C. M. (2012). Critical advocacy research: An approach whose time has come. In S. R. Steinberg & G. S. Cannella (Eds.), *Critical qualitative research reader* (pp. 2–13). New York, NY: Peter Lang.

Shupp, M. R., & Arminio, J. L. (2012). Synergistic supervision: A confirmed key to retaining entry-level student affairs professionals. *Journal of Student Affair Research and Practice, 49*(2), 157–174. doi: 10.515/jsarp-2012–6295.

Sipe, L., & Constable, S. (1996). A chart of four contemporary research paradigms: Metaphors for the modes of inquiry. *Taboo: The Journal of Culture and Education, 1,* 153–163.

Smith, J. K. (1990). Alternative research paradigms and the problem of criteria. In E. G. Guba, (Ed.), *The paradigm dialogue* (pp. 168–187). Newbury Park, CA: Sage.

———. (1993). *After the demise of empiricism: The problem of judging social and educational inquiry.* Norwood, NJ: Ablex.

Smith, J. K., & Deemer, D. K. (2000). The problem of criteria in the age of relativism. In N. K. Denzin & Y. S. Lincoln (Eds.), *Handbook of qualitative research* (2nd ed.; pp. 877–896). Thousand Oaks, CA: Sage.

Smith, J. K., & Hodkinson, P. (2008). Relativism, criteria, and politics. In N. K. Denzin & Y. S. Lincoln (Eds.), *Collecting and interpreting qualitative materials* (3rd ed.; pp. 411–434). Los Angeles, CA: Sage.

Smith, L. M. (1990). Ethics in qualitative field research: An individual perspective. In E. Eisner & A. Peshkin (Eds.), *Qualitative inquiry in education* (pp. 258–276). New York, NY: Teachers College Press.

Smith, W. A., Allen, W. R., & Danley, L. L. (2007). "Assume the position . . . You fit the description": Psychosocial experiences and racial battle fatigue among African American male college students. *American Behavioral Scientist, 51,* 551–578.

Solórzano, D. G., Ceja, M., & Yosso, T. (2000). Critical race theory, racial microaggressions, and campus racial climate: The experiences of African American college students. *Journal of Negro Education, 69*(1/2), 60–73.

Solórzano, D. G., Villalpando, O., & Osequera, L. (2005). Educational inequities and Latina/o undergraduate students in the United States: A critical race analysis of their educational progress. *Journal of Hispanic Higher Education, 4,* 272–294.

Solórzano, D. G. & Yosso, T. J. (2002). A critical race theory counterstory of race, racism, and Affirmative Action. *Equity & Excellence in Education, 35*(2), 155–168.

Soltis, J. F. (1990). The ethics of qualitative research. In E. Eisner & A. Peshkin (Eds.), *Qualitative inquiry in education* (pp. 247–257). New York, NY: Teachers College Press.

Spradley, J. (1979). *The ethnographic interview.* New York, NY: Holt, Rinehart and Winston.

———. (1980). *Participant observation.* New York, NY: Holt, Rinehart and Winston.

Stage, F. (Ed.). (2010). Using quantitative research to answer critical questions. (New Directions for Institutional Research, No. 33). San Francisco, CA: Jossey-Bass.

Stake, R. E. (1995). *The art of case study research.* Thousand Oaks, CA: Sage.

———. (2000). Case studies. In N. K. Denzin & Y. S. Lincoln (Eds.), *Handbook of qualitative research* (2nd ed.; pp. 435–454). Thousand Oaks, CA: Sage.

———. (2005). Qualitative case studies. In N. K. Denzin & Y. S. Lincoln (Eds.), *The Sage handbook of qualitative research* (3rd ed.; pp. 443–466). Thousand Oaks, CA: Sage.

Star, S. L. (2007). Living grounded theory: Cognitive and emotional forms of pragmatism. In A. Bryant & K. Charmaz (Eds.), *The Sage handbook of grounded theory* (pp. 75–94). Los Angeles, CA: Sage.

Steinberg, S. (2012). What's critical about qualitative research? In S. S. Steinberg & G. S. Cannella (Eds.), *Critical qualitative research reader* (pp. ix-x). New York, NY: Peter Lang.

Stewart, D.L. (2002). The role of faith in the development of an integrated identity: A qualitative study of Black students at a White college. *Journal of College Student Development, 43,* 579–595.

St. Pierre, E.A. (2011). Post qualitative research the critique and coming after. In N. K. Denzin & Y.S. Lincoln (Eds.), *Handbook of qualitative research* (4th ed.; pp. 611–625). Thousand Oaks, CA: Sage.

Strauss, A., & Corbin, J. (1990). *Basics of qualitative research.* Thousand Oaks, CA: Sage.

———. (1998). *Basics of qualitative research techniques and procedures for developing grounded theory* (2nd ed.). Thousand Oaks, CA: Sage.

Strayhorn, T. L. (2011). Singing in a foreign land: An exploratory study of gospel choir participation among African American undergraduates at a predominantly White institution. *Journal of College Student Development, 52,* 137–153.

Sue, D. W., Ivey, A. E., & Pederson, P. (1996). *A theory of multicultural counseling and therapy*. Pacific Grove, CA: Brooks/Cole.

Sze, M., & Wang, K. (1963). *The Tao of painting*. New York, NY: Pantheon Books. (Original work published 1701).

Talburt, S. (2004). Ethnographic responsibility without the "real." *Journal of Higher Education, 75,* 80–103.

Tashakkori, A., & Teddlie, C. (1998). *Mixed methodology combining qualitative and quantitative approaches,* Series # 46. Thousand Oaks, CA: Sage.

———. (2003). *Handbook of mixed methods in social & behavioral research.* Thousand Oaks, CA: Sage.

Taylor, E. (2009). The foundations of critical race theory in education: An introduction. In E. Taylor, D. Gillborn, & G. Ladson-Billings (Eds.), *Foundations of critical race theory in education* (pp. 1–13). New York, NY: Routledge.

Taylor, E., Gillborn, D., & Ladson-Billings, G. (Eds.). (2009). *Foundations of critical race theory in education.* New York, NY: Routledge.

Teddlie, C., & Tashakkori, A. (2011). Mixed methods research: Contemporary issues in an emerging field. In Denzin, N. K. & Lincoln, Y. S. (Eds.), *The Sage handbook of qualitative research* (4th ed.; pp. 285–300). Los Angeles, CA: Sage.

Tedlock, B. (2000). Ethnography and ethnographic representation. In N. K. Denzin & Y. S. Lincoln (Eds.), *Handbook of qualitative research* (2nd ed.; pp. 455–486). Thousand Oaks, CA: Sage.

Tierney, W. G. (1997). Organizational socialization in higher education. *Journal of Higher Education, 68,* 1–16.

Tierney, W. G., & Rhoads, R. A. (2004). Postmodernism and critical theory in higher education: Implications for research and practice. In J. C. Smart (Ed.), *Higher education: Handbook of theory and research* (Vol. 9). New York, NY: Agathon Press.

Torres, V. (2006). A Mixed method study testing data-model fit of a retention model for Latino students at urban universities. *Journal of College Student Development, 47,* 299–318.

Torres, V. (2009). The developmental dimensions of recognizing racist thoughts. *Journal of College Student Development, 50,* 505–520.

Torres, V., & Baxter Magolda, M. (2002). The evolving role of the researcher in constructivist qualitative studies. *Journal of College Student Development, 43,* 474–489.

Torres, V., & Hernandez, E. (2007). The influence of ethnic identity on self-authorship: A longitudinal study of Latino/a college students. *Journal of College Student Development, 48,* 558–573.

Torres, V., Howard-Hamilton, M., & Cooper, D. L. (2003). *Identity development for diverse populations: Implications for teaching and practice.* ASHE/ERIC Higher Education Report, Vol. 26, No. 6. San Francisco, CA: Jossey-Bass.

Torres, V., Martinez, S., Wallace, L., Medrano, C.I., Robledo, A.L. & Hernandez, E. (2012). The connections between Latino ethnic identity and adult experiences. *Adult Education Quarterly, 62*(1), 3–18.

Upcraft, M. L. (2003). Assessment and evaluation. In S. R. Komives & D. B. Woodard (Eds.), *Student services: A handbook of the profession* (4th ed.; pp. 555–572). San Francisco, CA: Jossey-Bass.

Upcraft, M. L., & Schuh, J. H. (1996). *Assessment in student affairs: A guide for practitioners.* San Francisco, CA: Jossey-Bass.

———. (2002). Assessment vs. research: Why we should care about the difference. *About Campus, 7,* 16–20.

Vaccaro, A., & Mena, J. A. (2011). It's not burnout, it's more: Queer college activists of color and mental health. *Journal of Gay & Lesbian Mental Health, 15,* 339–367.

Van Maanen, J. (1988). *Tales of the field: On writing ethnography.* Chicago, IL: University of Chicago Press.

———. (2011). *Tales of the field: On writing ethnography* (2nd ed.). Chicago, IL: University of Chicago Press.

van Manen, M. (1990). *Researching lived experience: Human science for an action sensitive pedagogy.* Albany, NY: SUNY Press.

Villalpando, O. (2003). Self-segregation or self-preservation? A critical race theory and Latina/o critical theory analysis of a study of Chicana/o college students. *Qualitative Studies in Education, 16,* 619–646.

Warner, L. R. (2008). A best practices guide to intersectional approaches in psychological research. *Sex Roles, 59,* 454–463.

Weber, M. (1958). Essays in sociology (H. H. Gerth & C. Wright Mills, Eds. & Trans.). New York, NY: Galaxy. (Original work published in 1946)

Weis, L., & Fine, M. (2000). *Speed bumps: A student friendly guide to qualitative research.* New York, NY: Teachers College Press.

Wertz, F. J. (2011). A phenomenological psychological approach to trauma and resilience. In F. J. Wertz, K. Charmaz, L. M. McMullen, R. Josselson, R. Anderson, & E. McSpadden (Eds.), *Five ways of doing qualitative analysis: Phenomenological psychology, grounded theory, discourse analysis, narrative research, and intuitive inquiry* (pp. 124–164). New York, NY: Guilford Press.

Winkle-Wagner, R. (2009). *The unchosen me: Race, gender, and identity among Black women in college.* Baltimore, MD: The Johns Hopkins University Press.

Wolcott, H. F. (2002) Writing up qualitative research . . . better. *Qualitative Health Research, 12*(1), 91–103.

———. (2010). *Ethnography lessons: A primer.* Walnut Creek, CA: Left Coast Press.

Woozley, A.D. (Ed.). (1964). *John Locke: An essay concerning human understanding.* New York, NY: Meridian.

Yin, R. K. (2008). *Case study research: Design and methods* (4th ed.). Thousand Oaks, CA: Sage.

———. (2009). *Case study research: Design and methods.* Applied Social Research Methods, Vol. 5. Los Angeles, CA: Sage.

Yosso, T. J., Parker, L., Solórzano, D.G., & Lynn, M. (2004). From Jim Crow to Affirmative Action and back again: A critical race discussion of racialized rationales and access to higher education. *Review of Research in Education, 28,* 1–25.

Zurita, M. (2001). La mojada y el coyote: Experiences of a wetback researcher. In B. M. Merchant & A. I. Willis (Eds.), *Multiple and intersecting identities in qualitative research* (pp. 9–32). Mahwah, NJ: Lawrence Erlbaum Associates.

Index

Note: Page numbers in *italics* indicate figures or tables.